STORMING

STORMING THE HEAVENS

The Soviet League of the Militant Godless

DANIEL PERIS

CORNELL UNIVERSITY PRESS

Ithaca and London

PUBLICATION OF THIS BOOK WAS ASSISTED BY A GRANT
FROM THE UNIVERSITY OF WYOMING.

First published 1998 by Cornell University Press.

Printed in the United States of America.

Library of Congress Cataloging-in-Publication Data

Peris, Daniel, 1964–
    Storming the heavens : the Soviet League of the Militant Godless / Daniel Peris.
        p.   cm.
    Chapters 3, 4, 7, and 8 were presented as papers at several conferences in 1994 and 1995.
    Includes bibliographical references and index.
    ISBN 0-8014-3485-8 (cloth : alk. paper)
    1. Atheism—Russia—History—20th century—Congresses.   2. Philosophy, Marxist—Study and teaching—Russia—History—20th century—Congresses. 3. Communist education—Russia—History—20th century—Congresses.   4. Soiuz voinstvuiushchikh bezbozhnikov SSSR—History—Congresses.   5. Russkaia pravoslavnaia tserkov'—History—Congresses.   6. Russia—Religion— Congresses.   I. Title.
    BL2765.R8P47   1998
    211'.8'06047—dc21   98-22595

Cornell University Press strives to use environmentally responsible suppliers and materials to the fullest extent possible in the publishing of its books. Such materials include vegetable-based, low-VOC inks and acid-free papers that are also either recycled, totally chlorine-free, or partly composed of nonwood fibers.

Cloth printing   10   9   8   7   6   5   4   3   2   1

**In Memory
of L.A.P.**

Contents

Illustrations   viii

Acknowledgments   ix

Glossary   xi

Introduction   1

1. Making Holy Russia Godless: Policies, Confusion, and Cadres, 1917–1925   19

2. Organized Atheism in the 1920s   47

3. Soviet Atheism?   69

4. "The Battle against Religion Is the Battle for Socialism"   99

5. The League of the Godless in Iaroslavl' and Pskov, 1926–1933   118

6. The League of the Godless, the Communist Party, and Bolshevik Political Culture   150

7. "Cadres Decide Everything"   174

8. The Second Coming? The League of the Godless in the Late 1930s   197

Epilogue and Conclusion   221

Selected Primary Sources   230

Index   235

Illustrations

A guided tour of the Central Antireligious Museum, Moscow   78

"Religion is poison. Protect your children"   80

"Religion is the enemy of industrialization"   113

Throwing the bell from the tower of the Cathedral
of the Assumption, Iaroslavl'   132

The destroyed bell from the Cathedral
of the Assumption, Iaroslavl'   133

Children with antireligious placards, Moscow   140

Delegates to the Second All-Union Congress
of the Godless, Moscow   154

"You are waiting in vain at the church door, priest"   218

Acknowledgments

It is my pleasure to thank those individuals who have helped me in my decade-long encounter with the Godless. They include Mary McAuley, Andrew Verner, Mark von Hagen, David Ransel, Lewis Siegelbaum, Gregory Freeze, Heather Coleman, and Ed Roslof. I am particularly grateful for the unstinting support and superb guidance of Diane P. Koenker. Although Bill Husband and I have disagreed on many points of interpretation, I have enjoyed enormously our many discussions about the Soviet antireligious effort. Similarly, I am grateful to Nikita Petrov, who generously shared with me the fruits of his many years of work in Soviet archives. Finally, I thank my wife, Irina, whose informed skepticism about chronicling the Godless and writing Soviet history in general has been the cause of many wonderful and salutary debates.

In Russia, I was aided by Galina Afanasievna Kazarinova (Iaroslavl'), Irina Viktorovna Poltavskaia (St. Petersburg), Irina Lints (Moscow), Mariia Rostislavovna Zezina (Moscow), the staffs of the former Central Party and Central State archives in Moscow, the former Leningrad Party Archive, the archive of the Museum of Religion (St. Petersburg), and the archival authorities in the cities of Iaroslavl' and Pskov. I am also grateful for the help of the staffs of the Slavic Library at the University of Illinois and the library of the Hoover Institution.

A version of Chapter 8 was presented at the spring 1994 meeting of the Midwest Slavic Historians' Colloquium. Chapters 3 and 4 were delivered as a conference paper at the 1994 AAASS convention in Philadelphia. Chapter 7 was presented to the Canadian Historical Association in Montreal in 1995. The International Research and Exchange Board, with

x   *Acknowledgments*

funds from the Department of State and the United States Information Agency, and the Fulbright-Hays program of the U.S. Department of Education made possible an extended research trip to Russia in 1991–1992. A Charlotte Newcombe Fellowship of the Woodrow Wilson National Fellowship Foundation provided support upon my return. Additional research was conducted in 1993 with a grant from the International Studies Program at the University of Illinois, and in 1994 on an NEH Summer Seminar for College Teachers. The University of Wyoming permitted me to accept a Title VIII Postdoctoral Fellowship, with funds from the Department of State, administered by the Hoover Institution.

The history department at the University of Wyoming provided a congenial setting and the additional financial support that allowed me to complete revision of this book. I am grateful to the department's chair, William Howard Moore, and to my former colleagues there.

Portions of Chapter 6 appeared originally in *Soviet Studies* (now *Europe-Asia Studies*) 43, no. 4 (July 1991): 711–732. I am grateful to Carfax Publishing Company, Abingdon, Oxfordshire OX14 3UE, for permission to reproduce them here.

D. P.

New York, N.Y.

Glossary

Geopolitical terms:
guberniia	province
gubkom	Communist Party committee of a province
obkom	Communist Party committee of an oblast
oblast	province (successor to *guberniia*)
okrug	region
okruzhkom	Communist Party committee of a region
raikom	Communist Party committee of a district
raion	district
uezd	county (predecessor to *raion*)
ukom	Communist Party committee of an *uezd*
volost'	subdivision of an *uezd*

Other terms:
agitprop	agitation propaganda; a department of all Party committees
aktiv	activist body
antireligioznik	antireligionist
apparat	administrative machinery
bezbozhie	godlessness
bezbozhnik	godless person
Glavpolitprosvet	Main Administration for Political Enlightenment, attached to the Commissariat of Enlightenment
Komsomol	Communist Youth League
OB	Obshchestvo Bezbozhnikov (Society of the Godless)
ODGB	Obshchestvo Druzei Gazety "Bezbozhnika" (Society of Friends of the Newspaper *Godless*)
OGPU, GPU	Soviet secret police

perebroska	administrative transfer of cadres
peregruzka	overextension, overwork of Party cadres
politprosvet	political education, or the relevant division of a local education authority
stikhiinost'	uncontrolled change

STORMING THE HEAVENS

Introduction

When the Bolsheviks came to power in 1917, they promised to sweep away all that was old in Russian society and to create an entirely new civilization. Although largely inchoate in 1917, the Bolshevik agenda was wide-ranging, concerning not only political and economic relations but also culture, education, women, family relations, and language. One of the most dramatic points on this agenda foresaw the metamorphosis of Holy Russia into an atheistic Soviet Russia. While the Bolsheviks ultimately attacked all religions and denominations with devastating effect, their main thrust was directed against the Russian Orthodox Church, which was still a vital force in Russian culture. As the established church, Orthodoxy claimed close to 100 million believers, over 40,000 functioning parish churches, and well over 100,000 parish clergy. The Orthodox hierarchy in 1917 consisted of 130 bishops presiding over 67 dioceses. More than a thousand monasteries and nunneries dotted the landscape.[1]

In the months immediately after the Revolution, the regime revoked the laws granting the Church a privileged position in the Russian Empire (some steps in this direction had been taken earlier by the Provisional Government), seized the Church's property, and for all intents and purposes prohibited religious education outside the home. Leading clergymen were imprisoned and killed during the campaign to "separate" Church and State and as a consequence of the Civil War (1918–1921).[2] Although

[1] Dimitry V. Pospielovsky, *The Russian Church under the Soviet Regime, 1917–1982* (Crestwood, N.Y.: St. Vladimir's Seminary Press, 1984), 20.
[2] For accounts of Bolshevik depredations against the Church, see Olga Vasil'eva, "Russkaia pravoslavnaia tserkov' i sovetskaia vlast' v 1917–1927 godakh," *Voprosy istorii*, 1993, no. 8:

1

the State security and administrative organs decimated the Orthodox Church and its clergy, these measures failed to eradicate popular Orthodox belief and practice, and this situation ultimately compelled the Communist Party leadership to launch a broadly based propaganda campaign against religion. Created in 1925, the League of the Militant Godless was the nominally independent organization established by the Communist Party to promote atheism.

By all outward appearances, the League seemed to succeed in its mission. In 1932, seven years after its creation, the League claimed 5.5 million members, 2 million more than the Communist Party itself.[3] The League's Central Council in Moscow published its own newspaper, *Bezbozhnik* (The Godless), several other Russian-language journals, and propaganda materials in many other languages of the Soviet Union. Antireligious pamphlets and posters were printed in large numbers. The League's far-flung network of cells and councils sponsored lectures, organized demonstrations, and actively propagandized against religious observance. Leading Bolshevik figures gave speeches at the League's national congress in 1929, at which the League officially became "Militant." The Communist Party, the Komsomol, the trade unions, the Red Army, and Soviet schools all conducted antireligious propaganda, but the League was the organizational centerpiece of this effort to bring atheism to the masses. By its size and its visibility, the League appeared to be motivating one of the most dramatic aspects of the "cultural revolution" promised by the Bolsheviks.

Despite the League's high profile and dramatic mandate, it has been accorded surprisingly little attention in the historical literature. That which exists is firmly rooted in the *kto kogo* (who prevails over whom) discourse that has dominated the discussion of religion in both the West and Russia. Soviet-era accounts are tendentious, accepting the rise of the League as a direct measure of atheism's increasing popularity, and depicting the League as an unmediated manifestation of effective Communist Party leadership and of the application of Bolshevik ideology. These accounts accept without question that a nationwide network of cells and councils was the appropriate and indeed the only means to achieve a broad secularization of society. Almost all of these works rely on central sources and do not consider the League's local functioning. Religion is treated nar-

---

40–55; V. A. Alekseev, *Shturm nebes otmeniaetsia?* (Moscow: Rossiia Molodaia, 1992) and *Illiuzii i dogmy* (Moscow: Politicheskoi Literatury, 1991); M. I. Odintsov, *Gosudarstvo i tserkov' (Istoriia vzaimootnoshenii, 1917–1938)* (Moscow: Znanie, 1991).

[3] Leonard Schapiro, *The Communist Party of the Soviet Union*, 2d ed., rev. and enl. (New York: Random House, 1970), 439. The Communist Party figure includes candidate members.

rowly, as an exploitative force and as the product of ignorance, and religious leaders in these accounts are plotting counterrevolutionaries. Similarly, the believing population is waiting to be enlightened by the Party and the State.[4] Post-Soviet Russian accounts have remained within an equally narrow but opposite framework, now committed to chronicling the regime's harsh assault on religion and basking in revelations from newly opened archives, such as Lenin's bloodthirsty letter ordering the arrest and execution of clergy in the town of Shuia in 1922. (This episode is discussed in Chapter 1.)[5] While some of this new scholarship, such as V. A. Alekseev's *Shturm nebes otmeniaetsia?* offers increasingly sophisticated analyses of the institutional politics of the time, post-Soviet Russian scholars are still at the stage of providing basic narratives of Church–State relations in the Soviet period and the regime's antireligious campaigns.

Until recently, Western historians of religion in Soviet Russia shared a limited agenda, detailing the assault on religion and portraying the victims, their suffering, and the resilience of their faith.[6] Scholars who have described the antireligious campaign usually mention the League, if only in passing, as part of the apparatus of persecution.[7] The exception among Western scholars was John Shelton Curtiss, who wrote after World War II and seemed highly sympathetic to an organized effort to counter religion. Curtiss openly lauded Soviet antireligious efforts and indicted the Orthodox Church whenever possible.[8] Relying on newspapers and other published accounts, Curtiss accepted Soviet statements about the activity of churchmen and implied that the regime had achieved its goals. Curtiss's ideological engagement and limited source base undermined his effort to provide a thorough account not only of religion in Soviet Russia but also of the League's role in that history.

Several institutional studies of the Soviet polity in the 1920s and 1930s have also briefly mentioned the League. In his classic account, Merle

---

[4] See, for example, G. V. Vorontsov, *Leninskaia programma ateisticheskogo vospitaniia v deistvii* (Leningrad: Leningradskii Gosudarstvennyi Universitet, 1973); V. N. Konovalov, "Soiuz voinstvuiushchikh bezbozhnikov," *Voprosy nauchnogo ateizma* 4 (1967): 63–93.

[5] For example, O. Iu. Vasilieva, "Russkaia pravoslavnaia tserkov' v 1927–1943 godakh," *Voprosy istorii*, 1994, no. 4, 35–46, and her "Russkaia pravoslavnaia tserkov' i sovetskaia vlast'"; Alekseev, *Illiuzii i dogmy*; Odintsov, *Gosudarstvo i tserkov'*; *Izvestiia TsK KPSS*, 1990, no. 4, 190–195.

[6] Pospielovsky, *Russian Church*; William C. Fletcher, *The Russian Church Underground, 1917–1970* (London: Oxford University Press, 1970). Dedicated to recounting the "magnificent resistance" of believers," Nicholas Timasheff's contemporary account, *Religion in Soviet Russia, 1917–1942* (New York: Sheed & Ward, 1942), remains a valuable analytical source.

[7] For example, Dimitry V. Pospielovsky, *A History of Soviet Atheism in Theory and Practice, and the Believer*, 3 vols. (New York: St. Martin's Press, 1987–1988).

[8] John Shelton Curtiss, *The Russian Church and the Soviet State* (Boston: Little, Brown, 1953).

Fainsod provided a partial account of the League's operations in Smolensk, and although he questioned its efficacy, Fainsod presented the League in the context of a totalitarian regime that successfully controlled and manipulated its citizens.[9] In a narrowly focused article, Joan Delaney linked an early conflict within the antireligious apparatus to high-level politics in the mid-1920s.[10] More recent Western scholarship has considered the antireligious campaign as part of the efforts in the 1920s to construct a new culture, but these treatments have not focused on the League.[11]

In view of the substantial lacunae in the existing scholarship, the first goal of this book is to provide a comprehensive account of the League. The opening of Party and State archives in Moscow and the provinces offers unparalleled opportunities to explore the League's local history and to consider many of the unanswered questions about an organization that contributed to perhaps the most dramatic period in twentieth-century Russian history. Beyond the League's impressive membership numbers and its well-developed publishing empire, the history of the institution remains virtually unknown. Uncovering its membership, its organization, and the functioning of its local councils is a high priority here. While drawing on materials involving the entire RSFSR, I focus on the League outposts in the industrial city of Iaroslavl' and the small town of Pskov to provide a range of contexts in which to consider the League's activities and challenges: large city and small town, rural agricultural-based community and urban industrial community, near center and definite periphery, but both overwhelmingly Russian and Orthodox.[12]

---

[9] Merle Fainsod, *Smolensk under Soviet Rule* (Cambridge: Harvard University Press, 1958), 430–444. Walter Kolarz, *Religion in the Soviet Union* (London: Macmillan, 1961), 6–15, also noted the League's failures, but looked no further than the assumed lack of appeal of atheism to explain them. Timasheff's *Religion in Soviet Russia*, 95–110, outlined the League's basic ineptitude.

[10] Joan Delaney, "The Origins of Soviet Antireligious Organizations," in *Aspects of Religion in the Soviet Union, 1917–1967*, ed. Richard Marshall Jr. (Chicago: University of Chicago Press, 1971), 103–130.

[11] Stefan Plaggenborg, "Volksreligiosität und antireligiöse Propaganda in der frühen Sowjetunion," *Arkhiv für Sozialgeschichte* 26 (1992): 95–130; Isabel Tirado, "The Revolution, Young Peasants, and the Komsomol's Antireligious Campaigns (1920–1928)," *Canadian-American Slavic Studies* 26, nos. 1–3 (1992): 97–117; Richard Stites, *Revolutionary Dreams: Utopian Vision and Experimental Life in the Russian Revolution* (New York: Oxford University Press, 1989). Glennys Young, in *Power and the Sacred in Revolutionary Russia: Religious Activists in the Village* (University Park: Penn State University Press, 1997), has sought to chronicle the Orthodox population's response to and engagement in the regime's effort to reconstruct the countryside.

[12] This book focuses on the Orthodox Church as the "majority" problem from the Bolshevik perspective, and includes sectarians where appropriate. As for the Jewish, Muslim,

The League's own institutional history, however, is only part of the story. The League occupied a front-rank position in the government-orchestrated effort to secularize Russia, but existing accounts provide inadequate insight into what the League actually did. Beyond the requisite sensational and cursory examples, there has been little analysis of the antireligious propaganda produced and distributed by the League. Through its changing forms and emphases, this propaganda broadly illuminated both the idea of atheism as it was understood by its promoters and the regime's vision of a society in the making in the 1920s and 1930s. Although atheism occupied an important place in this self-identity, it had to compete with many other agendas and organizations for symbolic prominence and material support. Atheism's position in the Bolshevik leadership's complicated propaganda agenda changed frequently, and being a "Godless" person was just one of numerous identities promoted in the 1920s and 1930s during construction of the oft-proclaimed New Soviet Man.

In addition to illuminating the regime's internal priorities, the League's history permits reconsideration of the "secularization" process long presumed to have accompanied "modernization" in European history. Secularization here signifies the rejection by increasing numbers of the population of specific beliefs in the transcendent and supernatural, and of the rituals, institutions, and personnel traditionally associated with those beliefs. Although the secularization thesis has come under fire from many quarters,[13] the Bolshevik Revolution and the subsequent reconfiguration of Russian society surely count as one of the great clashes of "modernity" and religion in European history. Whereas the terms of this debate are often abstract and ahistorical, study of the League provides a specific historical context in which to explore this issue.

How did secularization in Soviet Russia differ from the process as it unfolded in Western Europe (and North America)? With the short-lived exception of the French Revolution, programmatic secularization in Western Europe usually took mild forms amounting to an increasing distance between Church and State, most recently in France in 1905. Attempts to go further, such as Bismarck's *Kulturkampf* and the genteel free thought of the English National Secular Society under Charles Bradlaugh, stopped

---

Protestant, and Uniate populations, they and, more important, their social contexts differed sufficiently from the Orthodox case to warrant separate treatment.

[13] For an introduction to this voluminous literature, see Steve Bruce, ed., *Religion and Modernization: Sociologists and Historians Debate the Secularization Thesis* (Oxford: Clarendon, 1992).

well short of what later occurred in Russia.[14] Secularization in nineteenth- and early twentieth-century Western Europe is generally associated with urbanization, industrialization, and the spread of education. These were processes with indirect consequences for religion, rather than direct attacks on it. Although working-class hostility to religion became increasingly organized, especially in Germany, in the late nineteenth and early twentieth centuries, it did not acquire a separate organizational identity until 1925, when the International of Proletarian Freethinkers was created. Even then, the all but complete subordination of this organization's work to Comintern and intra-German politics limited its usefulness as a model for social engineering.[15]

In Russia, by contrast, secularization appeared late, hit hard, and came from the State itself. Having legally separated Church and State immediately after taking power, the Bolsheviks later embarked on a program of mass social engineering. The State closed churches, arrested priests, and forbade religious activities; it subjected the Soviet public to virulently atheistic propaganda on the streets and in the workplace. Perhaps the experience closest to Russia's was not in Europe but in similarly underdeveloped Mexico, where the revolutionary elite married coercion to mass indoctrination in the early 1930s.[16] In Soviet Russia, however, the regime's antireligious efforts complemented the effects of rapid industrialization, urbanization, and collectivization of agriculture beginning in the late 1920s.

Measuring the impact of these policies poses challenges. We need to distinguish between institutional religion and private religious beliefs and practices (which in Russia extended well beyond the churchyard gates).[17] The regime was clearly effective in limiting the activities of the first; assessing its impact on the second is far more problematic. Another distinction to keep in mind is the transformation of Orthodoxy that occurred in this period, no doubt traceable in part to persecution by the regime. For

[14] Suzanne Desan, *Reclaiming the Sacred: Lay Religion and Popular Politics in Revolutionary France* (Ithaca: Cornell University Press, 1990); Edward Royle, *Radicals, Secularists, and Republicans: Popular Freethought in Britain, 1866–1915* (Manchester: Manchester University Press, 1980); Albrecht Langner, ed., *Säkularisation und Säkularisierung im 19. Jahrhundert* (Munich: Paderborn, 1978).

[15] Jochen-Christoph Kaiser, *Arbeiterbewegung und organisierte Religionskritik: Proletarische Freidenkerverbände in Kaiserreich und Weimarer Republik* (Stuttgart: Klett-Cotta, 1981).

[16] Adrian A. Bantjes, "Idolatry and Iconoclasm in Revolutionary Mexico: The De-Christianization Campaigns, 1929–1940," *Mexican Studies/Estudios Mexicanos* 13, no. 1 (Winter 1997): 1–24.

[17] Moshe Lewin, "Popular Religion in Twentieth-Century Russia," in *The Making of the Soviet System: Essays in the Social History of Interwar Russia* (London: Methuen, 1985), 57–71.

instance, various Protestant sectarian groups flourished in the 1920s.[18] Orthodoxy itself was transformed; for a short time there was even a schismatic Renovationist or "red" church.[19] Numerous Orthodox believers continued their religious activity underground.[20] Other believers adopted a variety of strategies in response to the new conditions.[21] More generally, there is little way to trace the transformation of individual attitudes, given the highly subjective nature of religion and atheism and the politically charged atmosphere surrounding these associations in the 1920s and 1930s. Orthodoxy, including its many noncanonical elements, covered such a broad swath that often there was no clear line between the sacred and the profane,[22] and the categories of "atheist" and "believer" were imposed from without (if later internalized). These polarizations were useful for accounting purposes, but they did not necessarily describe how people actually behaved and thought.

If any secularization can be posited, it is equally difficult to determine which aspect of the regime's pressure on religion was responsible. Was it the persecution of believers, the arrest of clergy, and the closure of churches by the State? Was it the secular education in the schools, or indoctrination activity in the Red Army? Did responsibility lie with the League and the other institutions (the Party, the trade unions, the Komsomol) engaged in explicit antireligious propaganda? To the extent that secularization occurred, may it have stemmed not from the regime's antireligious efforts but from the dramatic social changes associated with forced modernization, the demographic upheaval of the First Five-Year Plan, the creation of new cities without churches, and the many other innovations that attended Soviet rule? A further methodological challenge arises when we consider that a possibly unique combination of such factors came into play for each individual. An important first step toward answers to these

[18] Aleksandr Etkind, "Russkie seky i sovetskii kommunism: Proekt Vladimira Bonch-Bruevicha," *Minuvshee: Istoricheskii al'manakh* 19 (1996): 275–319; Andrew Q. Blane, "The Protestant Sectarians," in Marshall, *Aspects of Religion;* A. I. Klibanov, *Religioznoe sektantstvo i sovremennost'* (Moscow: Nauka, 1969), 188–258; Kolarz, *Religion in the Soviet Union,* 286–298, 346–371.

[19] Edward E. Roslof, "The Renovationist Movement in the Russian Orthodox Church, 1922–1946," Ph.D. diss., University of North Carolina–Chapel Hill, 1994.

[20] For example, M. V. Shkarovskii, "Istinno-Pravoslavnye v Voronezhskoi Eparkhii," *Minuvshee: Istoricheskii al'manakh* 19 (1996): 320–358. For a general overview, see Fletcher, *Russian Church Underground.*

[21] Sheila Fitzpatrick, *Stalin's Peasants: Resistance and Survival in the Russian Village after Collectivization* (New York: Oxford University Press, 1994), 204–214, and Young, *Power and the Sacred.*

[22] Mircea Eliade, *The Sacred and the Profane: The Nature of Religion* (New York: Harcourt, Brace, 1961).

questions is to understand the mechanisms adopted by the regime to promote atheism.

Perhaps the most significant subjective factor in the Russian case concerns how atheism would be measured. Would it be simply by falling church attendance, closed churches, or active manifestations of atheism by the population? It is my belief that *how* the regime articulated this fundamentally vague goal profoundly shaped the nature of the resulting "Soviet atheism" in practice. There was a great distance between the intellectual atheism of Lenin or Trotsky and the bureaucratized version that filtered into local contexts.[23] This latter version amounted to a substantially form-bound construct—antireligion—that corresponded to certain basic presumptions and underlying commonalities in Bolshevik political culture in the 1920s and 1930s. In Bolshevik political culture, manifestations of a change in worldview were not left primarily to the believer (or nonbeliever), but had to be expressed and administered in bureaucratic forms such as the League. This culture equated the spread of atheism with the League's establishment of a quantifiable network of cells and councils, regardless of their level of activity. The creation of the League itself reflected an important component of Bolshevik political culture: unorganized sentiment was not acknowledged to exist. Because social transformation was defined in organizational terms, atheism was perceived to be flourishing only if the League prospered. For the individual, atheism and membership in the League were presumed to be the same.

Did secularization really require a separate institutional framework such as the League that would define, execute, and measure this transformation? There was certainly nothing inherently Marxist about having an organization to serve as evidence of atheism's success. Moreover, detailed examination of the League's operations in the provinces casts serious doubt on the efficacy of the League's network as an agent or reflection of social change. Throughout the country, local cells and councils of the Godless were founded, lapsed into desuetude, and were recreated when the next organizational wave struck. Membership usually amounted to little more than a name on a list. Ultimately, the organized form of atheism had substituted for genuine cultural change. Although fragmentary on this issue of the League's popular standing, archival materials limn a picture of a League dimly viewed by the Soviet population. A League of five million

[23] For examples of how ideology is transformed as it progresses from supposed author to presumed audience, see Desan, *Reclaiming the Sacred*; William Sheridan Allen, *The Nazi Seizure of Power: The Experience of a Single German Town, 1922–1945*, rev. ed. (New York: Franklin Watts, 1984); and David L. Hoffmann, *Peasant Metropolis: Social Identities in Moscow, 1929–1941* (Ithaca: Cornell University Press, 1994).

members served as evidence of the regime's success, but in fact it was largely a house of cards—a nationwide Potemkin village of atheism.[24]

While the Party and other institutions passed numerous resolutions in favor of the League and antireligious propaganda, these plans were rarely fulfilled to the letter or even in spirit. The League suffered tremendously from irregular support by its patron, the Communist Party, as well as tepid backing punctuated by occasional outright hostility from the Komsomol, unions, and educational authorities. When prompted, these institutions produced a cascade of insincere, unrealizable, and regularly ignored resolutions in favor of the League that fostered a rhetoric of social change well ahead of actual conditions. While acknowledging the need for antireligious work, these institutions usually pursued their own narrower agendas, all the while paying obeisance to "cultural revolution" and adhering to the Party line. In many cases, their contributions amounted to blaming one another for lapses in vigilance.

Because the League's goal of a broad and deep organizational network assumed the presence of large numbers of trained, competent cadres, the regime's chronic inability to meet this expectation became a defining characteristic of the League's history. The cadre problem lay at the heart of the League's organizational inconsistency and its endless campaigns. The available activists were of uncertain quality, most were poorly educated, and many did not even understand the ideology motivating their cause. Their actual behavior—often brutal, destructive, and counterproductive—was usually at odds with the stated purposes of the League and the explicit directives emanating from Moscow. The presence of so few women in the antireligious camp also posed obstacles when women were identified as the main carriers of religious belief. Under these conditions, the greatest challenge for the Godless was to put their own house in order, and the press and archival evidence indicates a continuous hectoring and cajoling of activists.

Mirroring the Bolshevik approach to social modernization and directly reflecting the League's organizational inconstancy, League propaganda shifted rapidly from one campaign to another. There was little everyday work, just campaigns strung together. Although containing the general outlines of a secular culture, League propaganda was mostly a negative assault on religion rather than an assertion of atheism. It focused on the outward manifestations of religion—clergy, churches, holidays—and largely ignored its subjective and emotional appeal. Moreover, much of

---

[24] Fitzpatrick also uses the idea of Potemkinism to describe the official view of the collectivized countryside in the 1930s in, *Stalin's Peasants*, 16–18.

this propaganda had nothing to do with religion or atheism. To justify its existence, the League participated in every major and minor campaign of the regime: collecting money for tanks and aircraft, hawking government bonds, promoting industrialization, and engaging in other actions that were distant from the League's purpose and for which it was ill suited.

Antireligion represented a bureaucratic, internal discourse, structured by a closed circle of rhetoric, organizational formalism, and institutional conflict. By the time it reached the propagandists in Iaroslavl' and Pskov, Soviet "atheism" had become this bureaucratic condition. Antireligion of course varied in its application from place to place and over time, but the Potemkinism in regard to social transformation remained widespread. Antireligion was markedly different from secularization, a process that, if it occurred, did not proceed directly from the League, the organization created specifically to promote atheism. In fact, the League tells us little directly about the workers' or the peasants' attitudes toward religion, though much can be inferred from the poor reception accorded the League and the substantial resistance that the regime encountered when it closed churches. The "propaganda state" described by Peter Kenez produced reams of printed materials in Moscow and an unceasing torrent of directives to the localities, but the efficacy of this official discourse was substantially less than its volume, and the entire effort was transformed by the bureaucratic understanding and execution of the task at hand.[25]

However bureaucratically laden and empty the official promotion of atheism, the regime's antireligious stance was not a mere formality. With only temporary respites, the Soviet regime attacked religion ruthlessly in the cities and later with even greater intensity in the countryside. These persecutions were the obverse of official Soviet atheism—the League was founded after direct confrontation with religion in the early 1920s had failed—but the link between the League itself and the direct persecution of Orthodoxy was tenuous. Indeed, the regime's failure to spread "atheism" through the League (granted, in unrealistically rapid plans and in extreme forms) was so undeniable that it quickly returned to purely "administrative measures" in the late 1920s to close churches and force clergy from their parishes. The League's explicit purpose was to persuade the population to demand the closure of churches. This project rarely proceeded as planned, and as a result, church closings were far from the smooth process envisioned in Soviet legislation and Party plans. The population widely re-

[25] Peter Kenez, *The Birth of the Propaganda State* (Cambridge: Cambridge University Press, 1985).

sisted these efforts, and in this actual conflict of church and state the League was rarely seen as a direct participant.

Because the conception of antireligion relies heavily on ideas of bureaucracy and political culture, let me briefly define these terms as I use them here. "Bureaucracy" is used here descriptively, as the series of offices, procedures, and positions through which complex organizations are administered. The original notion of the term—rule by individuals sitting behind cloth-covered desks in eighteenth-century France—retains some salience; the position precedes the individual, and this form of administration is closely associated with the emergence of impersonal rule in "modern" governments. It is characterized by explicitly defined rights and duties for officials, and an equally explicit hierarchical system of political and administrative offices.[26]

While the Soviet regime's bureaucracy was one of the weapons employed against the Orthodox Church, the bureaucracy extended to social relations, and had a particular impact on the execution of Bolshevik cultural plans.[27] The Bolsheviks' efforts to modernize society rapidly and by force necessarily required a large body of activists and the appropriate administrative apparatus to oversee this task. Indeed, the very forms I characterize as often empty conventions were hailed by the Bolsheviks as achievements necessary for the realization of a socialist society. Bolshevik modernity was heavily and self-consciously bureaucratic. But the question remains: How much administration is too much? However positive a virtue bureaucracy was for Bolshevik planners, and however natural a concomitant to most large governmental projects, it is not an environment conducive to social revolution. At what point did the means of promoting social transformation interfere with and limit actual change?

As for "political culture," it denotes the often unstated assumptions and methods of interaction that structure political activity. It refers as much to *how* things occurred in the political arena as what occurred, and it includes the rhetorical and administrative conventions that in the information age

[26] Michel Crozier, *The Bureaucratic Phenomenon* (Chicago: University of Chicago Press, 1964); Reinhard Bendix, "Bureaucracy," in *International Encyclopedia of the Social Sciences*, ed. David L. Sills, vol. 2 (New York: Macmillan, 1968), 206–217. Current pejorative definitions, including those specifically associated with the emergence of a ruling elite in communist societies, will not be directly employed here, though they lurk in the background.

[27] William Odom, *The Soviet Volunteers: Modernization and Bureaucracy in a Public Mass Organization* (Princeton: Princeton University Press, 1973), is the only study to consider seriously the interaction of bureaucracy and social mobilization in early Soviet history.

can be described as the "default" settings for political activity. In Lynn Hunt's examination of the French Revolution, it is "the common values and shared expectations of behavior."[28] Superficial elements of the political process may change rapidly; political culture (like culture generally) evolves much more slowly. While this usage presumes the existence of an underlying political culture, it is not intended to designate a singular and unchanging entity. It is instead the varied and evolving practices and conventions that constitute an interpretive context for Soviet history in the 1920s and 1930s.[29] This particular application of Bolshevik political culture focuses on social transformation. The Bolsheviks took power in 1917 promising to remake Russian society into a socialist utopia. Given the centrality of this task, Bolshevik political culture encompasses the often unstated assumptions about the definition, execution, and measurement of such change, as well as the language in which it is expressed.

Defining political culture in this manner and using the League to access it allow us to sidestep some of the more prominent pitfalls associated with limning political cultures in modern Eastern Europe and Russia. The troubling distinction between behavior and attitudes and the inability to assess attitudes objectively when compulsion limits open political behavior are less relevant here because our main focus is on the apparatus of ideology promotion itself. The League's archival and published records lay bare the process by which supposedly canonical stances were transformed as they were transmitted from agency to agency and to the population. Although these materials must be used with care, they are rich veins for exploration of local procedures, language, and practices that reveal the tension between the "official" form of Soviet atheism and its realization locally. David Hoffmann has stressed how official culture was transformed as it was received and understood by its intended Muscovite audience;[30] local concerns also proved as powerful as central ideological dictates in Smolensk in the 1920s.[31] Soviet atheism clearly meant something far different outside the rarefied realm of Bolshevik intellectuals in Moscow than it did within the Kremlin's walls. Study of the League also makes it obvious that in a polity as large as Soviet Russia, the official political culture of

---

[28] Lynn Hunt, *Politics, Culture, and Class in the French Revolution* (Berkeley: University of California Press, 1984), 10.

[29] Among the few scholars who have cast their research in this perspective are Moshe Lewin, *The Making of the Soviet System: Essays in the Social History of Interwar Russia* (London: Methuen, 1985), and Mark von Hagen, *Soldiers in the Proletarian Dictatorship: The Red Army and the Soviet Socialist State, 1917–1930* (Ithaca: Cornell University Press, 1990).

[30] Hoffmann, *Peasant Metropolis*.

[31] William G. Rosenberg, "Smolensk in the 1920s: Party-Worker Relations and the 'Vanguard' Problem," *Russian Review* 36, no. 2 (April 1977): 127–150.

atheism through the 1920s remained multifaceted and far from unanimous at the points of production.

As an institution and as the Bolshevik version of secularization, the League offers insight into the politics of social transformation during three distinct periods: the New Economic Policy (NEP, 1921–1928), the First Five-Year Plan and its concomitant "cultural revolution" (1928–1932), and the prewar period of High Stalinism (1937–1941). Examining the League at these three very different stages permits us to trace the enduring characteristics of Bolshevik political culture against the backdrop of the highly dramatic changes occurring in Soviet society. The League was founded at the high point of the NEP, and although the League in part reflected the utopianism characteristic of NEP cultural and social policies, this utopianism was the work of limited numbers of interested intellectuals and the occasional local zealot. The League's history demonstrates the divisions in the mid-1920s among bureaucratic groups over ideology, the leadership of the antireligious campaign, and its practical application. Utopia in practice looked a great deal like traditional bureaucratic infighting. These divisions in turn reflected fundamental uncertainties throughout the Party over its goals and relationship with society.[32] The disjuncture between the League's radical goals and Party backing on the one hand and its nominal status as an independent volunteer society on the other casts doubt on the stability of the NEP order that produced such an arrangement. The League's very existence suggested ideological continuity—a bridge between the periods of revolutionary intensity. Ironically, despite its threatening-sounding name, the League (at least at the higher levels) generally adhered to a go-slow policy that conflicted with the impulses of both the Civil War and Cultural Revolution periods.

The League experienced its greatest growth during the years of the First Five-Year Plan and the so-called Cultural Revolution. With its aggressive agenda the League seemed to reflect the spirit of the times, that of an impatient younger generation motivated to fulfill the promises of the Revolution.[33] The Cultural Revolution should have been the League's heyday, but there was a basic contradiction between the upheaval of those times and the League's organizational ethos. The League was a NEP-vintage organization, bureaucratically top-heavy, that measured social change by the activities of its rigidly organized network. As a result, the League was vulnerable to the dramatic social and demographic upheaval that began in

[32] These questions are raised more broadly in Lewis Siegelbaum, *Soviet State and Society between Revolutions, 1918–1929* (Cambridge: Cambridge University Press, 1992).
[33] See Sheila Fitzpatrick, *The Cultural Front: Power and Culture in Revolutionary Russia* (Ithaca: Cornell University Press, 1992).

the late 1920s. The rapid, uncontrolled growth of the League in this period actually reflected the League's institutional weakness, for it resulted from mass conscription rather than genuine social change. This method not only did not reflect secularization, it simply did not work well. By 1933, when some order began to return to Soviet society, the League was in shambles and receding quickly. The League's experience suggests that we need to exercise great care when we are tempted to consider a bureaucracy such as the League as evidence of a radical cultural transformation.

Having declined rapidly in the early 1930s, the League briefly reappeared at the end of the decade, seemingly reanimated by the Great Terror. In comparison with its earlier existence, the League was nearly a phantom organization, recalled from the dead for its putative ideological vigilance. Yet the task of cultural transformation was absent from this period, despite abundant evidence in 1936 and 1937 that many Russians still clung to their religious beliefs. In its relationships with other institutions, however, the League's return suggested important continuities from the mid-1920s to the late 1930s in forms of expression and in the manner of institutional interaction, though the superficial discourse (as well as the stakes) was quite different. The League was even less visible in the suppression of religion now than it had been from 1928 to 1932. There was little pretense that the government was spreading atheism; this was the exercise of naked power.

Through three distinct phases over sixteen years, the League's history suggests underlying continuities in Bolshevik political culture, a distinct posturing in regard to the challenges facing the regime, and a likelihood of adopting certain strategies in response. Beyond relying on external, form-oriented manifestations of the regime's activity, this culture was characterized by a high degree of institutional and linguistic conflict in the contest over ideology and, more important, resources.[34] In this light, the "Great Turn" (*Velikii perelom*) of 1929 was less of a watershed in Soviet history than has been assumed. Although what happened in 1929 was indeed a dramatic change, *how* it happened was quite familiar. The approaches to problems and the rhetoric changed little, if at all. The continuities in the application of ideology, rather than the ideology itself in the hands of Lenin or Stalin, proved crucial because of the degree to which "official" ideologies in Moscow were completely transmuted by the many layers of competing bureaucratic forces charged with presenting them to the popu-

[34] For evidence of this culture at work in higher education, see Michael Fox, "Political Culture, Purges, and Proletarianization at the Institute of Red Professors, 1921–1929," *Russian Review* 52, no. 1 (January 1993): 20–42.

lation. It would be misleading to suggest that ideology "moved" in only one direction; knowledge of both the shortcomings of the regime's cadres and the resilience of popular religion influenced the makers of official culture at the center. The focus here is on the process of presentation. In this practice, the tremendous gap between the regime's goal of militant atheism, however it may have been understood, and the regime's ability to achieve that goal given its limited resources and the inherited Orthodox culture was vitally important. Roger Pethybridge's formulation of this problem captures the challenges facing the regime: "large-scale theories versus small-scale realities."[35] Although Pethybridge used this model to explain the emergence of the Stalinist political system, it also describes how form overwhelmed function in the narrower promotion of atheism. Similar bureaucratic obstacles were encountered in other social realms as the promises of 1917 gave way to institutionalized interests and bureaucratic conflicts.[36] By the mid-1930s, some of the Revolution's promises had been fulfilled, but much more remained undone. Instead of heaven on earth, denizens of the Soviet Union were left with a wasteful and brutal example of authoritarian modernization.

Much of the administrative material presented in this book is drawn from Iaroslavl' and Pskov provinces. The 1897 census recorded Iaroslavl' Province's population as 1,071,355, of whom only 146,310 were considered urban. The population of Iaroslavl' itself—250 kilometers northeast of Moscow—was 71,616, including suburbs.[37] Iaroslavl' grew rapidly in the early twentieth century, to 125,194 inhabitants by 1917. After declining as a result of the Civil War, Iaroslavl''s population stood at 114,282 in 1926, and rose to 134,407 in 1929.[38] Considered a part of the Russian industrial heartland, Iaroslavl' was the location of a key railroad junction and the home of significant industry, including the Bol'shaia Manufaktura textile works across the Kotrosl' River, which became the Krasnyi Perekop complex in the Soviet period. The city also had a tobacco plant employing

---

[35] Roger Pethybridge, *The Social Prelude of Stalinism* (New York: St. Martin's Press, 1974).

[36] Hugh D. Hudson Jr., *Blueprints and Blood: The Stalinization of Soviet Architecture, 1917–1937* (Princeton: Princeton University Press, 1994); Wendy Z. Goldman, *Women, the State, and Revolution* (Cambridge: Cambridge University Press, 1993); Larry Holmes, *The Kremlin and the Schoolhouse* (Bloomington: Indiana University Press, 1991); Christopher Read, *Culture and Power in Revolutionary Russia: The Intelligentsia and the Transition from Tsarism to Communism* (New York: St. Martin's Press, 1990); Stites, *Revolutionary Dreams*.

[37] F. A. Brokgauz and I. A. Efron, eds., *Entsiklopedicheskii slovar'*, 41 vols. (St. Petersburg: Brokgavz & Efron, 1890–1904, 1911–16), 41:817, 819, 824.

[38] *Bol'shaia sovetskaia entsiklopediia*, 65 vols. (Moscow, 1926–47), 65:771.

940 workers, a chemical works with 440 employees, and a match factory with 350 laborers.[39] By 1929, 30,204 industrial laborers worked in Iaroslavl', with 12,000 employed at Krasnyi Perekop alone.[40] Construction of the large Resino-Asbestos Kompleks (RAK) began in 1929 on the north side of the city and was completed in 1932.

Literacy in Iaroslavl' Province was relatively high by the turn of the century. For the urban population, the reported literacy rate in 1897 was 54.3 percent—65 percent for males and 43 percent for females. Rural literacy stood at 50 percent and 22 percent, respectively. These rates placed the province fourth overall in European Russia.[41] At the turn of the century, there were 23 monasteries in the province and 841 parishes. More than 1,500 churches dotted the landscape, 70 in the town of Iaroslavl' alone, which was the seat of the archbishop and was known for its seventeenth-century ecclesiastical architecture.[42] In 1918, in response to an uprising in Iaroslavl', Bolshevik forces surrounded the city and shelled it. Most of the churches in the town's center were damaged or destroyed.

Unlike Iaroslavl', Pskov entered the twentieth century as a sleepy provincial town whose greatest years in the medieval period were but a distant memory. Two hundred and fifty kilometers southwest of St. Petersburg in the marshes near Estonia, the province had a population of 1,425,000 in 1914. Only 6.5 percent (92,625) lived in towns. On the eve of the war, Pskov had 34,100 residents and 2,000 "industrial" workers.[43] After dropping during the Civil War, the province's population grew by 1926 to 1,674,000, with 8 percent (134,192) categorized as urban.[44] The city's population in 1939 was 59,900.[45]

The Pskov region's economy was based on the production of flax, and there were only a few industrial enterprises in the town itself. The Metallist factory, originally opened in 1897, made farm machinery. The Proletariat tannery also dated from the late nineteenth century and had been operated by Belgians in the early twentieth. The Shpagat factory produced twine, and the Uritskii mill processed lumber.[46] Pskov's relatively undevel-

[39] *Entsiklopedicheskii slovar'*, 41: 818.

[40] *Bol'shaia sovetskaia entsiklopediia*, 65:772.

[41] *Entsiklopedicheskii slovar'*, 41: 827; *Pervaia vseobshchaia perepis' naseleniia rossiiskoi imperii, 1897*, vol. 50, *Iaroslavskaia guberniia* (St. Petersburg, 1904), 1.

[42] *Entsiklopedicheskii slovar'*, 41: 817, 827.

[43] *Pskovskii krai v istorii SSSR* (Pskov: Lenizdat, 1970), 177; *Entsiklopedicheskii slovar'*, 25: 698, 707.

[44] *Pskovskii krai v istorii SSSR*, 247. See also *Pskovskii nabat*, 19 November 1920, and *Pskov: Ocherki istorii* (Pskov: Lenizdat: 1990), 218.

[45] *Bol'shaia sovetskaia entsiklopediia*, 20:588.

[46] *Pskovskii krai v istorii SSSR*, 251; *Pskov: Ocherki istorii*, 219.

oped status was indicated as well by one of the lowest literacy rates in Europ鈥俷 Russia. At the turn of the century, only 14.6 percent (50.4 percent in the towns; 12.1 percent in the countryside) of the total population were recorded as literate.[47] Pskov Province encompassed 361 parishes, more than 500 churches, and 12 monasteries and convents, including the famous Mirozhskii Monastery, dating from the thirteenth century.[48] Immediately before the League's appearance in the town, Pskov's Bishop Varlaam (Riashentsev) and twenty other clergy and laity were arrested and charged with arranging the "fraudulent renovation" of icons. Popular belief held that tarnished icons could miraculously regain their luster, and after the Revolution, the Bolsheviks charged church leaders with having staged various renovations. The accused were tried in December 1924, and several, including Varlaam, were sent to prison.[49]

This book first establishes the central context for the development of antireligious policy and propaganda. Chapter 1 follows the regime's changing policies toward religion in the years before the League's founding and assesses the legacy of this period for the League. Chapter 2 presents an overview of the Communist Party's antireligious propaganda apparatus, including the creation of the League itself. Chapters 3 and 4 examine the League's printed propaganda to illuminate the regime's official culture of atheism.

I then turn to the League's local operations, mostly in Iaroslavl' and Pskov, to explore how the regime's official message of atheism was actually manifested in practice—that is, the League's real story. Chapters 5 through 7 track the bureaucratization of the antireligious campaign in Iaroslavl' and Pskov between 1926 and 1933. Organized thematically, these chapters emphasize the introspective, form-oriented elements of the antireligious campaign, and particularly the continuity in Bolshevik political culture across the presumed great divide of 1929. Chapter 5 details wave after failed wave of League council and cell creation and decay. It chronicles the League's failure to establish a genuinely popular base of support, and the resulting compulsion of the secularization process during the First Five-Year Plan. Chapter 6 focuses on the Communist Party's inconstancy in matters of antireligious propaganda and on other obstacles

---

[47] *Pervaia vseobshchaia perepis'*, *34*, pt. 1: 1; pt. 2: xi.

[48] *Entsiklopedicheskii slovar'*, 25: 698.

[49] Oblastnoi Tsentral'nyi Arkhiv Dokumentov Partii i Obshchestvennykh Dvizhenii (Pskov Party Archive; hereafter PPA), f. 1, op. 1, d. 386, ll. 58鈥?1, 85鈥?9, 94鈥?9; *Pravda*, 1 January 1925. On Varlaam's background, see Lev M. Regel'son, *Tragediia russkoi tserkvi, 1917鈥?945* (Paris: YMCA Press, 1977), 585.

to the League's effective operation. Chapter 7 takes up the issue of cadres, its centrality to the League's discourse, and the efforts to train antireligious activists. Chapter 8 stands alone to review the fate of the League in the late 1930s. Having nearly disappeared in the mid-1930s, the League was revitalized in 1937, well after the visible manifestations of organized religion had disappeared. The Epilogue and Conclusion chronicle the demise of the League during World War II and speculate on the origin and evolution of those features of Bolshevik political culture observed in the League, those that preceded the Soviet era and those that can serve as a basis for understanding post-Soviet Russia.

1

Making Holy Russia Godless: Policies, Confusion, and Cadres, 1917–1925

The abolition of religion as the illusory happiness of the people is a demand for their true happiness.

—Karl Marx, "A Contribution to the Critique of Hegel's *Philosophy of Right*," 1844

In the aftermath of the Soviet regime's decades-long opposition to religion, it would be easy to assume that the Bolsheviks held to a firm course of action against the Orthodox Church from the very moment they took power. While the regime certainly maintained a general hostility motivated by ideology and immediate political concerns, its policy progressed through several broad stages early in the Soviet period. Until 1922, the thrust of the Bolshevik effort was directed against the Orthodox Church as an institution. The regime's leaders sensed little need for systematic propaganda while they optimistically expected religion to collapse in the postrevolutionary order. The regime changed course in late 1922 and early 1923 to reflect changing political circumstances and the persistence of popular belief, and complemented its policy of selective direct repression with broad antireligious propaganda targeted at belief per se. The League of the Godless was one visible manifestation of this new approach. (I discuss the return to a more forceful intervention against the Church in the late 1920s in Chapter 5.) Crucial in determining the regime's strategy toward religion were deeply held concerns about the ability of local cadres to fulfill the regime's basic ideological goals. These activists seemed ill prepared to carry out or even understand the Party's central dictates, or to follow Moscow's numerous shifts in policy. The cadres represented just one example of the broader difficulties the regime encountered in realizing the slogans that brought it to power in 1917. The move from intervention to propaganda only heightened the expectations placed on local cadres, and left a troubling legacy for the League when it appeared in the mid-1920s.

19

The Religious Challenge

The Bolsheviks' initial approach to religion was conditioned by the pervasiveness of popular religious belief and the power of the Orthodox Church as an institution. Although by 1917 the Bolshevik leaders and increasing numbers of their working-class supporters either were avowedly atheistic or at least no longer accepted Orthodox beliefs or rituals,[1] the country at large remained profoundly Orthodox. Even after the regime decimated the Orthodox Church as an institution, it remained into the 1920s the only broadly based organization not clearly controlled by the regime. Moreover, the regime's efforts to undermine the visible church only addressed part of the religious challenge. Orthodoxy was deeply rooted in popular culture and extended far beyond the church gates. Popular Orthodoxy was reflected in the presence of icons in most believers' homes; chapels (*chasovni*) dotted the countryside, and "renovated" icons became minor pilgrimage sites. Most of these forms of Orthodox expression required neither the services of a priest nor a church. Beyond Orthodoxy strictly defined, numerous noncanonical beliefs and practices characterized rural religion well into the twentieth century. Peasants celebrated local pagan deities (either directly or under a thin Christian veneer), observed pre-Christian rites, took for granted the presence of evil and benevolent spirits, and employed fortune-tellers and would-be sorcerers. Whether or not popular religion was a dual faith (*dvoeverie*), part pagan and part Christian, or, in the words of Moshe Lewin, "an amalgam of Christian symbolism welded onto a bedrock of an old agricultural civilization,"[2] this admixture of traditions left much of what amounted to an individual's religion beyond the immediate reach of the new urban-based state. Simply closing churches and arresting clergy would not be sufficient. As Lewin wrote, "the official church can in this context be dispensed with, and peas-

---

[1] For a discussion of the extent of secularization among the working class, see Deborah Pearl, "Tsar and Religion in Russian Revolutionary Propaganda," *Russian Review* 20 (1993): 94–107. See also Reginald E. Zelnik, "'To the Unaccustomed Eye': Religion and Irreligion in the Experience of St. Petersburg Workers in the 1870s," *Russian History* 16, nos. 2–4 (1989): 297–326.

[2] Moshe Lewin, "Popular Religion in Twentieth-Century Russia," in *The Making of the Soviet System: Essays in the Social History of Interwar Russia* (London: Methuen, 1985), 70; Eve Levin, "*Dvoeverie* and Popular Religion," in *Seeking God: The Recovery of Religious Identity in Orthodox Russia, Ukraine, and Georgia*, ed. Stephen K. Batalden (De Kalb: Northern Illinois University Press, 1993), 29–52; Pierre Pascal, *The Religion of the Russian People* (Crestwood, N.Y.: St. Vladimir's Seminary Press, 1976), 3–15; S. A. Tokarev, *Religioznye verovaniia vostochnoslavianskikh narodov XIX—nachala XX vekov* (Moscow: Izdatel'stvo Akademii Nauk SSSR, 1957).

ants can fall back on other resources when they find the Church wanting or persecuted and when the churches are being closed. . . . They can retreat into their own shell, opt out of the 'larger society', ensconce themselves in their own 'world'. . . ."[3] The peasantry's ability to isolate itself economically and politically motivated the regime's collectivization policy in the late 1920s. Similarly, transforming rural religion would require that popular culture be comprehensively recreated, a challenge not lost on revolutionaries in France and Mexico, where Catholicism extended beyond canonically Catholic institutions and practices. Most modernizing revolutionaries have found that their intention to overcome religion has required them to recreate popular culture, especially rural culture.

Faced with the challenge of an omnipresent, culturally diffuse religion, the Bolsheviks initially appeared woefully unprepared to fulfill even the vague promises inherent in their ideology. Beyond monopolizing power and offering general slogans such as "Bread, Land, and Peace" in 1917, the Bolsheviks provided few details of their plans for the transformation of Russia. This was particularly the case in a variety of socio-ideological matters—women's liberation, education, culture, and the arts—where the Bolsheviks had come to power "without an authentic domestic plan."[4] Religion was no exception; there was ample hostility, but little in the way of concrete guidance. The growing association of socialism with atheism during the nineteenth century represented more a means of opposing established churches than a precise plan for disseminating atheism. Marx and Engels offered critiques of religion, not a plan to combat religion in the postrevolutionary order. Indeed, they expected the masses to be well alienated from religion by the time the Revolution came, and they dismissed the promotion of atheism as a sideshow to the main conflicts between the working class and the bourgeoisie.[5]

In Russia the Orthodox Church had been closely identified with the tsarist regime, which the revolutionaries were dedicated to destroying. Even before the Bolsheviks took power, the Russian intelligentsia long had had a troubled relationship with Orthodoxy, and the revolutionary intelligentsia did not hide its dislike for the Orthodox Church. Much of the working class in whose name power had been seized also was estranged

[3] Lewin, *Making of the Soviet System*, 70.

[4] Stephen F. Cohen, *Bukharin and the Bolshevik Revolution: A Political Biography, 1888–1938* (New York: Knopf, 1973), 129.

[5] David McLellan, *Marxism and Religion: A Description and Assessment of the Marxist Critique of Christianity* (Houndsmills, Hants.: Macmillan, 1987); Owen Chadwick, *The Secularization of the European Mind in the Nineteenth Century* (Cambridge: Cambridge University Press, 1975), 48–87.

from the Orthodox Church, having become secularized or having entered the orbit of sectarian groups. Although Christian socialism had been popular across much of Western Europe in the nineteenth and early twentieth centuries, its appeal in Russia was more limited, because Orthodoxy's close relationship with the State and its inherent temporal passivity made it an unlikely vehicle for a revolutionary ideology.[6] Early in the century, some Russian revolutionaries, most notably the future commissar of enlightenment, Anatolii Lunacharskii, had gravitated toward a form of Christian socialism, so-called God-building, but Lenin furiously repudiated any merging of Christianity and socialism for the Bolshevik Party as a whole.[7] More immediately after the Revolution, the Orthodox Church represented to many Bolsheviks a direct political threat as a potential nationwide rallying point for their opponents. Finally, many Bolshevik leaders associated Orthodoxy with the severe Russian cultural "backwardness" that hindered Bolshevik plans for the creation of a socialist society.

What to Do?

However clear the hostility to religion was among the Bolshevik leaders, this legacy did not translate into a specific program for disseminating atheism. Recent European history provided them little guidance. The legislative separation of Church and State increasingly common in Western Europe was deemed insufficient and a bourgeois deception, and the facile creation of a secular religion in the tradition of the French revolutionaries was unacceptable, although many facets of one later appeared in the Soviet Union.

Lenin himself provided little explicit direction. His writings on religion were few, dated from well before the Revolution, and most often dealt with immediate political or philosophical issues within the Social Democratic camp.[8] After the Bolshevik takeover in 1917, Lenin joined his stri-

---

[6] Christopher Read, *Culture and Power in Revolutionary Russia* (London: Macmillan, 1990) and *Religion, Revolution and the Russian Intelligentsia* (London: Macmillan, 1979); V. Prokof'ev, *Ateizm russkikh revoliutsionerov-demokratov*, 2d ed., rev. (Moscow: Gosudarstvennoe Izdatel'stvo Politicheskoi Literatury, 1955). See also George L. Kline, *Religious and Antireligious Thought in Russia* (Chicago: University of Chicago Press, 1968).

[7] Richard Stites, *Revolutionary Dreams: Utopian Vision and Experimental Life in the Russian Revolution* (New York: Oxford University Press, 1989), 101–105; Read, *Religion, Revolution and the Russian Intelligentsia*; Jutta Scherrer, "Intelligentsia, religion, révolution: Premières manifestations d'un socialisme chrétien en Russie, 1905–1907," *Cahiers du monde russe et soviétique* 17, no. 4 (1976): 427–466, and 18, nos. 1–2 (1977): 5–32.

[8] "Sotsializm i religiia," *Novaia zhizn'*, no. 28, 3 December 1905; "Ob otnoshenii rabochei partii k religii," *Proletarii*, no. 45, 13 May 1909; "Klassy i partii v ikh otnoshenii k religii i

dency in policy matters with his often-expressed admiration for the intellectual atheism of the eighteenth-century philosophes. Moreover, Lenin was highly inconsistent in his occasional references to religion. While he regularly warned that believers should not be threatened by regime activists, in 1919 he insisted on an extreme program, which stated that the Party would not be satisfied with the mere separation of Church and State. Three years later, he wrote of the need to publish the works of eighteenth-century materialists, while at the same time he ordered the arrest and execution of churchmen in connection with the Shuia incident.[9]

The other leading Bolshevik thinkers had little to add beyond a shared contempt for the Church and a belief in the ability of education to overcome religious convictions. Lev Trotsky believed that religion would be eradicated over time by education and new diversions, particularly the cinema. The integration of believers into communal activities (such as clubs and collective dining facilities) also would erode the "fictional knowledge" upon which religion relied.[10] Nikolai Bukharin held that scientific knowledge "slowly but surely undermines the authority of all religions."[11] Commissar of Enlightenment Anatolii Lunacharskii characterized religion as a matter of superstition and ignorance that would be overcome in the schools through the teaching of science and history.[12]

There was another, more fundamental reason for the absence of a detailed plan. Revolutionaries inspired by Marxism were not supposed to have to contend with religion after a proletarian revolution. Bolshevik policy makers were operating within an ideological framework theorized for an industrialized nation with an already secularized working class. The Revolution, however, took place in the still largely rural, agrarian, and Holy Russia. While political aspects of Marxism had been modified (if not fully reversed) by Lenin to justify a takeover in Russia, the revisionary

---

tserkvi," *Sotsial demokrat*, no. 6, 4 June 1909. For an exhaustive treatment of Lenin's views on religion, see Mikhail Shakhnovich, *Lenin i problemy ateizma* (Moscow/Leningrad: Akademiia Nauk, 1961). See also Iosif Aronovich Kryvelev, *Lenin o religii* (Moscow: Akademiia Nauk SSSR, 1960); McLellan, *Marxism and Religion*, 95–105.

[9] V. I. Lenin, "O znachenii voinstvuiushchego materializma," *Pod znamenem marksizma*, 1922, no. 3: 5–12. The Shuia episode is discussed below.

[10] Baruch Knei-Paz, *The Social and Political Thought of Leon Trotsky* (Oxford: Clarendon, 1978), 285; Lev Trotskii, *Voprosy byta*, 2d ed. (Moscow, 1923) and "Leninizm i rabochie kluby," *Izvestiia*, 23 July 1924.

[11] Nikolai Bukharin and Evgenii Preobrazhenskii, *Azbuka kommunizma: populiarnoe obiasnenie programmy Rossiiskoi kommunisticheskoi partii bolshevikov* (Moscow: Gosudarstvennoe izdatel'stvo, 1920), 216.

[12] A. V. Lunacharskii, "Ob antireligioznoi propagande," *Revoliutsiia i tserkov'*, 1919, no. 1: 13–16.

process had not extended to cultural transformation, and certainly not to the dissemination of atheism.[13] Direct antireligious propaganda, however framed, amounted to ideological voluntarism, and Bolshevik leaders repeatedly stated that the ultimate "liquidation of religion" would require the completed construction of socialism.

While some Bolsheviks, such as Aleksandra Kollantai, did argue for immediate and radical cultural change soon after the Revolution, the regime either rejected their programs or abandoned them after brief experimentation.[14] Even in this initial "heroic phase" of the Revolution,[15] transforming the religious worldview of millions of peasants and many workers into a scientific-materialist outlook was too much to envision. The immediate task after 1917 remained that of contending with the Orthodox Church as an institution and the clergy as a social category, and this was the thrust of the regime's policy through 1922. An obvious first step in this direction was the separation of Church and State.

Separate and Divide

The complete disestablishment of Orthodoxy soon after the Bolsheviks took power was not designed primarily to promote atheism in Russian society. Rather it was one of a series of political measures aimed at dismantling the old regime in which the Church increasingly had become an administrative and even political department.[16] The Bolsheviks' social isolation, and the fact that most clergy were hostile to the new regime, led

[13] Soviet scholars hedged their bets by attempting to argue that the peasantry on the eve of the Revolution was highly anticlerical and increasingly hostile to religion generally. See L. I. Emel'iakh, *Krest'iane i tserkov' nakanune oktiabria* (Leningrad, 1976) and "Ateizm i antiklerikalizm narodnykh mass v 1917 g.," in *Voprosy istorii religii i ateizmag* 5 (1958): 64–72; D. A. Garkavenko, "Rost ateisticheskikh i antiklerikal'nykh nastroenii v armii i flote v 1917 godu," in *Voprosy istorii religii i ateizma* 8 (1960): 193–218.

[14] Lynn Mally, *Culture of the Future: The Proletcult Movement in Revolutionary Russia* (Berkeley: University of California Press, 1990); Stites, *Revolutionary Dreams*; Abbott Gleason, Peter Kenez, and Richard Stites, eds., *Bolshevik Culture: Experiment and Order in the Russian Revolution* (Bloomington: Indiana University Press, 1985); William G. Rosenberg, ed., *Bolshevik Visions: First Phase of the Cultural Revolution in Soviet Russia* (Ann Arbor: Ardis, 1984); Beatrice Farnsworth, *Aleksandra Kollantai* (Stanford: Stanford University Press, 1980); Nils A. Nilsson, ed., *Art, Society, Revolution: Russia 1917–1921* (Stockholm: Almqvist & Wiksell International, 1979).

[15] The phrase is from Lev Kritsman, *Geroicheskii period Velikoi russkoi revoliutsii*, 2d ed. (Moscow, 1926).

[16] For a differing view of the Church, see Gregory L. Freeze, "Handmaiden of the State? The Church in Imperial Russia Reconsidered," *Journal of Ecclesiastical History* 36, no. 1 (January 1985): 82–102.

the revolutionaries to use whatever limited means were at their disposal to support their struggle for political survival. Thus, under the cloak of a supposedly disinterested separation of Church and State, the Bolsheviks arranged the legal evisceration and financial decimation of the Orthodox Church.

In the weeks and months after the Bolsheviks seized power, the State transferred all Church-run educational institutions to the newly formed Commissariat of Enlightenment. Church holdings were included in the general nationalization of all property. The State no longer recognized the validity of social functions long performed by the Church, and withdrew its financial support of clergy, churches, and the public performance of religious rituals.[17] These incremental measures were encapsulated in a comprehensive decree issued on 23 January 1918: "On the Separation of Church from State and School from Church." This decree confirmed Russia as a fully secular state, denied the Church legal standing, and for all intents and purposes forbade instruction of religion outside the home. By the terms of the RSFSR Constitution adopted in July 1918, the clergy were classified as second-class citizens, in the same category as "capitalists, merchants, former members of the police, criminals, and imbeciles." The constitution also equated antireligious propaganda with that of religious expression, making it a constitutionally protected behavior.[18] These measures sent a clear signal that, despite the nominal separation of Church and State, the new regime in fact would be aggressively and intimately involved in overseeing the Church's demise. This intention was symbolized by the term commonly used for the authorities overseeing the separation decree—the Commissariat of Justice's "liquidation" department and local "liquidation" commissions.

The local separation of Church and State occurred during the Civil War, when the clergy repeatedly engaged in direct conflict with representatives of the new regime. Even before the outbreak of organized fighting in the summer of 1918, Patriarch Tikhon (Belavin) publicly anathematized those Bolsheviks who were, if in name only, Orthodox. Later that year, in October, he issued another public denunciation of the Bolsheviks for the ruin they were bringing upon Russia. During the war, most of the higher clergy openly sided with the Whites, and over the next three years,

[17] The Provisional Government had already taken the first steps to loosen the tight bonds of Church and State. See V. A. Alekseev, *Illiuzii i dogmy* (Moscow: Izdatel'stvo Politicheskoi Literatury, 1991), 10–17.

[18] Joshua Rothenburg, "The Legal Status of Religion in the Soviet Union," in *Aspects of Religion in the Soviet Union, 1917–1967*, ed. Richard Marshall Jr. (Chicago: University of Chicago Press, 1971), 63–65.

many clergymen were arrested and executed.[19] The legacy of the Civil War for subsequent Soviet history has long been debated, with many scholars focusing on the militarized context in which the new regime developed its social, administrative, and political relationships. The League's Civil War legacy is more difficult to judge. On one level, League propaganda frequently evoked the Civil War, but there is little direct evidence linking the brutality of this period with the later emergence of the League or its manner of operation. Indeed, the League was often cast, however ironically, as a moderate force against the Komsomol. Civil War lore may have perpetuated this impression, but in fact the Party's young enthusiasts regularly ran headlong into the League's bureaucrats.

After years of warfare, economic ruin, and disease, drought struck the lower Volga region and parts of the Ukraine in the summer of 1921, and quickly produced a famine. Although the Orthodox Church was active in the relief effort and donated its own financial resources, including church treasures, for famine relief, the regime saw the famine as another opportunity to assault the Church.[20] In February 1922, the Soviet government ordered the seizure of all church valuables, including sacramental items. Opposition was widespread, and in the town of Shuia, northeast of Moscow, the Soviet effort resulted in a violent confrontation with the local population. When news of the conflict reached Moscow, Lenin personally ordered the arrest and execution of as many clergy and active laity in Shuia as possible.[21] Throughout Russia, churchmen were arrested, and after a well-publicized trial, the metropolitan of Leningrad, Veniamin, among others, was executed for resisting the collection. In May 1922, Patriarch Tikhon also was seized for his alleged role in resisting the seizure of church valuables. Friction between Church and State in this period was aggravated by an ongoing assembly of émigré Orthodox churchmen in Serbia—the Karlovci Council—which called upon the Orthodox to overthrow the Communists.[22]

The "church valuables" crisis was not about the additional resources for famine relief that might have been garnered from sacramental vessels.

[19] Alekseev, *Illiuzii i dogmy*, 41–72, 100–168; Vladimir Stepanov (Rusak), *Svidetel'stvo obvineniia: Tserkov' i gosudarstvo v Sovetskom soiuze* (Moscow, 1980), pt. 1; Lev M. Regel'son, *Tragediia russkoi tserkvi, 1917–1945* (Paris: YMCA Press, 1977), 223–278; A. Valentinov, *Chernaia kniga* (Paris: Russkago Natsional'nago Studencheskago Ob'edineniia, 1924), 24–53.

[20] Alekseev, *Illiuzii i dogmy*, 191–200.

[21] N. N. Pokrovskii, "Dokumenty Politbiuro i Lubianki o bor'be s tserkov'iu v 1922–1923 gg.," *Uchenye zapiski Rossiiskogo pravoslavnogo universiteta*, 1 (Moscow, 1995), 125–174; *Izvestiia TsK KPSS*, 1990, no. 4: 190–195; Alekseev, *Illiuzii i dogmy*, 200–210.

[22] John Shelton Curtiss, *The Russian Church and the Soviet State* (Boston: Little, Brown, 1953), 108–118.

Indeed, there is no evidence that the treasures collected from the churches were ever used for famine relief. The real issue was political. Victorious in the Civil War, the Bolsheviks sought to use their growing strength, and the famine, to move against their only remaining institutional opponent with national stature—the Orthodox Church. By seizing its treasures and arresting Patriarch Tikhon, the state symbolically subjugated the Church, and further sapped its financial resources. To complement this assault, in 1922 the regime promoted a schism in the Church and supported the "Renovationist" movement, openly loyal to the Bolsheviks. True, pressure for reforming the Orthodox Church administration had existed for over twenty years, but recently opened Party archives indicate that the Renovationist Church was thoroughly controlled by the Bolsheviks.[23] While the regime hoped to undermine Orthodoxy in general through the fall of the Tikhonite church, the immediate goal remained that of institutional division.

Early Propaganda

The regime's initial institutional approach to religion did not preclude some use of propaganda. Nevertheless, such propaganda was far from systematic and took a subordinate position to execution of the Separation Decree, the prosecution of the Civil War, and the ongoing conflict with the Church. Perhaps the most developed antireligious propaganda occurred within the Red Army as part of its general indoctrination efforts.[24] Beyond the garrison, antireligious propaganda from 1918 to 1922 was limited to simple events, most notably the widely publicized openings of reliquaries (*moshchi*) of Orthodox saints, whose bodies the faithful believed were incorruptible. The regime targeted the reliquaries of the most venerated saints, such as Sergei Radonezhskii, whose sarcophagus was opened on 11 April 1919.[25] At this early stage, the Bolshevik leadership still believed

[23] The protocols of the Central Committee's Antireligious Commission from 1922 and 1923 (RTsKhIDNI, f. 17, op. 112, dd. 443a, 565a) indicate this control.

[24] See I. Struchkov, "Antireligioznaia rabota v Krasnoi armii," in *Voinstvuiushchee bezbozhie v SSSR za 15 let*, ed. M. Enisherlov (Moscow, 1932), 412–426. On the Red Army's general impact on Soviet social development, see Mark von Hagen, *Soldiers in the Proletarian Dictatorship: The Red Army and the Soviet Socialist State, 1917–1930* (Ithaca: Cornell University Press, 1990).

[25] *Revoliutsiia i tserkov'*, 1919–1920, nos. 9–12: 72; Mikhail Gorev, *Troitskaia lavra i Sergei Radonezhskii* (Moscow: Narodnyi Kommissariat Iustitsii, 1920); F. Garkavenko, ed., *O religii i tserkvi: sbornik dokumentov* (Moscow: Izdatel'stvo Politicheskoi Literatury, 1965), 105–109; G. V. Vorontsov, *Leninskaia programma ateisticheskogo vospitaniia v deistvii* (Leningrad: Leningradskii Gosudarstvennyi Universitet, 1973), 72–74.

that "opening" the population's eyes to the Church's "machinations" would dispel popular belief by desacralizing central elements of the faith. Speeches by officials of the commissariats of Enlightenment and Justice were another form of antireligious propaganda during the Civil War.

These propaganda forms were limited also in that they assumed an easy and inevitable victory over religion. Defeating the Whites and their clerical allies, vigorously executing the Separation Decree, seizing whatever substantial financial sources might remain in the Church's possession by 1922—these measures in no way assumed the need for or even the desirability of launching a comprehensive antireligious propaganda campaign. They certainly revealed no expectation of having to create a separate antireligious bureaucracy. As suggested by the title of a pamphlet published by the People's Commissariat of Justice—"Why Belief Is Falling and Unbelief Is Growing"—the peasants were expected simply to cease believing in God and the Orthodox Church once they learned the truth about religion.[26] The subsequent emergence of a fully developed antireligious propaganda apparatus was a reaction to circumstances—the population's "failure" to abandon religion—rather than the execution of a well-prepared plan.

Change of Course

In late 1922 and early 1923, the regime shifted strategies by launching a widespread, systematic propaganda campaign targeted at popular religious belief, not just at the Church. During the Civil War and famine years, such propaganda was deemed unnecessary, and, in any case, the regime had few resources to dedicate to such an effort. This shift to a nationwide propaganda campaign reflected an alteration of the regime's relation to society, especially the peasantry, inherent in the adoption of the New Economic Policy.[27] The ravages of Civil War and famine were receding. Small producers and traders were returning to activity. The regime's embrace of the peasantry at its Thirteenth Party Congress in 1924, and its "face to the countryside" campaign later that year, entailed the rejection of measures that would alienate the rural population.[28] In accord with this

---

[26] I. Stepanov, *Pochemu padaet vera i narostaet bezverie?* (Moscow: Narodnyi Komissariat Iustitsii, 1920).

[27] For an overview of this transition, see Lewis Siegelbaum, *Soviet State and Society between Revolutions, 1918–1929* (Cambridge: Cambridge University Press, 1992), 85–126.

[28] Stephan Merl, *Der Agrarmarkt und die Neue Ökonomische Politik* (Munich: R. Oldenbourg, 1981), 40–49; Cohen, *Bukharin and the Bolshevik Revolution*, 161ff.

"soft" line, non-Bolshevik groups were to be permitted to operate in non-political spheres.[29] With regard to religion, the nearly constant conflict of Church and State during the Civil War, and the church valuables crisis, were over. The establishment of diplomatic relations with Western powers, beginning at the Genoa Conference in 1922, increased foreign pressure on the regime to ease its attacks on the Church. Calls from England are credited with facilitating the release of Patriarch Tikhon in 1923 in return for Tikhon's statement of loyalty and his condemnation of Russian émigré organizations.

Despite some officials' references to a "religious" NEP, the use of this term is quite misleading. In August 1923, the League's future leader, Emel'ian Iaroslavskii, denied the existence of any such plan, but stated that the regime would now focus on confronting popular religious beliefs, not just discrediting religious leaders.[30] Although persecutions and administrative pressure would continue, atheistic propaganda was given new prominence. If not exactly gentle persuasion, this effort was at least nominally designed more to win over minds with a positive program of culture building than to coerce behavior through attacks on the clergy. Ironically, the rollback of the Bolshevik presence in the countryside, associated with the introduction of the NEP, made propaganda campaigns more likely than direct pressure, and the Bolsheviks created an array of social organizations and launched multiple propaganda campaigns over the next several years. It was a period given to vivid imagining about the future of a socialist society, not just the demolition of the old world.

The second reason for the shift to a broad campaign of antireligious propaganda was simple: religion remained a popular force. The previous policy was acknowledged implicitly to have failed: Orthodoxy among the population had survived both the regime's propaganda ploys and its decimation of central Church institutions. Although anticlerical sentiment was strong in places (the Church's own cadres problem),[31] Orthodoxy still retained a hold on much of the population, particularly in the countryside. Indeed, popular religion outside the bounds of the Orthodox Church appeared resurgent in the 1920s. Calls for antireligious propaganda at that time revealed concern about the growing popularity of sects, especially

[29] Sheila Fitzpatrick, "The Soft Line on Culture and Its Enemies," in *The Cultural Front: Power and Culture in Revolutionary Russia* (Ithaca: Cornell University Press, 1992), 91–95.
[30] RTsKhIDNI, f. 89, op. 4, d. 9, l. 12.
[31] Gregory L. Freeze, "A Case of Stunted Anticlericalism: Clergy and Society in Imperial Russia," *European Studies Review* 13, no. 2 (April 1983): 177–200. For the more tendentious Soviet view, see L. I. Emel'iakh, *Krest'iane i tserkov' nakanune oktiabria* and "Ateizm i antiklerikalizm narodnykh mass v 1917 g."; Garkavenko, "Rost ateisticheskikh i antiklerikal'nykh nastroenii v armii i flote v 1917 godu."

rationalistic Western Protestant groups. How much this perception corresponded to reality and how much was self-justifying rhetoric is hard to gauge. Benefiting from a fractured Orthodox Church, and enjoying religious freedom denied them under tsarism, sectarian groups spread rapidly in the 1920s, though their precise size remained unclear.[32] Whatever the reality, the rhetorical threat of an ever-increasing upward spiral of sectarian and continued Orthodox activism was used to justify a confrontation with religious belief. Although religion no longer was considered a direct political threat, it was now a pressing cultural concern, part of Russia's backwardness, to be countered, at least in part, by propaganda campaigns initiated by the regime.

Central authorities repeatedly called for greater antireligious propaganda in the early 1920s. The same Party congress that introduced the NEP in early 1921 also listed antireligious propaganda among the tasks of the newly created Main Administration for Political Enlightenment (Glavpolitprosvet), the political education department of the Commissariat of Enlightenment.[33] As in other realms, abandonment of Civil War–era direct intervention in society was balanced by the regime's more aggressive propaganda agenda. The pressure for antireligious propaganda mounted during 1922. In February the Central Committee issued a directive calling for antireligious propaganda, and in the March issue of *Pod znamenem marksizma*, Lenin expressed his hope that the journal would become an organ of militant atheism.[34] The popular resistance to the seizure of church valuables in the spring, and the failure of the Komsomol's Christmas campaign later that year brought home to the regime's leadership the need to alter its policy.

[32] See Aleksandr Etkind, "Russkie sekty i sovetskii kommunizm: Proekt Vladimira Bonch-Bruevicha," *Minuvshee: Istoricheskii Al'manakh* 19 (1996), 298; Alekseev, *Illiuzii i dogmy*, 272ff; Aleksandr Klibanov, *Religioznoe sektantstvo i sovremennost'* (Moscow: Nauka, 1969), 188–258; Donald Treadgold, "The Peasant and Religion," in *The Peasant in Nineteenth-Century Russia*, ed. Wayne Vucinich (Stanford: Stanford University Press, 1968), 81, 93; Walter Kolarz, *Religion in the Soviet Union* (London: Macmillan, 1966), 286–298, 346–371.

[33] Garkavenko, *O religii i tserkvi*, 57. On Glavpolitprosvet, see Peter Kenez, *The Birth of the Propaganda State* (Cambridge: Cambridge University Press, 1985), 123–128; I. E. Rozanova, "Glavpolitprosvet RSFSR v sisteme rukovodstva kul'turnym stroitel'stvom v 1920–1930 gg.," in *Gosudarstvennye uchrezhdeniia i obshchestvennye organizatsii SSSR: Problemy, fakty, issledovaniia*, ed. T. P. Korzhikhina (Moscow: Moskovskii Gosudarstvennyi Istoriko-arkhivnyi Institut, 1991), 69–78.

[34] *Izvestiia TsK VKP(b)*, 1922, no. 2: 35; N. Lenin, "O znachenii voinstvuiushchego materializma," *Pod znamenem marksizma*, 1922, no. 3. The editors did not heed their master's call, placing only occasional and highly scholastic antireligious articles on their pages throughout the 1920s.

These pressures culminated in a resolution at the Twelfth Party Congress, in April 1923, the first to be concerned solely with antireligious propaganda.[35] The resolution stated that although the final demise of religion required the completed economic transformation of society, the Party required in the meantime "intensified, systematic propaganda, graphically and convincingly revealing to every worker and peasant the lie and contradiction to his interests of any religion." The resolution offered few details, merely criticizing the lack of literature appropriate for a mass readership, and calling for propaganda and large-scale training of antireligious activists. On cue, a Komsomol congress in June called for "more profound and systematic [antireligious] propaganda" to be included in regular Komsomol political education.[36] The Trade Union Central Council followed suit the same month with a circular calling for "a prolonged educational culture" of antireligious work.[37] The ideological mandate implicit in Bolshevism had been made explicit at the highest levels. Exactly how it would be realized remained to be seen.

Cadres

The issue of execution was vital because of concerns about repeated "excesses" (arbitrary church closings, summary arrests of clergy, illegal seizure of religious items, and the like) by local Communists and Soviet officials that jeopardized the regime's new relationship with the peasantry. Moreover, Soviet officials in the provinces, many non-Communists among them, did not necessarily concur with the leadership in Moscow on numerous issues, including religion. Indeed, not all Communists in the years immediately after the Revolution shared or even understood the regime's agenda as articulated at the highest levels, or its many shifts of focus. This confusion affected basic administrative matters, such as the distribution of food.[38]

Amidst this chaos, the Separation Decree placed a tremendous burden on local Soviet and Party officials, requiring extensive involvement in

[35] "O postanovke antireligioznoi propagandy," *Dvenadtsatyi s'ezd RKP(b): Stenograficheskii otchet* (Moscow: Gosudarstvennoe Izdatel'stvo Politicheskoi Literatury, 1968), 716–717.
[36] Tsentr Khranenia dokumentov molodezhnykh organizatsii (Center for the Preservation of Documents of Youth Organizations, formerly the Central Archive, All-Union Leninist Communist Union of Youth, TsA VLKSM; hereafter TsKhDMO), f. 1, op. 3, d. 6, ll. 107–108.
[37] RTsKhIDNI, f. 89, op. 4, d. 163, ll. 1–3.
[38] Lars T. Lih, *Bread and Authority in Russia, 1914–1921* (Berkeley: University of California Press, 1990).

Church-related matters: administering agreements with believers to lease church buildings from the state (free of charge), cataloging church property, conflicts over marriage and divorce, the transfer of schools to state control. The People's Commissariat of Justice repeatedly criticized local authorities during the Civil War for not understanding either the letter or the purpose of the Separation Decree.[39] The liquidation department's journal, *Revoliutsiia i tserkov'* (Revolution and Church), apparently was created in response to the shortcomings of local officials, and much of it was given over to resolving conflicts, explaining policy to local officials, and answering their questions. Rampant local confusion and the central authority's very real frustration over its cadres became the leitmotif of Soviet antireligious policy.

The cessation of the Civil War did not end the cadres problem. Indeed, it may have exacerbated it. A multitude of sins in local administration could be explained away by wartime conditions, but the challenge of peacetime administration revealed the critical personnel shortcomings of a regime that intended to transform the lives and thinking of every citizen. In February 1922, the Central Committee issued a circular that explicitly directed cadres not to engage in insulting forms of antireligious agitation that would strengthen religious convictions.[40] At the party's Twelfth Congress, in April 1923, the resolution calling for greater antireligious propaganda specifically cautioned against aggressive methods that would make martyrs of believers and "lead only to the strengthening of religious fanaticism."[41] Subsequent directives in 1923 warned that uncontrolled church closings were a boon to anti-Soviet forces and were to stop immediately; in October the Central Party's agitprop department commented that "debates, trials of religion, and so forth are transforming our battle with religion into a sport" that only insulted and alienated believers. A Central Committee document from 1925 characterized "the homegrown rural godless [as agitating] more against themselves than for themselves."[42] In all these cases, the central authorities feared that the antireligious work of local cadres was intensifying religious feelings recently liberated from the stultifying tsarist embrace. These concerns were aired publicly at the Thirteenth Party Congress, in the spring of 1924, when delegates cited many incidents of unacceptable antireligious behavior. Among

[39] According to one Soviet scholar, the difficulties in the separation of school and Church stemmed from the failure of local cadres to "explain" properly the intention of the decrees. V. A. Kozlov, *Kul'turnaia revoliutsiia i krest'ianstvo, 1921–1927* (Moscow: Nauka, 1983), 22.
[40] Alekseev, *Illiuzii i dogmy*, 271.
[41] "O postanovke antireligioznoi propagandy," *Dvenadtsatii s"ezd*, 716–717.
[42] RTsKhIDNI, f. 17, op. 60, d. 723, l. 125; d. 509, ll. 3–4; Alekseev, *Illiuzii i dogmy*, 277.

the congress's resolutions was a statement that "it is necessary to liquidate decisively the efforts to battle religion using administrative measures [such as arbitrary closings]. Antireligious propaganda in the countryside should consist exclusively of materialistic explanations of phenomena of nature and social life." Special care should be taken not to insult believers. Victory would come only through "years and decades" of enlightenment work.[43] Such decrees, repeated throughout the 1920s, indicated the seriousness and extent of the problem and the regime's inability to decree it away.

A genuine social revolution in a less developed country such as Russia would have to be made by its individual representatives at every level. Russia in the 1920s and early 1930s did not have the mass media infrastructure that permitted Nazi Germany to control and homogenize its message. If the cultural revolution was to occur in Russia, it would require far more trained cadres than the Party had in the early 1920s. "Revolutionary Russia simply lacked an adequate complement of personnel for the tasks at hand, or the resources to support them."[44] This weakness was particularly evident with regard to bureaucratic matters requiring literate, cooperative officials in general agreement with the regime's agenda. The Bolshevik leadership was painfully aware that its success depended on local cadres, and the result was a comprehensive public discourse about the need for quality cadres throughout the 1920s and 1930s. A similar phenomenon was observed in both Mexico and France. The teachers who spearheaded the dissemination of revolutionary ideology in Mexico were subjected to intense scrutiny, their commitment to the revolution ever suspect.[45] The de-Christianization campaign in revolutionary France assumed a variety of local forms over which the leaders of the revolution had little control, and many of the most fanatic de-Christianizers were "adventurers on the margins of power."[46] The League's cadres are discussed at length in Chapter 7, but it is important to

[43] *Trinadtsatyi s"ezd RKP(b) (mai 1924): Stenograficheskii otchet* (Moscow, 1963), 450, 471, 642–643.

[44] William Rosenberg, "Conclusion: Understanding NEP Society and Culture in the Light of New Research," in *Russia in the Era of NEP: Explorations in Soviet Society and Culture,* ed. Sheila Fitzpatrick, Alexander Rabinowitch, and Richard Stites (Bloomington: Indiana University Press, 1991), 311.

[45] Adrian A. Bantjes, "Burning Saints, Molding Minds: Iconoclasm, Civil Ritual, and the Failed Cultural Revolution," in *Rituals of Rule, Rituals of Resistance: Public Celebrations and Popular Culture in Mexico,* ed. William Beezley, Cheryl Martin, and William French (Wilmington, Del.: SR Books, 1994), 274–276.

[46] John McManners, *The French Revolution and the Church* (New York: Harper & Row, 1969), 87.

note here that the League emerged in an atmosphere of chronic concern over cadres throughout the Soviet realm.[47]

The problem was twofold: quantity and quality. Given that Russian society in the 1920s remained overwhelmingly rural, substantially illiterate outside the cities, and with few means of mass communication, the numerous NEP-era social campaigns launched by the Bolsheviks required labor-intensive efforts by large numbers of skilled staff.[48] The dissemination of atheism was no exception. There were far too few of Trotsky's cinemas to accomplish the task; not even the mass publication of antireligious tracts that developed in the mid-1920s obviated the need for cadres. The regime's rollback from the countryside during NEP only aggravated the dearth of skilled cadres in rural areas. The Rybinsk Party organization reported to the Central Committee in March 1922 that "antireligious propaganda among the masses is not conducted because there are no staff sufficiently prepared for that purpose."[49] In Iaroslavl' Province, the "shift to new forms of antireligious propaganda is being blocked by the absence in sufficient measure of qualified propagandists."[50] Similarly, reports from the Pskov provincial party in 1924 and 1925 cited the absence of cadres as a major obstacle to combating religion. The dearth of activists was compounded by the fact that available cadres—the regime's public face—were overwhelmed with work.[51]

---

[47] This broader shortage was such that the Bolsheviks, however unwillingly, welcomed back the so-called bourgeois specialists who occupied administrative and technical positions under the Old Regime. See von Hagen, *Soldiers in the Proletarian Dictatorship*; Siegelbaum, *Soviet State and Society*; Moshe Lewin, "The Civil War: Dynamics and Legacy," in *Party, State and Society in the Russian Civil War*, 407–411; Sheila Fitzpatrick, "New Perspectives on the Civil War," in *Party, State, and Society in the Russian Civil War: Explorations in Social History*, ed. Diane P. Koenker, William G. Rosenberg, and Ronald Grigor Suny (Bloomington: Indiana University Press, 1989), 15–17, and "The Problem of Class Identity in NEP Society," in *Russia in the Era of the NEP*, 20.

[48] The most comprehensive and successful effort was the campaign against illiteracy. See von Hagen, *Soldiers in the Proletarian Dictatorship*, 95–99; Kenez, *Birth of the Propaganda State*, 70–83; Kozlov, *Kul'turnaia revoliutsiia*; Sheila Fitzpatrick, *Education and Social Mobility in the Soviet Union, 1921–1934* (Cambridge: Cambridge University Press, 1979), 168–176; Roger Pethybridge, *The Social Prelude to Stalinism* (New York: St. Martin's Press, 1974), 61–92; V. A. Kumanev, *Revoliutsiia i prosveshcheniia* (Moscow: Nauka, 1973); T. A. Remizova, *Kul'turno-prosvetitel'naia rabota v RSFSR (1921–1925)* (Moscow: Izdatel'stvo Akademii Nauk, 1962).

[49] RTsKhIDNI, f. 17, op. 60, d. 347, l. 24 ob. In 1923, Rybinsk Province was merged with Iaroslavl' Province.

[50] Tsentr Dokumentatsii Noveishei Istorii Iaroslavskoi Oblasti (Center of Documentation of Contemporary History of Iaroslavl' Oblast, formerly the Iaroslavl' Party Archive and cited hereafter as IaPA), f. 1, op. 27, d. 1733, l. 39.

[51] PPA, f. 1, op. 1, d. 386, ll. 64, 129.

When the League began organizing locally in 1925 and 1926, the lack of cadres was regularly blamed for the League's poor performance. Even with a sharp increase in Party membership in 1924—the so-called Lenin levy—numerous rural counties through the mid-1920s had no more than one or two Party cells.[52] The shortage of rural cadres was severe even in "developed" areas such as Iaroslavl' Province. As of 1 November 1926, there were 7,927 full and candidate members (about half fell into the latter category) in the entire provincial party organization. Most were new to the Party, having joined in 1925 or 1926. The majority— 5,164 (over 65 percent)—lived and worked around the city of Iaroslavl'. That left 2,763 Communists facing a rural population of 1,079,015 (80 percent of the province's population), or one Communist for every 390 people.[53] A report from Iaroslavl' Province concluded that "in the countryside, the almost complete absence of even a few qualified propagandists remains particularly acute."[54] Even when the rural Komsomol membership was considered, the Bolsheviks' reach clearly exceeded their grasp.[55]

However inadequate these numbers may have been, Iaroslavl' was a centrally located industrial province and therefore was relatively well provisioned with cadres. Rural Pskov had far fewer agents of modernization available. Even after the Lenin draft of 1924, there were still only 4,695 Communists facing a total population of 1,788,418. The Party's agitprop apparatus consisted of only seven employees in Pskov and twenty-eight at the *uezd* (or county) level. Because the Communists were concentrated in the province's few towns, the imbalance was even greater in the villages, where 91.2 percent of the population resided. As in Iaroslavl', the presence of a larger number of Komsomol members—15,500 in 1925 after several years of rapid growth—still left a serious dearth of cadres.[56]

[52] Kozlov, *Kul'turnaia revoliutsiia*, 39; Pethybridge, *Social Prelude to Stalinism*, 207.
[53] *Vsesoiuznaia perepis' naseleniia 1926 g.*, vol. 2, pt. 1 (Moscow: 1928), 108. Of the 1,343,159 inhabitants, 1,079,015 were classified as rural and 264,144 as urban. *Iaroslavskaia guberniia v tsifrakh (statisticheskii spravochnik)* (Iaroslavl', 1927), 2; and *Otchet Iaroslavskogo gubernskogo komiteta VKP'b) za period dekabria 1925–dekabria 1926* (Iaroslavl', 1926), 84.
[54] IaPA, f. 1, op. 27, d. 1733, l. 38.
[55] Komsomol membership in Iaroslavl' Province in December 1925 stood at 17,000. Half were identified as workers and one-third as peasants. *Ocherki istorii Iaroslavskoi organizatsii KPSS* (Iaroslavl': Verkhne-Volzhskoe Knizhnoe Izdatel'stvo, 1967), 239–240.
[56] *Vsesoiuznaia perepis' naseleniia 1926 g.*, vol. 1, pt. 1, 96; total population of Pskov Province: 1,788,418; rural 1,630,249 (91.2%); urban 158,169 (8.8%). *Ocherki istorii Pskovskoi organizatsii KPSS* (Leningrad: Lenizdat, 1971), 176, 190; *Otchet Pskovskogo gubkoma RKP(b) k XV gubpartkonferentsii* (Pskov, 1924), 34–35.

What of the other possible agents of modernization? These too were thinly dispersed around the country, especially in rural areas. By 1923, literacy "points" (*likbezpunkty*) had been cut back sharply, to only 3.8 percent of their peak number in 1921. There were only 16.1 percent of the former number of reading huts, and only 47.7 percent of libraries. Rural schools had been cut back around 30 percent.[57] In the existing rural schools, teachers could not be counted on to attack religion because many were the children of clergy.[58] Even those with radical political sympathies were not necessarily prepared to become conduits of atheism.[59] As a result of these pressures and the nominal legal separation of Church and State, the Commissariat of Enlightenment initially adhered, at least in theory, to a policy of neutrality in regard to religion until 1929.[60]

The available cadres presented additional problems. The regime's ambitious goal of replacing a traditional religious worldview with a comprehensive, materialistic one required much of its activists. Despite the regime's effort to simplify and popularize its ideology—as in the mass tract prepared by Bukharin and Evgenii Preobrazhenskii, *Azbuka kommunizma*[61]—this program still demanded prepared, skilled propagandists. They needed to be familiar with both religion and atheism and to have the ability to express their views in lectures, discussions, and debates in a manner likely to be well received by a possibly uncomprehending and probably hostile audience. Lenin's scholasticism and Trotsky's intellectual bullying would not go far under these circumstances.

Against the backdrop of these high expectations, the educational level of local Bolsheviks was a constant source of concern. Through the 1920s, over 90 percent of Party members had only a primary school education.[62] Urbanized Iaroslavl' Province was in a slightly better position,

---

[57] Kozlov, *Kul'turnaia revoliutsiia*, 55–56.

[58] Before 1914, one-third (32.6%) of rural women teachers were the daughters of clergy. Ben Eklof, *Russian Peasant Schools* (Berkeley: University of California Press, 1986), 189.

[59] On the political orientation of teachers before 1917, see ibid., 243–247. For their relationship with central authorities after 1917, see Larry Holmes, "Fear No Evil: Schools and Religion in Soviet Russia, 1917–1941," in *Religious Policy in the Soviet Union*, ed. Sabrina Ramet (Cambridge: Cambridge University Press, 1993), and *The Kremlin and the Schoolhouse: Reforming Education in Soviet Russia, 1917–1931* (Bloomington: Indiana University Press, 1991); and Sheila Fitzpatrick, *The Commissariat of Enlightenment: Soviet Organization of Education and the Arts under Lunacharskii, October 1917–1921* (Cambridge: Cambridge University Press, 1970), 34–43.

[60] Holmes, "Fear No Evil," 138–142.

[61] N. Bukharin and E. Preobrazhenskii, *Azbuka kommunizma: Populiarnoe ob"iasnenie programmy Rossiiskoi Kommunisticheskoi Partii Bol'shevikov, priniatoi na 8-m s"ezde* (Moscow: Gosizdat, 1920).

[62] Pethybridge, *Social Prelude to Stalinism*, 156.

but just 380 of 4,376 Communists (16.6 percent) in 1924 had some training beyond primary school.[63] Basic literacy alone certainly did not guarantee competence in ideological matters. Some familiarity with Bolshevik principles and policies, known as political literacy, was also necessary, but the Party's periodic reviews of political literacy among its members were alarming. The survey of 1923, which included Iaroslavl'-area Communists, found that 70 percent of rural Party members and 50 percent of urban members were politically "illiterate."[64] Good cadres were even rarer in Pskov. In 1923, the Pskov provincial party's agitprop department estimated that 85 percent of its rural members were politically illiterate.[65] Political literacy schools existed throughout both provinces in the early 1920s, and while these programs were a testament to the Bolshevik training process, their very existence underscored the lack of individuals who had more than just a "slogan understanding" of Bolshevism.

In its most extreme form—the phenomenon of Communists who attended church and participated in religious rites—the political illiteracy problem revealed the complexity of rural life in early Soviet Russia. Hostility toward religion was implicit in even the most general understanding of Bolshevism, and in any case the Party made it clear in its program of March 1919. Point 13 stated that the Communists needed to go beyond the mere separation of Church and State to become a force for liberating the masses from religion.[66] Despite this condition of Party membership, numerous Communists continued to observe religious rites. In May 1921, the Iaroslavl' party reported that "religious prejudices" in its organization "have not been eliminated and are even strengthening."[67]

The phenomenon of religious Communists was sufficiently common to be discussed openly in the Party press in early 1921, when the Central Committee called for the views and experiences of local Communists in this matter.[68] Letter writers most frequently cited Communists who passively condoned or participated in rites under severe pressure from family

[63] "Iaroslavskaia oblastnaia organizatsiia KPSS v tsifrakh, 1917–1990," *Vremia i my: Zhurnal ideologicheskogo otdela Iaroslavskogo obkoma*, 1990, nos. 5–6 (May): 29.

[64] N.K., "Likvidatsiia politnegramotnosti v partii," *Kommunisticheskaia revoliutsiia*, 1923, no. 8 (15 April): 83–85. Standards varied by province.

[65] RTsKhIDNI, f. 17, op. 60, d. 629, l. 38.

[66] *Kommunisticheskaia partiia Sovetskogo Soiuza v resoliutsiiakh i resheniiakh s"ezdov, konferentsii i plenumov TsK* (Moscow, 1953), pt. 1, 420–421.

[67] GARF, f. a-353, op. 5, d. 262, l. 3.

[68] *Pravda*, 31 March 1921. The statement was signed by Emel'ian Iaroslavskii in his capacity as secretary of the Central Committee, a position he held briefly in 1921.

and community.[69] Other Communists were actively religious and declared their belief in God. In September 1921, the Central Committee issued guidelines that confirmed and clarified Point 13 of the program. Although the policy held that no clergy or active believers could become or remain members of the Party, it permitted passive participants in religious rituals who were reacting to acute "social/family" conditions to become and remain Communists while they struggled to overcome religion in their midst.[70] Making a virtue of necessity, the regime accepted supporters even if they did not know what their support actually entailed on a personal or professional level.

Reports of religiousness among Communists and Komsomol members continued throughout the 1920s. In 1923, the Central Committee found "as a mass phenomenon . . . the church marriage of rural and even sometimes urban Communists, including workers, and the baptism of children in the countryside."[71] According to *Revoliutsiia i tserkov'*, Communists from Tver' would go "on assignment" to other towns for confession or to be married in a church. "Religion and Communism get on together excellently in the countryside," the journal noted. One Communist was married in a church under a banner reading "Proletariat of the world unite!"[72] The vision of a Communist marrying in a church festooned with revolutionary banners evoked the conflicting loyalties and social pressures on local cadres, and also demonstrated that while communism and the Church each demanded exclusive allegiance, prevailing conditions produced compromises and intermediate degrees of commitment. Even in urban, sophisticated Leningrad, a Party official stated in April 1926 that fifty candidate members had already left the Leningrad organization that year for religious reasons; fifty more had broken Point 13 and left as a result of actions initiated by local Party control commissions. He added to these numbers the approximately 25 percent of Communists who left the Party without explanation, who were believed to have done so for reli-

---

[69] RTsKhIDNI, f. 17, op. 60, d. 52. Some of the letters are excerpted in Vorontsov, *Leninskaia programma*, 46–48.

[70] "O postanovke antireligioznoi propagande i o narushenii punkt 13 programmy," *Izvestiia TsK RKP(b)*, 1921, no. 33 (October): 32–33; Vorontsov, *Leninskaia programma*, 48; Alekseev, *Illiuzii i dogmy*, 268.

[71] RTsKhIDNI, f. 17, op. 60, d. 442, l. 78. Additional anecdotal evidence is presented in Glenny Young, *Power and the Sacred in Revolutionary Russia: Religious Activists in the Village* (University Park: Penn State University Press, 1997), 87–89.

[72] *Revoliutsiia i tserkov'*, 1922, nos. 1–3: 64–65. Church weddings of Communist and Komsomol grooms to non-Communist brides were also noted at the League's congress in 1925. GARF, f. r-5407, op. 1, d. 5, l. 25. I did not encounter any discussion of atheist brides and believer grooms.

gious reasons. He concluded gravely that these numbers were not decreasing over time.[73]

The shortcomings of its cadre base was a major obstacle for the Bolshevik leadership in all spheres, and throughout the 1920s, the Communist Party held regular purges and reregistrations of its membership primarily to rid itself of "problem" members.[74] While these measures often were undertaken for political purposes, they also were genuinely directed against those who, in the terminology of the time, were too passive, too careerist, too drunk, or otherwise inappropriate for the Party's public face. Party documents are particularly replete with discussion of members' excessive drinking, offering further evidence that the Bolshevik construction of New Soviet Man was less directly ideological than cultural.

Short on skilled Communists, the regime was forced to rely on the enthusiasm of the local Komsomol members, whose ardor often exceeded their judgment,[75] and as a result the Komsomol leadership was compelled to issue numerous warnings about local Komsomol antireligious behavior throughout the 1920s. Directives to limit the Komsomol's planned anti-Christmas carnival of 1923 to Moscow and Petrograd were ignored, and Komsomol Christmas in Pskov consisted of a street procession with torches, automobiles, an orchestra, the burial of "counterrevolution," and the incineration of gods, all to the reported delight of large crowds.[76] One of the initiators of the Komsomol Christmas campaign, Ivan Stepanov, later admitted that "in many cases [it] turned into Komsomol mischief."[77] Referring to the Komsomol, Stalin commented in the spring of 1924 that "hooliganish escapades under the guise of so-called antireligious propaganda—all this should be cast off and liquidated immediately."[78] Nevertheless, a report in 1925 found that atheistic propaganda in many areas consisted of Komsomol members "getting drunk—brawling and having a good time fighting."[79] In Pskov, an investigation in 1925 concluded that the peasantry would not participate in antireligious circles

---

[73] RTsKhIDNI, f. 17, op. 60, d. 791, l. 77.
[74] T. H. Rigby, *Communist Party Membership in the USSR, 1917–1967* (Princeton: Princeton University Press, 1968), 70, 77, 96–100, 128, 172, 176–177; Leonard Schapiro, *The Communist Party of the Soviet Union* (New York: Random House, 1971), 236–237, 324.
[75] For further general evidence of Komsomol exuberance and associated shortcomings, see Young, *Power and the Sacred*, 92–110.
[76] RTsKhIDNI, f. 17, op. 112, d. 443a, l. 19; "Komsomol'skoe rozhdestvo," *Izvestiia*, 3 January 1923, 4; "Komsomol'skoe rozhdestvo," *Izvestiia*, 6 January 1923, 2, and 10 January 1923, 4.
[77] GARF, f. r-5407, op. 1, d. 6, l. 5.
[78] Alekseev, *Illiuzii i dogmy*, p. 280.
[79] TsKhDMO, f. 1, op. 23, d. 392, l. 9.

"as long as the fervent Komsomol spirit is not eliminated."[80] Party authorities criticized the Komsomol in Nekouz volost' (Iaroslavl' Province) for engaging in "outrageous forms" of godlessness, such as destroying cemeteries and disrupting church services.[81] In the course of the 1920s, the Komsomol Christmas and Easter campaigns became, at least officially, more muted and less physically aggressive, though the authorities' constant pleading suggests that local activists turned a deaf ear to calls for restraint.[82] In many rural corners of the Soviet Union, the *komsomol'tsy* were the regime's most visible representatives, and their behavior often discredited the Bolshevik program. The Revolution put power in the hands of teenagers, compounding the challenge to traditional authority associated with adolescence. Their largely uncontrolled antireligious activities made the regime's propaganda agenda all the more difficult to realize.

Mixed Signals, Many Signals

Although much of the concern over the execution of the regime's policy reflected genuine questions about the "quality" of local cadres, some blame must be assigned to the regime's inconsistency in such matters. Local Party, Komsomol, and Soviet cadres had to struggle with ever-changing and often confusing central policies. Even after the Civil War ended, mixed signals continued to come from Moscow. In 1921, the Central Committee issued a statement that antireligious propaganda should not occupy the leading position on the propaganda agenda. The Party leadership backtracked a few months later, however, saying that this did not mean that antireligious propaganda should be ignored.[83] In 1923, the Twelfth Party Congress adopted a resolution specifically encouraging antireligious propaganda, but the following year at its Thirteenth Congress, the Party downplayed the campaign against religion when it adopted the pro-peasant, "face to the countryside" policy.[84] A Central Committee report on antireligious propaganda in 1925, however, pointed out that the Thirteenth Party Congress's injunction to be careful in matters of religion

---

[80] PPA, f. 1, op. 1, d. 386, l. 65.

[81] IaPA, f. 1, op. 27, d. 2234, l. 20.

[82] On the Komsomol's general approach to the antireligious campaign, see Isabel Tirado, "The Revolution, Young Peasants, and the Komsomol's Antireligious Campaigns (1920–1928)," *Canadian-American Slavic Studies* 26, nos. 1–3 (1992): 97–117.

[83] *Vestnik Agitatsii i Propagandy*, 1921, no. 19; *Izvestiia TsK*, 1922, no. 2: 35; RTsKhIDNI, f. 17, op. 60, d. 158, ll. 17–18.

[84] *Dvenadtsatyi s"ezd RKP (b)*, 716–717; *Trinadtsatyi s"ezd RKP (b)*, 642–643.

did not mean to do nothing.[85] To complicate matters, the Party issued statements through the early 1920s suggesting support for certain sectarian groups, including a provision in 1919 for exemption from military service on the basis of conscientious objection, and assistance to some sectarians in establishing agricultural communes.[86] The regime's support for the Renovationists could easily have confused local cadres not fully initiated into the regime's divide-and-conquer policy.[87] Different secularization strategies existed simultaneously within the Soviet Union. A fully distinct policy in the 1920s in Central Asia focused on women as a "surrogate proletariat" in order to undermine the political power of the male clergy in Islamic society.[88]

Shifting policies and their varied application remained a problem throughout the 1920s. A uniform policy on religious organizations was promulgated only in 1929; before that, policy and legislation emanated from various quarters. In the early 1920s, there existed numerous short-lived commissions, subcommittees, and working groups concerned with religion within the Central Committee alone.[89] They were joined in 1922 by a special group headed by Trotsky to oversee the seizure of church valuables.[90] Another body, headed by Petr Germanovich Smidovich, concerned itself with sectarian matters. The Commissariat of Justice, the secret police (OGPU), the Central Executive Committee of Soviets (VTsIK), and the Ministry of Internal Affairs (NKVD) also played roles.

The regime was aware of this disorder, and the shift toward systematic propaganda in the early 1920s included a partial simplification of this apparatus that also reflected a sorting out of power relations at the highest echelons, to Trotsky's detriment. In the autumn of 1922, the Central Committee

---

[85] RTsKhIDNI, f. 17, op. 60, d. 723, ll. 121–122.

[86] *Spravochnik partiinogo rabotnika*, vyp. II (Moscow, 1922), 93–94; Petr Krasikov, "Trudovoe sektantstvo," *Revoliutsiia i tserkov'*, 1922, nos. 1–3: 26–30. See Etkind, "Russkie seky i sovetskii kommunism," 275–319; M. I. Odintsov, *Gosudarstvo i tserkov': Istoriia vzaimootnoshenii, 1917–1938* (Moscow: Znanie, 1991), 27; Alekseev, *Illiuzii i dogmy*, 72, 274–275; Arto Luukkanen, *The Party of Unbelief: The Religious Policy of the Bolshevik Policy, 1917–1929* (Helsinki: Societas Historica Finlandiae, 1994), 181–186.

[87] The temptation to establish a modern counterchurch also briefly seduced the Mexican revolutionary leadership, which created the Iglesia Católica Apostólica Mexicana. See Adrian Bantjes, "Idolatry and Iconoclasm in Revolutionary Mexico: The De-Christianization Campaigns, 1929–1940," *Mexican Studies* 13, no. 1 (Winter 1997): 13.

[88] Gregory Massell, *The Surrogate Proletariat: Moslem Women and Revolutionary Strategies in Soviet Central Asia, 1919–1929* (Princeton: Princeton University Press, 1974).

[89] Odintsov, *Gosudarstvo i tserkov'*, 28–29; RTsKhIDNI, f. 17, op. 60, d. 158.

[90] *Russkaia pravoslavnaia tserkov' i kommunisticheskoe gosudarstvo, 1917–1941: Dokumenty i fotomaterialy* (Moscow: Bibleisko-bogoslovskii Institut Sviatogo Apostola Andreia, 1996), 67–145.

unified its disparate voices on religious policy into one standing commission "with full authority in general leadership of policy in regard to religion and the Church and the development of Party directives on issues of antireligious propaganda, and [ended] the work of all other such commissions."[91] This body was formally titled the "Committee on the Execution of the Decree Separating Church and State," but was better known as the Antireligious Commission. A core of prominent Bolsheviks served on the commission throughout the 1920s: Petr Krasikov; the Central Committee propaganda official Konstantin Popov (added in 1924); the OGPU official V. R. Menzhinskii; P. G. Smidovich; and the commission's long-time secretary, Evgenii A. Tuchkov, who headed the OGPU's Sixth Department, in charge of religious affairs.[92] Although Trotsky had headed the campaign to seize church valuables and had been active in previous Central Committee working groups on religion, he was not appointed to the new commission. Instead, a presumptive ally of Stalin, Emel'ian Iaroslavskii, was appointed chairman in early 1923, effectively ending Trotsky's direct influence on antireligious matters. Until its dissolution in 1929, the Antireligious Commission oversaw all aspects of Church–State relations and antireligious propaganda, including the League's activities. The commission had only limited direct authority, however, because its resolutions and requests became authoritative only with the sanction of the Central Committee's Secretariat, Orgbiuro, or Politbiuro.[93] It remains unclear to what degree this structure was replicated locally outside Moscow—the large Moscow Party Committee had its own Antireligious Commission—but there is no evidence of standing antireligious Party commissions in Iaroslavl' or Pskov.

Early Organizational Efforts

Having streamlined its antireligious apparatus, the regime then created the structures necessary for a propaganda campaign. Organized manifesta-

---

[91] Vorontsov, *Leninskaia programma*, 59.

[92] RTsKhIDNI, f. 17, op. 60, d. 158, l. 14; op. 112, d. 367, l. 3; op. 112, d. 378, ll. 60–61, op. 112, d. 443-a. Other occasional participants included T. D. Deribas (OGPU), Vladimir Bonch-Bruevich (Lenin's former personal secretary and a specialist on sects), Fedor Putintsev (sects), Ivan Skvortsov-Stepanov, Fedor Oleshchuk (League), Aleksandr Lukachevskii (League), Anatolii Lunacharskii (Narkompros), Anton Loginov (Moscow Party Committee), and Mariia Kostelovskaia (Moscow Party Committee).

[93] The Commissariat of Justice's "liquidation" department was itself liquidated in 1924 during an administrative reorganization. In late 1929, many of the functions of the former Antireligious Commission were shifted to the newly created (April 1929) Permanent Commission on Questions of Cults of the Presidium of the All-Russian Central Executive Committee

tions of revolutionary sentiment were deeply rooted in Bolshevik political culture, as Bolshevism fully accepted modernist assumptions about planning a socialist society. With this orientation, publishing media, particularly newspapers, took on crucial importance. In addition to promoting the regime's ideology, these media provided vital information to local officials, activists, and sympathizers in the absence of other forms of communication. This was the case in 1922 in Soviet Russia, when the regime's reach into the countryside and the reliability of its cadres remained questionable. These print sources also served as direct propaganda organs, supplying material for activists and, in theory, attracting new adherents to the cause. Finally, the print media provided a foundation upon which to rally the cause's followers. Lenin's famous statement of 1901, "The newspaper is not only a collective propagandist and a collective agitator, it is also a collective organizer," had already become axiomatic in Bolshevik political culture.[94] (The press was similarly important in Nazi Germany.)[95] When, in November 1922, the newly created Antireligious Commission asked the Central Committee's agitprop department to create an antireligious newspaper for national distribution, the cause of atheism had been judged sufficiently important to merit its own newspaper, and thus the means of organizing, controlling, and promoting Soviet atheism. The first issue of *Bezbozhnik* (Godless) appeared in late December 1922 with a print run of 15,000,[96] and a new era of Soviet atheism began.

The logical next step in the apotheosis of the antireligious movement was the formation of an organization to manifest and promote the achievements of Soviet atheism. Although Lenin had identified the importance of

---

(Postoiannaia komissiia po voprosam kul'tov pri Prezidiume VTsIK, 1929–1934), which was reorganized in 1934 as the Permanent Commission on Questions of Cults of the Presidium of the Central Executive Committee of Soviets (Postoiannaia komissiia po kul'tovym voprosam pri prezidiume TsIK SSSR, 1934–1938).

[94] Kenez, *Birth of the Propaganda State*, 26.

[95] The literature on Nazi propaganda techniques is voluminous, but for a concise presentation of Nazi use of newspapers in a local context, see William Sheridan Allen, *The Nazi Seizure of Power: The Experience of a Single German Town, 1922–1945*, rev. ed. (New York: Franklin Watts, 1984), 202–206.

[96] RTsKhIDNI, f. 17, op. 112, d. 443a, ll. 10, 16. Although nominally edited by Emel'ian Iaroslavskii, *Bezbozhnik* relied on Mikhail Gorev for its early day-to-day operations. *Bezbozhnik*'s print run jumped to 210,000 by February 1925 before slipping back to less than a 100,000 until the end of the 1920s, when it grew rapidly again to over 500,000. The appearance of *Bezbozhnik* in late 1922 was preceded by several short-lived publications produced by dedicated individuals without the full backing of authoritative institutions. These included in 1922 *Ateist* and *Nauka i religiia* in Moscow and *Vavilonskaia bashnia* in Petrograd. RTsKhIDNI, f. 17, op. 60, d. 182, ll. 103, 116; op. 112, d. 367, l. 3; op. 112, d. 443a, l. 10.

revolutionary organizations in his *What Is to Be Done?* (1902), there was nothing inherently Marxist about this form of historical agency; it was instead largely the product of the Russian revolutionary experience and the bureaucratic nature of the tsarist period in which the revolutionary culture had developed. According to the internal logic of this culture, atheism could flourish only if it were guided. An organization of atheists would promote, control, and measure the dissemination of atheism in society. Pressure to "organize" atheism was particularly great by the mid-1920s in light of the counterproductive Komsomol campaigns, the apparent religious renaissance, and the increasing realization that the Renovationist Church was unable to influence Orthodoxy.

Not surprisingly, the means chosen to organize atheism grew out of *Bezbozhnik*. In October 1923, in a front-page editorial, Iaroslavskii called for the formation of a national League of the Godless. Given the brief retreat from direct attacks on the Church during the summer of 1923, this proposal had little resonance at the time, but less than a year later, on 27 August 1924, the newspaper established a lesser Society of Friends of the Newspaper *Bezbozhnik* (Obshchestvo druzei gazety "Bezbozhnika," abbreviated ODGB), a sort of nationwide fan club.[97] Soviet histories claim that this organization emerged from below in response to popular demand. While a few local initiatives were taken to organize the ODGB outside of Moscow, they were exceptions to the generally observed pattern of organization "from above."[98] The ODGB remained loosely organized until April 1925, when a congress of *Bezbozhnik* correspondents and ODGB members met in Moscow and reorganized the ODGB into an All-Union League of the Godless (Vsesoiuznyi soiuz bezbozhnikov).[99]

What, precisely, was the League? In theory, it was a voluntary association of individuals seeking to combat the influence of religion in all its forms and to promote "scientific materialism." Like the other voluntary societies founded in the 1920s, the League was subordinate to the regime, with a core

[97] On 13 November 1924, the Antireligious Commission approved the creation of an all-union, unified, antireligious society with *Bezbozhnik* as its central organ and the ODGB as its organizational base. *Bezbozhnik*, 7 October 1923 and 31 August 1924; V. N. Konovalov, "Soiuz voinstvuiushchikh bezbozhnikov," *Voprosy nauchnogo ateizma* 4 (1967): 67–68; RTsKhIDNI, f. 17, op. 112, d. 775, l. 15.

[98] Several small-scale, short-lived atheist groups appeared in the early 1920s in Voronezh, Severodvinsk, and Moscow. Somewhat more enduring, the Moscow Society of Godless (Obshchestvo bezbozhnikov) was created by the Moscow Party Committee in the autumn of 1923. See Konovalov, "Soiuz voinstvuiushchikh bezbozhnikov," 67; RTsKhIDNI, f. 89, op. 4, d. 158 ll. 32–36; V. Shishakov, "Soiuz voinstvuiushchikh bezbozhnikov," in *Voinstvuiushchee bezbozhie v SSSR za 15 let*, ed. M. Enisherlov (Moscow, 1932), 324.

[99] The use here of the term "League" rather than the more narrowly correct "Union" follows the existing practice of translation for this organization's name.

of members and leadership provided by the Communist Party. According to its first charter, membership in the League required USSR citizenship, complete civil rights,[100] "open and sincere breaking with any cult or religious society with belief in God and subtle forms of religiosity, and active work in a League cell."[101] Those cells were to promote atheism by selling subscriptions to League periodicals and through lectures, discussions, tours of museums, reading circles, demonstrations (direct agitation), and the rest of the panoply of propaganda methods employed by the regime.

Individuals under eighteen could participate on a consultative basis, and the League later created a special organization for Young Godless. The League very much resembled the Party in structure: individual members were organized into cells based at the workplace. In the cities, League cells formed in stores, offices, factory sections, railroad depots, and schools. In the countryside, the League appeared at cooperatives and reading huts, and later at collective farms and machine tractor stations. Individual cells were overseen by councils organized at the level of the *uezd* (or *raion* [district]), *okrug* (region), or *guberniia* (province) or oblast, as it was now called. This network had its headquarters in Moscow.

Cells with more than ten members were to elect a bureau of at least three individuals. Councils of five to seven individuals ran *uezd* and *raion* League organizations. Larger councils headed provincial League organizations. Each council was to be elected at regularly scheduled conferences, and was divided internally according to functional responsibilities such as sects, agitation, research, international work, youth. Depending on its size and prosperity, a council might have a chairman, a deputy chairman, an executive secretary, and instructors, and several of these positions might be full-time paid jobs. The League's activities were supposed to be financed with income from dues and the sale of propaganda materials. Dues were initially set at 5 kopeks a year for urban members, and 2 for rural Godless. The unemployed, Red Army soldiers, and students were exempted from dues. One half of the collected dues was to remain in the cell to finance its activities. Of the remainder, 10 percent each went to the *volost'* and *uezd* councils, 20 percent to the provincial council, and 10 percent to the Central Council in Moscow.[102]

The eight years between the Bolshevik takeover in 1917 and the League's appearance in 1925 left the antireligious propaganda campaign a

---

[100] By the constitution of 1918, many individuals, including clergy and former clergy, were denied the franchise and numerous other civil rights.

[101] *Ustav Soiuza bezbozhnikov SSSR* (Moscow, 1925).

[102] Over the years, the amount of dues and their distribution changed frequently. This schematic is for 1925.

complicated legacy. In the absence of an overall plan and with a shifting policy record, a substantial burden was placed on local cadres. Their low numbers, inadequate education, and religiosity kept the cadres issue at the forefront of the antireligious campaign, and also contributed to the regime's broader need to engage in a comprehensive process of state building. Ironically, in this context the regime launched a propaganda effort that depended on the presence of a large number of qualified cadres. The regime was aware of this difficulty; the very decree approving the formation of a national antireligious organization in November 1924 specifically stated that a high-quality membership must be guaranteed.[103] Yet the regime needed to establish central institutions to oversee and control the effort to build that membership. As we will see in Chapter 2, the regime's activists were not of one mind concerning these developments.

[103] RTsKhIDNI, f. 17, op. 112, d. 775, l. 15.

2

Organized Atheism in the 1920s

We want to sweep away everything that claims to be supernatural and super-human. . . . For that reason, we have once and for all declared war on religion and religious ideas and care little about whether we are called atheists or anything else.

—Friedrich Engels, "Die Lage Englands,"
in *Deutsch-Französische Jahrbücher, 1844*

Almost immediately after its creation, the League found itself embroiled in a series of controversies that lasted until the end of the decade. These years witnessed an open struggle for leadership of the antireligious campaign, as well as disagreements in the Bolshevik Party over how an atheistic society would be defined, measured, and achieved. Throughout these debates, the dearth of quality cadres regularly emerged as a source of conflict and a fundamental obstacle to achieving the regime's goals, however defined. Although these conflicts were to some extent related to political maneuvering within the Kremlin, they also constituted ample evidence of a broader uncertainty in the identity and purpose of the Party in the mid-1920s. Institutional, personal, and ideological cleavages characterized the Bolshevik polity and boded ill for the long-term viability of the NEP.[1]

The vast Western secondary literature on the NEP has focused on several issues. The most important of these is the coherence, extent, and—crucially—viability of the NEP between the perceived "revolutionary" periods of the Civil War and Stalin's Great Turn at the end of the 1920s. Earlier generations tended to downplay the NEP's significance, casting it as a minor respite in the regime's committed policy of radical intervention to create its version of a socialist society. In Western scholarship, this consensus began to crack with the publication of Stephen Cohen's biography

[1] The high-level maneuvering is recounted in Stephen F. Cohen, *Bukharin and the Bolshevik Revolution: A Political Biography, 1888–1938* (New York: Knopf, 1973); the broader social divisions are discussed in Lewis H. Siegelbaum, *Soviet State and Society between Revolutions, 1918–1929* (Cambridge: Cambridge University Press, 1992).

of Nikolai Bukharin in 1973,[2] which cast the NEP as a functional, theoretically justified, and viable alternative to the path of forced industrialization and collectivization that was ultimately adopted. Since then, a cottage industry of sorts concerning the NEP has sprung up, and most recently has been able to take advantage of greater access to source materials. This scholarship has focused attention on NEP society—its contours, strength, and relative autonomy. In his overview of this literature, Lewis Siegelbaum limns a State/society relationship in the 1920s characterized by flexible boundaries, mutual interaction, and constant redefinition.[3] To the extent that there is a consensus in this literature, it concerns the highly conflicted nature of NEP society. And as William Rosenberg has argued, there were few means to mediate conflicts within NEP society that would have undermined the regime's justification for intervention late in the decade.[4] While study of the League of the Godless cannot resolve all of the debates concerning NEP society, it can provide one more piece of the NEP puzzle, particularly in the area of voluntary organizations and the regime's pursuit of its social agenda.

Publications, Personalities, and Programs

The first clash concerned publications. Even before *Bezbozhnik* appeared in December 1922, signs of tension between its backer, the Antireligious Commission, and the Moscow Party organization were apparent. In early December, the Antireligious Commission criticized as unnecessary a potentially competitive journal planned by the Moscow group. Nevertheless, in January 1923, the journal, also called *Bezbozhnik*, appeared under the editorship of a Moscow Party activist, Mariia Mikhailovna Kostelovskaia. Although the Antireligious Commission failed in its initial effort in early 1923 to have the new journal merged into Iaroslavskii's newspaper, the Moscow publication either was compelled or chose to add *u stanka* (at the workbench) to its title to differentiate it from the newspaper *Bezbozhnik* and to suggest an urban worker orientation.[5]

The conflict may have been a personal struggle between the two editors, Iaroslavskii and Kostelovskaia. Iaroslavskii was born Minei Izrailovich

[2] Cohen, *Bukharin and the Bolshevik Revolution.*

[3] Siegelbaum, *Soviet State and Society between Revolutions.*

[4] William G. Rosenberg, "Introduction: NEP Russia as a 'Transitional' Society," and "Conclusion: Understanding NEP Society and Culture in the Light of New Research," in *Russia in the Era of NEP: Explorations in Soviet Society and Culture,* ed. Sheila Fitzpatrick, Alexander Rabinowitch, and Richard Stites (Bloomington: Indiana University Press, 1991), 1–11, 310–320.

[5] RTsKhIDNI, f. 17, op. 112, d. 443a, ll. 19, 28.

Gubel'man in 1878 in the Siberian town of Chita, where his father had been exiled. His involvement in the revolutionary movement began before the turn of the century, and in 1917 he participated in the Bolshevik takeover of Moscow and was the first commissar of the Moscow Military District. After serving briefly in 1921 as secretary of the Central Committee, Iaroslavskii worked throughout the 1920s as secretary of the Party's Central Control Commission, as well as in numerous other Party and government positions.[6] Iaroslavskii sat on the editorial board of many newspapers and journals, and was intimately involved in several prominent Bolshevik historical projects. In addition to heading the League of the Godless, he also led the Society of Old Bolsheviks and was the elected elder (*starosta*) of the Society of Political Exiles. Iaroslavskii was a wide-ranging intellectual who can fairly be considered a graphomaniac, even if many of his writings did little more than articulate the prevailing political line. Although criticized by Stalin in his famous "Letter to the Editors of *Proletarian Revolution*" in 1931, Iaroslavskii remained one of Stalin's second-rank deputies throughout the 1930s.

Iaroslavskii's qualifications to lead the regime's antireligious apparatus were limited but probably sufficient, given the dearth of skilled cadres at all levels of the Bolshevik apparatus. In 1907, Iaroslavskii had penned an antireligious tract under the name "Social Democrat Volodia." In 1918, he was among the troika of high officials directed to stir up opposition to the Orthodox clergy, and the following year he co-authored the provision exempting certain sectarians from military service as conscientious objectors.[7] More important, in 1921, as a Central Committee secretary he had overseen the discussion of religiousness among Party cadres. Iaroslavskii served as editor of the main antireligious newspaper, *Bezbozhnik* (to 1941), chairman of the Antireligious Commission (to 1929), and leader of the League (to 1943). For almost two decades he was the Soviet Union's most visible atheist and public spokesman on Church–State relations.

Kostelovskaia lacked Iaroslavskii's stature in the Bolshevik hierarchy, but she still occupied influential positions. A Communist since 1903, Kostelovskaia arrived in Moscow in 1916 and participated in the Bolshevik uprising there. At that time, she would likely have come into contact

[6] S. N. Savel'ev, *Emel'ian Iaroslavskii—propagandist marksistskogo ateizma* (Leningrad: Leningrad State University, 1976); D. I. Antoniuk, "E. M. Iaroslavskii," *Voprosy istorii KPSS*, 1978, no. 3, 98–102; *Bol'shaia sovetskaia entsiklopediia*, 65 vols. (Moscow, 1926–47), 65:778–780.
[7] V. A. Alekseev, *Illiuzii i dogmy* (Moscow: Izdatel'stvo Politicheskoi Literatury, 1991), 72; *Izvestiia TsK KPSS*, 1989, no. 4, 147; RTsKhIDNI, f. 89, op. 4, d. 9, l. 13.

with Iaroslavskii, who was one of the leaders of the Moscow revolt. After serving in the South during the Civil War, Kostelovskaia returned to Moscow and headed the Party Life department of *Pravda*, serving simultaneously as the secretary of the Baumanskii District Party Committee. Kostelovskaia was delegated to the Antireligious Commission from the Moscow Party organization in December 1922, and from then until 1926 she and several Moscow-based colleagues were in almost constant conflict with Iaroslavskii and the institutions aligned with him.[8] Although these conflicts suggested some personal enmity, there is also evidence of clashing ideological views and institutional associations.

The two groups had strongly contrasting views of religion and how to achieve an atheistic society. Iaroslavskii understood religion to be a complex cultural phenomenon reflecting both production relations within society and the Russian peasantry's centuries-old isolation and subservience to nature. Ultimately, the victory of a scientific-materialist worldview required transformation of "rural production relations" and the peasantry's relationship to nature and technology. In the meantime, antireligious propaganda, carefully explaining what religion was and how it harmed believers, was necessary. Such a statement of ideological voluntarism was contradictory to orthodox Marxism, but it was compatible with the actual conditions in Russia during the NEP. This approach entailed certain specific policies. First, great care would have to be exercised when one confronted religion. The arbitrary closing of churches and arrest of clergy would simply alienate the population and delay cultural transformation. Iaroslavskii was ruthless in persecuting the Orthodox hierarchy but his view on cultural transformation was decidedly more moderate, emphasizing long-term educational propaganda. Although confident of the regime's ability to transform the peasantry, Iaroslavskii and his supporters showed a much greater awareness of peasant resistance to external intervention, as well as of the complexities of a government-sponsored program of radical social transformation. This "culturalist"[9] approach also implied the need for trained cadres with some knowledge of Orthodox history, other religions, and mythology, in addition to science and technology. Finally, Iaroslavskii and his allies supported a process of secularization to be ad-

---

[8] RTsKhIDNI, f. 17, op. 60, d. 294, l. 76; *Soratniki: Biografii aktivnykh uchastnikov revoliutsionnogo dvizheniia v Moskve i Moskovskoi oblasti* (Moscow: Moskovskii Rabochii, 1985), 218–220.

[9] The terms "culturalist" and "interventionist" are taken from my earlier analysis of this conflict. See Daniel Peris, "The 1929 Congress of the Godless," *Soviet Studies* 44, no. 3 (July 1991): 711–732.

ministered through educational propaganda and discreet pressure on both the institutional Orthodox Church and the various sects.

Kostelovskaia and her supporters held a simpler, more mechanistic, and even impatient view of social transformation. According to them, Orthodoxy was a direct manifestation of exploitation in Russia and warranted immediate intervention to close churches and rid the landscape of clergy. Kostelovskaia's side envisioned the process of eliminating religion as a series of battles, presumably borrowing from the imagery of the Civil War. These idealistic "interventionists" acknowledged few limitations on their ability to transform society. They evinced an extreme materialism and anti-intellectualism, and they believed that general Party cadres would be sufficient for antireligious work. The Party (along with the Komsomol) would be the agent of social change, not the ever-proliferating State and State-associated bureaucracies (or voluntary societies) that harbored nonparty specialists of questionable loyalty. The interventionists shared the Komsomol's impatience for achieving social transformation—recalling that "heroic stage" of the Civil War. And when Kostelovskaia's group was defeated in 1926, the Komsomol took up the mantle as the radical challenger to the League's putative moderation.

After the initial internal conflict, the struggle moved to the general Party press.[10] The first fusillade was fired in early 1924, when Stepan Polidorov, a Kostelovskaia lieutenant, attacked *Bezbozhnik* in a journal published by the Moscow Party Committee, *Sputnik kommunista*. He wrote of *Bezbozhnik*'s "permissive attitude" toward the Renovationists and its unnecessarily complex criticisms of religion based on a comparison of myths. The deputy chairman of the League, Mikhail Gorev, responded in *Bezbozhnik*, and Iaroslavskii offered his own retort in a later issue of *Sputnik kommunista*.[11] While the public polemic continued, conflict in Moscow Province between the ODGB and a Society of Godless (Obshchestvo Bezbozhnikov, or OB) created by the Moscow Party unfolded in late 1924 and early 1925. ODGB activists wrote to Iaroslavskii complaining

[10] For a more detailed discussion of the published debate over antireligious propaganda, see (the highly pro-Iaroslavskii) S. N. Savel'ev, "Em. Iaroslavskii i preodolenie anarkhistskikh vliianii v antireligioznoi rabote v SSSR," in *Ezhegodnik muzeia istorii religii i ateizma 7* (1963): 36–50; and Joan Delaney, "The Origins of Soviet Antireligious Organizations," in *Aspects of Religion in the Soviet Union, 1917–1967*, ed. Richard Marshall Jr. (Chicago: University of Chicago Press, 1971), 103–130.

[11] S. Polidorov, "Antiklerikaly i bezbozhniki," *Sputnik kommunista*, 1924, nos. 2–3, 47–53; M. Gorev, "Kak *Bezbozhnik* 'Zhivuiu tserkov' zashchishchal," *Bezbozhnik*, 29 June 1924; and E. Iaroslavskii, "Marksizm i anarkhizm," *Sputnik kommunista*, 1924, nos. 4–5, 42–55.

of pressure from the Moscow Party. One organizer, a candidate Party member, was directed to reorganize his ODGB group into the OB. Although he preferred the ODGB, he was not in a position to refuse the directive of his Party superior.[12] Out in the provinces, this conflict produced a faint but certain echo. The charter of the Pskov ODGB included the statement that ODGB members were distinguished from members of other antireligious groups by their complete support for the newspaper *Bezbozhnik*, and at the first Pskov ODGB conference in January 1925, one of the main speakers told the delegates about the two methods of antireligious propaganda, one careful and one not, being championed in Moscow by competing organizations.[13]

After the exchanges in the Party press, in late 1924 the conflict again reached the Central Committee in a series of investigations and reports featuring both Kostelovskaia and Iaroslavskii. Iaroslavskii attacked the "uncontrolled amateurishness" of the current antireligious scene and wrote emphatically that it would be foolish to limit an antireligious organization to Party and Komsomol members (Kostelovskaia's wish). Kostelovskaia, in turn, disparaged the available propaganda materials as third-rate German translations and mythology. She defended the Moscow organization's selective membership, and charged that the ODGB admitted anyone who would pay dues. Despite Kostelovskaia's efforts, in December 1924 the Orgbiuro approved the ODGB's plan to hold a congress of *Bezbozhnik* correspondents in February 1925.[14]

The League's new status did not put an end to the ODGB/OB conflict. Kostelovskaia raised the level of confrontation in an article in *Pravda* on 25 January 1925, in which she linked the recent growth of sects to the failure of Bolshevik antireligious propaganda.[15] Among the numerous shortcomings in antireligious work that she cited were too much clergy bashing (*popoedstvo*), a crude substitution of revolutionary symbols for religious ones, and the mixing of religious and revolutionary terminology, giving the impression that communism was a religion. She explained this last point by noting that the earliest antireligious activists were those who at one time had been close to religion, such as clergymen and God-seekers. Because of their influence, "Godlessness . . . [was] built in the manner of a religion, only a religion of a particular type . . . Communist religion." The prevailing Godlessness shared the scholasticism of religion and its idealism by calling for the personal asceticism of League members, in particular ab-

[12] RTsKhIDNI, f. 89, op. 4, d. 147, l. 1.
[13] PPA, f. 1, op. 4, d. 161, ll. 4, 19.
[14] RTsKhIDNI, f. 17, op. 112, d. 620, ll. 2–3, 15–72.
[15] "Ob oshibkakh v antireligioznoi propagande," *Pravda*, 25 January 1925.

stinence from alcohol.[16] These tendencies in antireligious propaganda, she charged, were grist for the sectarian mill. To improve antireligious propaganda, she concluded, it should be removed from the control of specialists and imbued with a class emphasis rather than a scientific or mythological orientation.

Four days later, Iaroslavskii responded with a blistering attack on Kostelovskaia in *Pravda*.[17] Reviewing their skirmishes of the previous year, he blamed Kostelovskaia for reopening the conflict and making charges against him personally. Iaroslavskii defended ODGB and *Bezbozhnik*'s appeal to nonparty members and maintained that *Bezbozhnik u stanka* was far more narrowly anticlerical, referring specifically to the content of recent issues. He also accused Kostelovskaia of lacking a basic understanding of how individuals understood religion and reacted to antireligious propaganda.

In February the Antireligious Commission condemned Kostelovskaia for failing to discuss her concerns within the commission, and asked the Central Committee and the Moscow Party Committee to replace her on the Antireligious Commission.[18] In a three-page statement appended to the official protocol, Kostelovskaia furiously responded to the charges leveled against her. She claimed that Iaroslavskii's published attacks against her were far more personal than hers against him. She recalled her many appeals to the Central Committee to resolve this problem once and for all. She also noted that the Antireligious Commission's purpose was not to concern itself with the methodology and content of antireligious propaganda but to attend to the administrative matters suggested by its formal title, the Committee on the Execution of the Decree on Separation of Church and State, and she pointed out that its core staff consisted of administrators.[19] Kostelovskaia further pointed out that her appointment to the commission had been approved by the Politbiuro in June 1923, but that in the course of the following eighteen months, the commission had not met once in plenary session. The group that convened regularly, she charged, was a "presidium" constructed to exclude her. In nearly two years, she had managed to participate in only four meetings.

[16] Apparently this condition for membership in the League had been proposed; it was not adopted.

[17] "O metodakh antireligioznoi propagandy—vynuzhdennyi otvet tov. Kostelovskoi," *Pravda*, 29 January 1925.

[18] RTsKhIDNI, f. 89, op. 4, d. 14, l. 13.

[19] Of the hundred or so protocols of this body that I was able to examine in the Central Party Archive in Moscow, all but a handful were headed "Committee on the Separation of Church and State." In almost every other instance, in both personal and official documents, the body was referred to as the Antireligious Commission.

These statements were to no avail. The Moscow Party Committee removed Kostelovskaia from the Antireligious Commission on 28 February 1925 and ordered the merger of the Moscow Society of Godless and the ODGB.[20] With the first organizational battle over, a congress of *Bezbozhnik* correspondents and ODGB members met in Moscow from 19 to 26 April 1925. The conflict still served as a leitmotif for the speakers at the congress, but Iaroslavskii sought to downplay its importance, confirming that agreements had been reached and that the Moscow Society of Godless was the division of the ODGB in Moscow Province.[21]

The 1926 Central Committee Conference

The charges and countercharges begun late in 1922 culminated formally in a special Central Committee conference (*soveshchanie*) on antireligious propaganda in April 1926.[22] Fifty-five activists attended, thirty from Moscow and twenty-five from the provinces. Although Kostelovskaia had already been removed from the Antireligious Commission, fundamental issues remained unresolved. What would Soviet atheism look like? Who would be responsible for it now that cultural transformation was nearing the top of the regime's ideological agenda?

Anton Loginov delivered the main report on the task and methods of antireligious work. A Party member of twenty years' standing, Loginov had been an early activist for *Bezbozhnik u stanka*, and at the April 1925 congress he had justified the journal's extreme caricatures, though he backed off from defending the entire *Bezbozhnik u stanka* program.[23] The Moscow Party had appointed Loginov to Kostelovskaia's place on the Antireligious Commission in March 1925, and by 1926 he was a leading League official and writer for *Bezbozhnik*. In his report, Loginov staked out a conciliatory middle position, which at times amounted to fence-sitting. He outlined both religion's immediate political threat and the importance of science and long-term education in overcoming religion. Similarly, Loginov spoke in favor of both antireligious specialists and the use of general cadres, thereby glossing over another point of conflict. The tone of Loginov's report, however, clearly was critical of Kostelovskaia's stridency and views.[24]

[20] RTsKhIDNI, f. 89, op. 4, d. 116, l. 20.
[21] GARF, f. r-5407, op. 1, d. 5, l. 32.
[22] The conference's stenographic report and resolutions are preserved in RTsKhIDNI, f. 17, op. 60, dd. 791–793.
[23] GARF, f. r-5407, op. 1, d. 5, l. 23.
[24] RTsKhIDNI, f. 17, op. 60, d. 791, ll. 7–28.

Kostelovskaia immediately attacked Loginov for his "sauce vinai-grette," his theoretical eclecticism, and his "utmost abstraction and ut-most scholasticism." Religion was an immediate threat to workers; sects were no different. It was ridiculous to emphasize that religion contradicted science, she continued, because all the best scientists in Western Europe were believers: "Aren't you ashamed to say such nonsense, that religion is the realm of ignorance, as if the matter lay only in enlightenment. Because of this, our staff are extremely surprised when they find out that the work-ers in Western Europe believe in God." The target of their efforts, she pressed, ought to be the core of society—the workers—and antireligious work should be administered directly by Party agitprop departments. The League of the Godless was fine as a limited voluntary association, but by no means should it be strongly centralized.[25] The workers and their party should remain in the forefront of social change, not the ever-expanding bureaucracy of State and non-State organizations.

Discussion of Kostelovskaia's comments was heated.[26] Kostelovskaia had her supporters, among them a Komsomol activist, M. Galaktionov, who charged that *Bezbozhnik* represented the enlightenment approach to religion, against which Comrade Lenin had warned. He saw no evidence of the class approach in *Bezbozhnik,* and claimed that it coddled former priests.[27] The League official Anatolii Lukachevskii refuted Galaktionov's accusations and labeled the other side narrow and overly abstract in its methods. Lukachevskii also accused Kostelovskaia's camp of an utter lack of realism in respect to the way antireligious propaganda had to be pre-sented to be accepted by the population. V. G. Knorin, of the Central Committee, interjected that the debate was too broad and too concerned about the past. He also reminded the interventionists that workers were no longer subjected to capitalist exploitation in Soviet Russia. Ending the first day's discussion, Iaroslavskii declared victory and consensus, though he added none too subtly that Kostelovskaia had been wrong on most points.

The second day of debate featured a report on the League of the Godless by Fedor Oleshchuk.[28] The son of a priest, Oleshchuk later stated that he had "learned to doubt religion" as a youth. Having joined the Party in 1921, he served in various capacities as an antireligious instructor for the

[25] RTsKhIDNI, f. 17, op. 60, d. 791, ll. 29, 33, 35, 42.

[26] RTsKhIDNI, f. 17, op. 60, d. 791, ll. 45–114.

[27] This is a reference to Gorev and another prominent League staff member, Ivan Brikhnichev, who were former priests. See Daniel Peris, "Commissars in Red Cassocks," *Slavic Review* 54, no. 2 (Summer 1995): 340–364.

[28] RTsKhIDNI, f. 17, op. 60, d. 792, ll. 33–52.

Moscow Party until 1925, when, apparently befriended by Iaroslavskii, he joined the ODGB Central Council as its executive secretary. He remained in that position until the outbreak of World War II.[29] At the League's First Congress in 1925, Oleshchuk still showed some allegiance to the Moscow organization, but by 1926 he had become a key League bureaucrat squarely in Iaroslavskii's camp. In his presentation, Oleshchuk argued that the League ought to be moderately centralized. He also supported a proposal to open the League to nonparty members as a means of spreading antireligious propaganda broadly in society.

The final session met on 29 April to hammer out the conference's resolutions.[30] The resolution on Loginov's main report pointed to both the objective and subjective—the very word "subjective" had sent Kostelovskaia into a frenzy—sides of religion. Discussion of Oleshchuk's report turned on the League's centralization. Oleshchuk offered a compromise that would have limited the League's organizational development above the provincial level, but this highly decentralized version, leaving the central body as little more than an information clearinghouse, was criticized by Knorin and Iaroslavskii. The structure finally adopted featured a stronger League central council, though one dedicated more to coordination than to leadership. In his closing remarks, Iaroslavskii artfully claimed that the conference had begun with the antireligious camp divided and had ended in unanimity.[31] This was wishful thinking. Fundamental divisions remained, and *Bezbozhnik u stanka* continued to exist as a platform for opposing views.

The League's Second Congress (1929)

Did the divisions in evidence at the 1926 Central Committee conference extend beyond the closed doors of high-level activists? The League's Second All-Union Congress, held three years later, suggested the existence of similar divisions among the lower- and middle-level cadres. By June 1929, when hundreds of League delegates gathered in Moscow at the House of the Red Army, public forums for the discussion of policy issues were already largely scripted in terms of official agendas and resolutions,[32] but a

---

[29] Abstracts on Oleshchuk's career provided by the Central Party Archive and the Moscow Party Archive, the latter with reference to TsGAOD g. Moskvy, f. 4, op. 2, d. 98, ll. 137–138, as well as an interview with his son Iurii Fedorovich Oleshchuk, 25 May 1992, Moscow.

[30] RTsKhIDNI, f. 17, op. 60, d. 792, ll. 145–190; *Antireligioznik*, 1926, no. 8, 62–79.

[31] RTsKhIDNI, f. 17, op. 60, d. 792, ll. 187–190.

[32] The following section is excerpted from Peris, "1929 Congress of the Godless."

close reading of the congress's stenographic report reveals a replay of the 1926 and even 1924 conflicts. Despite Iaroslavskii's victories in these earlier engagements, by 1929 the political context had altered to such a degree that it allowed the conflict to resurface. The regime's renewed direct assault on religion, launched in early 1929 (discussed in chapter 5), and the generally radicalized political climate emboldened the interventionists to reassert their claims during the congress.

Iaroslavskii maintained his culturalist approach, citing the *"bezkultur'e* [that] still plays an enormous role" in peasant religion. He also warned against arbitrary church closings that might lead to "a bitter battle with at least 60 to 70 million toilers." Commissar of Enlightenment Lunacharskii stated that "we should not undertake to make priests martyrs and have peasants turn against us."[33]

Riding the waves of the Cultural Revolution, the interventionists, now led by the Komsomol, believed that their time had come. A Komsomol spokesman argued that religion was the ideology of the class enemy, and that, among other measures, they must clearly uncover the class essence of religion and prove that the Church was a political organization of the class enemy, and that its primary weapon was deception of the masses. These latter-day interventionists also derided enlightenment strategies against religion and welcomed "administrative measures." One Komsomol radical argued that such measures were necessary to give an "irreconcilable, Bolshevik, clear class rebuff to the assaulting *popovshchina.*"[34] At one point in the debate, the cauldron of passions boiled over. A rampage by the interventionist I. Bukhartsev against Iaroslavskii's emphasis on culture was interrupted by hissing from the audience. Bukhartsev shot back, "What are you cackling about? Really, this is not a meeting of kulaks." According to the official stenographic report, the ensuing noise in the hall cut off the speaker.[35]

As in 1926, Iaroslavskii's control of the apparatus allowed him to ride out the rebellion of the radicals, and the congress adopted resolutions tending to support the culturalist program. Although the main resolution opened with fire and brimstone—religious organizations were calculating counterrevolutionary groups actively seeking to depose the Bolsheviks—the resolution then hailed the progress made in the Soviet period and proceeded to address specific issues, such as combating religious holidays,

---

[33] *Stenograficheskii otchet vtorogo vsesoiuznogo s'ezda Soiuza Voinstvuiushchikh Bezbozhnikov,* 2d ed. (Moscow, 1930), 55, 82, 161.

[34] *Stenograficheskii otchet,* 149, 242, 259. *Popovshchina* combines the colloquial, somewhat contemptuous term for priests, *popy,* with a suffix suggesting a menacing or marauding presence.

[35] *Stenograficheskii otchet,* 152.

propaganda work among women and youth, better training of activists, and further development of propaganda forms such as art, film, lectures, and museums. These were all points on the culturalist agenda. The resolutions on sects, peasants, women, and national minorities adopted similar approaches. The culturalists may have won the battle at this congress, but they lost the larger war. Changes in the legal status of religion in April 1929 and the forced closing of churches and persecution of priests during collectivization and dekulakization struck a tremendous blow against popular religious expression. More broadly, the turmoil of the Cultural Revolution, in which the Komsomol played a leading role, meant that the League's nominal "moderation" would be tested as local activists were caught up in the antireligious fervor.[36]

High Politics and Ideology

The debate over the best means to pursue antireligious propaganda and the struggle for leadership of the antireligious movement must be seen on several levels. First, scholars have placed the debates in the context of high-level maneuvering for power, particularly in the years from 1923 to 1926. Arto Luukkanen depicts a clear power shift in religious matters in 1922–23, from Trotsky to Stalin's Iaroslavskii. Concrete evidence linking Kostelovskaia to Trotsky would buttress this interpretation. Nonetheless, some commonality can be seen in their view of religion as a superficial cultural phenomenon atop an institutional infrastructure that posed a direct political threat to the regime.[37]

V. A. Alekseev made a similar argument, but cast Bukharin as Iaroslavskii's target. In February 1923 Bukharin had published an article in *Bezbozhnik u stanka* opposing Iaroslavskii's condemnation of the new journal, and he "did everything he could so that the journal could continue to come out in its initial form." In early 1925, Bukharin allowed Kostelovskaia to express her views in *Pravda*, which he edited. After publication of that article, Iaroslavskii asked the Central Committee to investigate the matter of Kostelovskaia and "her protector Bukharin." The members of the Antireligious Commission who removed Kostelovskaia in

---

[36] V. A. Alekseev, *Shturm nebes otmeniaetsia?* (Moscow: Rossiia Molodaia, 1992), 81–131.

[37] Some two decades earlier, Joan Delaney speculated that Iaroslavskii's inability to have *Bezbozhnik u stanka* shut down in 1923 and Kostelovskaia removed from the upper reaches of the antireligious apparatus was due to Trotsky's influence. See Delaney, "Origins of Soviet Antireligious Organizations." See also Arto Luukkanen, *The Party of Unbelief: The Religious Policy of the Bolshevik Party* (Helsinki: Societas Historica Finlandiae, 1994), 96–207.

February also complained to the Politbiuro about Bukharin's "excessive sympathies for the leadership of *Bezbozhnik u stanka*."[38] Alekseev argues that Stalin was directly responsible for several of the Orgbiuro directives of 1923 and 1924 that criticized antireligious "excesses," particularly those by the Komsomol, one of Bukharin's political bases. Alternatively, Iaroslavskii may have been attacking Bukharin for reasons related to his own political standing.

These relationships are not substantially clarified even when we consider their possible ideological motivations. Stalin and Iaroslavskii were both ideological chameleons, and at mid-decade Bukharin was in transition from his early radicalism to a more moderate position. By 1929 and the League's Second Congress, Bukharin had arrived at a position close to that of the culturalists. The political battle, however, had already been fought and all but won by Stalin, who had come to favor the rapid social transformation to which the interventionists subscribed. At a combined plenum of the Central Committee and the Party Control Commission in April 1929, Bukharin was relieved of his duties as editor of *Pravda* and as secretary of the Comintern. When Bukharin addressed the League of the Godless in June as the official representative of the Central Committee and the Politbiuro (from which he would be removed in November 1929), his slide from power and the rejection of the gradualism associated with him could not have gone unnoticed by the delegates.

Although the development of the antireligious campaign was closely tied to high-level personal politics, it may have been even more dependent on high-level decisions concerning rural economic policy. Whatever general policy the Party adopted toward the countryside would directly determine the nature of antireligious activity. In that regard, Kostelovskaia's shrill attitude in the mid-1920s did not correspond to that of a regime whose face was "to the countryside." By mid-1929, however, that policy appeared all but abandoned, and the interventionists understood the mounting pressure to collectivize agriculture as authorizing them to eradicate religion any way they could. In January 1929, an explicit Politbiuro directive to increase antireligious agitation compounded these expectations. The First Five-Year Plan, as presented to the Party in April 1929, envisioned moderate growth of cooperative and collective farms, though highly taxed individual farming was to have remained an important element of the rural economy.[39] The threshold to a new policy of substantially greater intervention seems to have been crossed at the end of June,

[38] Alekseev, *Illiuzii i dogmy*, 264–290.
[39] Moshe Lewin, *Russian Peasants and Soviet Power: A Study of Collectivization* (New York: Norton, 1975), 351–357.

some two weeks after the congress closed, when the Central Committee issued new policy guidelines that extended control over the peasantry and strengthened the collective farm movement. During the summer reports of locally initiated forced collectivization began to circulate, but the *sploshnaia kollektivizatsiia* (total collectivization) was yet to come. This was the uncertain but highly suggestive context in which the League's activists gathered.

Debating Secularization

For better or worse, the sparring between the culturalists and interventionists also constituted the first reflective debate about religion and secularization during the Soviet period. As suggested earlier, the regime's earliest policies toward religion—during the separation of Church and State, the Civil War, the seizure crisis, and even the promotion of the Renovationist Church—had been largely derivative of other, generally political agendas. Similarly, the regime's unmitigated attack on popular religion during collectivization just a few years later was mostly a consequence of other policies. This debate was the last such semipublic discussion of religion (the public sphere limited here to the Communist community) until the Khrushchev period.[40] Although divisions in the antireligious camp were manifest, certain basic assumptions about the secularization process can be discerned. Whether these assumptions grew out of the conflicts of the Civil War and famine periods or were attributable to the regime's basic motivating ideology, all of the activists considered religion to be a hostile force to be countered. Even though a policy of accommodation had been advocated from time to time by individual regime figures (Vladimir Bonch-Bruevich, Ivan Skvortsov-Stepanov)[41] and had even been instituted briefly for certain sects and as short-term support for the Renovationists, the regime clearly was intent on ultimately eliminating religion from Soviet Russia.[42] None of the leading figures publicly doubted the long-term success of this project. Despite nearly a decade of often disillusioning experience, the regime's leading atheists remained optimistic about a complete victory. Their confidence may have been based on the general cul-

[40] For these discussions, see John Anderson, *Religion, State and Politics in the Soviet Union and Successor States* (Cambridge: Cambridge University Press, 1994), 6–67.

[41] Luukkanen, *Party of Unbelief*, 181–186.

[42] For Luukkanen, an end to the lenient policy toward sectarian groups and renewed hostility toward Muslim clergy were the major consequences of the 1926 conference. See ibid., 201–202.

tural utopianism of the NEP period, the more focused enthusiasm of the Cultural Revolution, or perhaps the narrower successes against the Orthodox Church as an institution.

The two major camps took a similar view of agency. With few exceptions, everyone involved agreed that secularization would be achieved as a conscious, deliberate process imposed by the regime on the masses. In this view, the masses were largely passive vessels to be transformed by direct intervention or extensive education. Secularization meant not the gradual transformation of attitudes observed in Western Europe but the measurable results of explicit government policies, which were reflected in both the physical diminution of the Church and the religious activities of believers. Despite an insistence on the material decline of religious institutions, both sides in the antireligious camp realized by the mid-1920s that the time had come to address individual believers and their attitudes. The Church as an institution had been decimated, but popular religious expression appeared to be flourishing. Even the statements of Kostelovskaia and her supporters demonstrated that the cavalier dismissals of popular religion that characterized the Civil War period had given way to acknowledgment of the need for propaganda and policies directed against religion itself, not just against the clergy.

Beyond illuminating Kremlin intrigues and specific policy issues, this debate had a broader significance as the Party struggled to determine its postrevolutionary identity. Rehearsing a debate that had plagued the Social Democratic movement from its inception, the Party was once again divided over conflicting visions of its membership and its mission. These disagreements had caused the Menshevik/Bolshevik split in 1903, and had hounded the Bolsheviks through the Revolution, the Civil War, and the introduction of the NEP. These challenges amounted, in essence, to the question of how the vague utopian ideology of the Bolsheviks would actually be implemented. Utopia in power meant making choices, abiding by promises, making compromises, or moving on.[43] After the pressing political concerns of the Civil War, the regime now had to face the question of what the Revolution really meant. That the 1920s presented a period of options for the ultimate direction of Soviet society is widely accepted among Western historians.[44] This conclusion, however, has not generally been extended to all parts of the social realm, particularly religion and atheism, where the creation of the League in 1925 is taken as a sign of new

[43] Siegelbaum, *Soviet State and Society*, esp. chap. 4.

[44] This view is due largely to Cohen's *Bukharin*. For more recent examples, see Richard Stites, *Revolutionary Dreams: Utopian Vision and Experimental Life in the Russian Revolution* (New York: Oxford University Press, 1989), and Siegelbaum, *Soviet State and Society*.

militancy. It may have been, of course; this was only part of the story. Here, too, options existed.

The antireligious debate, at least at the 1926 conference, clarified several important matters. First, the battle between competing organizations was definitively resolved in favor of Iaroslavskii's League. There would be one League and a "mono-organizational culture" of Soviet atheism.[45] Similarly, after the 1926 meeting, the officially sanctioned methods of promoting atheism would correspond roughly to Iaroslavskii's culturalist vision of secularization, at least for the foreseeable future. Whatever that meant for actual conditions on the ground (very little after 1928, despite Iaroslavskii's efforts at the 1929 congress), an "authoritative [monologic] discourse" had been established.[46] This particular discourse was not surprising, of course, given the regime's nominally restrained methods of social transformation during the high NEP period, but such restraint was misleading; the promotion of a single, official view of religion united with the long-term goal of atheism established the basis for the regime's subsequent assault on religion. The revolutionary agenda was merely on hold, boding ill for the long-term viability of the NEP.

Other Societies, Same Issues

The outcome was equally ominous in a parallel debate in the mid-1920s over voluntary societies in which the League was a minor participant. Compared with the brawling in the antireligious camp, this disagreement was mild, but the issues were similar. NEP society was distinguished by numerous voluntary societies, characteristically identified by acronyms:

- MOPR (1922): International Organization to Assist Revolutionaries
- ODN (1923): Down with Illiteracy Society
- ODVF (1923): Society of Friends of the Air Force
- Liga "Vremia" (1923): League of Time
- ODD (1924): Society of Friends of Children
- ODGB (1924): Society of Friends of the Newspaper *Godless*

---

[45] The term is borrowed from T. H. Rigby, *The Changing Soviet System: Mono-Organizational Socialism from Its Origins to Gorbachev's Restructuring* (Aldershot, Hants.: Edward Elgar, 1990). Katerina Clark traces a similar "normalization" in culture and the arts that amounted to an end to revolutionary instability and the beginning of cultural management. See Clark, "The 'Quiet Revolution' in Soviet Intellectual Life," in Fitzpatrick et al., *Russia in the Era of NEP*, 211.

[46] Jeffrey Brooks, "Socialist Realism in *Pravda*: Read All about It!" *Slavic Review* 53, no. 4 (Winter 1994): 975.

- DobroKhim (1924): Friends of Chemistry
- OSO: Society to Assist Defense; in 1927, OSO merged with ODVF and DobroKhim to form OSOAviaKhim
- ODSK (1925): Society of Friends of Soviet Film
- ODR: Society of Friends of Radio
- Down with Crime Society
- Town and Country Society
- Technology to the Masses Society (1927)
- Battle with Alcohol Society (1928)

In addition to these organized groups, the *shefstva* (oversight groups) and the correspondent and *delegatki* movements reflected the regime's attempt to extend its reach into society, even though the introduction of the NEP had compelled it to adopt a lower social profile.[47]

Single-issue voluntary societies offered the Bolsheviks numerous advantages. They harnessed the energies of persons sympathetic to a part but not all of the Bolshevik program. Voluntary societies also brought individuals into the Bolshevik orbit, built social support for the regime, and provided possible recruits for the Party. Bukharin viewed the voluntary organizations as a potential counterbalance to the burgeoning Party bureaucracy, although these groups themselves offered ample evidence of the "organized chaos" that Bukharin saw emerging in the Soviet system by the late 1920s.[48] Voluntary societies also were as much reflections of Bolshevik political culture as they were conscious agents of change. Like the League, they manifested and justified the social transformation presumed to have been achieved. Moreover, voluntary societies channeled and controlled social change, countering the unacceptable notion of *stikhiinost'* (spontaneity).

Beyond these general parameters, however, many of the details of voluntary societies remained to be determined: How closely should the Communist Party supervise their activities? Were these groups to extend the

---

[47] There is little literature in English on the voluntary societies. William Odom's study of OSOAviaKhim, *The Soviet Volunteers: Modernization and Bureaucracy in a Public Mass Organization* (Princeton: Princeton University Press, 1973), is rich from the perspective of organizational theory and modernization studies. See also Charles Clark, "Literacy and Labor: The Russian Literacy Campaign within the Trade Unions, 1923–1927," *Europe-Asia Studies* 47 (December 1995): 1327–1342. Among post-Soviet scholarship in Russian, see T. P. Korzhikhina, ed., *Gosudarstvennye uchrezhdeniia i obshchestvennye organizatsii SSSR: Problemy, fakty, issledovaniia* (Moscow: Moskovskii Gosudarstvennyi Istoriko-arkhivnyi Institut, 1991), and *Dobrovol'nye obshchestva v Petrograde-Leningrad v 1917–1937 gg.: Sbornik statei* (Leningrad: Nauka, 1989).

[48] Cohen, *Bukharin and the Bolshevik Revolution*, 206–208; Moshe Lewin, *Russia/USSR/Russia: The Drive and Drift of a Superstate* (New York: Free Press, 1995), 177–181.

Party's reach into the nonparty masses or simply to consolidate the ideo-logical gains among those already generally sympathetic to the regime? Questions of membership, structure, function, and interaction among or-ganizations remained undecided. Moreover, the rapid growth of voluntary societies in the 1920s had itself become problematic. The Soviet political landscape had become a patchwork of overlapping single-issue organiza-tions demanding ever more time and support from a limited pool of ac-tivists. (This frenzy of NEP-era particularism extended to nationalities policy, creating an often senseless administrative mosaic.)[49] According to a report presented to the Central Committee's Orgbiuro in December 1924, the Party had lost control of the mass societies and could not provide the necessary attention to each one. The pressure for rapid growth had often resulted in compulsory collective enrollments and the automatic withhold-ing of dues from wages. Some people misunderstood or simply did not know the objectives of organizations they had joined; others did not know which societies they belonged to. Too many societies had little interaction with the masses, and were preoccupied with commercial fund-raising ac-tivities. The societies also were developing central bureaucracies rather than focusing activity at the local level.[50] An article in early 1925 in the Pskov Party paper criticized the proliferation of social organizations from the standpoint of dues and energy. These groups "destroy the united front in the countryside, and every one of [these] . . . societies has as its pressing task the recruitment of the peasantry."[51]

In February 1925, the Orgbiuro issued a resolution prohibiting coerced collective membership in voluntary societies. Dues were to be limited and could not be automatically deducted from wages. In the countryside, only those societies relevant to the interests of rural people should be estab-lished. Bureaucratic centralization must be avoided, and emphasis should be on attracting a nonparty *aktiv*.[52] Despite this high-level mandate, arti-cles in the Party press in 1925 and 1926 suggested that the effort to vivify the voluntary societies was not successful. In November 1925, a Central Committee official wrote in *Pravda* that "in a word, many of our volun-tary societies . . . lack the main thing—society."[53] At the 1926 antireli-

---

[49] Yuri Slezkine, "The USSR as a Communal Apartment, or How a Socialist State Promoted Ethnic Particularism," *Slavic Review* 53, no. 2 (Summer 1994): 414–452.

[50] "O rabote massovykh obshchestvennykh organizatsii," *Izvestiia TsK RKP(b)*, 5 January 1925, 1–2.

[51] *Pskovskii nabat*, 7 February 1925.

[52] "O dobrovol'nykh massovykh organizatsii," *Izvestiia TsK RKP(b)*, 2 February 1925; "O formakh massovykh organizatsii," *Pravda*, 25 February 1925.

[53] K. Mal'tsev, "O massovykh dobrovol'nykh obshchestvakh," *Pravda*, 1 November 1925. See also A. Lebzin, "K itogam raboty massovykh dobrovol'nykh obshchestv," *Kommunis-*

gious conference, one delegate commented that in response to a good speech, one hundred people might join an organization but only five really understood what their membership entailed. "As a result, as fast as they spring up, the organizations die off."[54] Investigations into textile plants in Iaroslavl' in 1928 and 1929 found that "voluntary societies, in most cases, [exist] only on paper." Workers complained that "you join a voluntary society but absolutely no work goes on. You only pay dues; it's better not to join at all."[55]

Although it arrived on the scene later than most of the other mass voluntary societies, the League suffered many of the ills associated with them. Despite the Central Committee's prohibition, the League owed its growth to collective enrollment. It also suffered from bureaucratization and the sense that it did little. Other problems appeared to be specific to the League. Speaking at the 1926 conference, Oleshchuk cast the League as a voluntary body at the Party level, whereas ODR, AviaKhim, ODN, and others were associated with the system of soviets.[56] This proximity caused a variety of problems. Atheism was, after all, an integral part of the Bolshevik ideological package, at least on the rhetorical level, so antireligious propaganda was already an explicit responsibility of Party agitprop departments. Seen in this light, the League was denied an exclusive mandate. The overlap of League and Party responsibilities (as well as those of the Komsomol, unions, and educational authorities) exacerbated the lack of cadres available in the countryside.

The resolution of the cadre problem, as far as the regime's leaders could see, was to involve nonparty activists in the regime's circle. Lenin had argued in favor of a limited "open tent" policy as early as 1922: "Without an alliance with noncommunists in the widest range of activities, there can be no talk at all of a successful construction of communism. . . . For a long time to come Russia will have many noncommunist materialists."[57] Two years later Petr Smidovich added that because Party bodies in the countryside were already seriously overloaded, they should welcome the services of nonparty activists.[58] Despite these statements, local Party leaders in

---

ticheskaia revoliutsiia, 1925, no. 24 (December), 111–125; I. L. "Zapisi dnia," *Kommunisticheskaia revoliutsiia*, 1926, no. 23, 51–55; *Izvestiia TsK RKP(b)*, 1926, no. 29–30, 13–14. See also A. Lebzin, "Dobrovol'nye obshchestva pered novym periodom raboty," *Kommunisticheskaia revoliutsiia*, 1926, no. 20, 47–50.

[54] RTsKhIDNI, f. 17, op. 60, d. 792, ll. 53–54.

[55] RTsKhIDNI, f. 17, op. 60, d. 829, l. 300; IaSA, f. 2410, op. 1, d. 1, l. 32.

[56] RTsKhIDNI, f. 17, op. 60, d. 792, l. 47.

[57] V. I. Lenin, "O znachenii voinstvuiushchego materializma," *Pod znamenem marksizma*, 1922, no. 3, 5.

[58] RTsKhIDNI, f. 17, op. 112, d. 620, ll. 42–44.

Ukraine and parts of Russia, as well as the Red Army, initially banned establishment of the League. These leaders feared, so it was said, the League's vulnerability to political and ideological aliens. Like Kostelovskaia, they wished antireligion to remain a Party monopoly.[59] One also suspects that local officials were concerned that the presence of an organization with the League's name and declared intentions would further alienate the population.

These tensions were manifest in debates over the League's membership. At the First Congress in 1925, one delegate argued that it was senseless to take in only Komsomol and Party members. Indeed, he thought the League in theory ought to be open to believers, should they care to join![60] If the League were exclusively the preserve of the Party and Komsomol members who joined as a matter of course, membership would have no significance. The possibility that Komsomol members might be forced to join as a group led the Komsomol Central Committee to direct the Pskov Komsomol to see that, although participation in the League was encouraged, "under no circumstances should recruitment occur through 'naked agitation' or calls for *levées en masse*."[61] One concerned League official at the congress in 1925 spoke in favor of requiring members to be active, "otherwise we would have to include . . . all Party members and all Komsomol members. Every member should be obligated to perform at least a little work."[62] The League's charter indicated that members must "actively [work] in a cell of the League of the Godless."[63] Ultimately, the League did not find a satisfactory balance in its membership. Local League organizations that had few Party and Komsomol members found themselves outside the arena of power and resources; those that had many such members lost the opportunity for activism among the population.

As emphasis on economies of scale pushed Soviet planners toward ever larger enterprises, the idea of merging the voluntary societies into larger groups was suggested several times in the late 1920s. A specific plan in 1929 proposed reducing the mass societies from sixteen to five.[64] And in 1930, Iaroslavskii fended off another proposal to merge the League, ODN, and the Society to Battle Alcoholism. He believed that none of the

---

[59] RTsKhIDNI, f. 17, op. 60, d. 723, ll. 121–122; d. 793, l. 97; GARF, f. r-5407, op. 1, d. 11, l. 17.

[60] GARF, f. r-5407, op. 1, d. 8, ll. 27–29.

[61] PPA, f. 2496, op. 1, d. 161, l. 138.

[62] GARF, f. r-5407, op. 1, d. 8, l. 43.

[63] *Ustav Soiuza bezbozhnikov SSSR* (Moscow, 1925), 3.

[64] *Kommunisticheskaia revoliutsiia*, 1927, no. 5, 72–73; *Izvestiia TsK VKP(b)*, 1927, no. 20–21, 8; B. Spektor, "O ratsionalizatsii raboty dobrovol'nykh obshchestv," *Kommunisticheskaia revoliutsiia*, 1929, no. 2, 83–89, and no. 5, 92–97.

individual tasks would be achieved and, shamelessly invoking the Bible, compared the Party aktiv to "Martha of the Gospels," who "took on so many concerns that she was unable to resolve any of them."[65] Although the megamergers never took place, increasingly in the late 1920s voluntary societies were placed under greater and greater control until their capacity for mobilization, once hailed, was transformed into utter bureaucratic submission.[66] Most voluntary societies were disbanded—"liquidated," in the expressive Bolshevik lexicon—in the early 1930s as their perceived usefulness came to an end. Only a few, including the League of the Godless, survived until World War II.

Throughout the debates on the voluntary societies, neither the propriety of using them as a means of spreading the Bolshevik gospel nor the belief that such societies should be administratively uniform and subject to one oversight policy was ever questioned. One standard of organization and internal operation was posited by the regime for all voluntary societies, however nominally nonideological. This homogenization served the additional purpose of banishing large-scale spontaneous developments (*stikhiinost'*) from the Soviet scene. Katerina Clark, Hugh Hudson, and Christopher Read find a similar routinization in the arts and creeping conformism among the intelligentsia's organizations in the 1920s.[67] Yet what the Bolshevik leadership considered *stikhiinost'* could also be interpreted as evidence of a functioning civil society. In the Soviet case, however, the potential of voluntary societies to serve as the "institutional core of civil society"—that is, outside the regime and its control—had been consciously thwarted.[68] While the presence of numerous voluntary societies may have represented one outward manifestation of a dynamic, multifaceted society, the uniformity imposed on these groups made it a mock civil society at best, with each group having the same agenda and in one voice proclaiming the social unity so long sought. This administrative homogenization may not have directly undermined the eclecticism that was presumed to underpin NEP society, but it suggested a certain hollowness in

[65] GARF, f. r-5407, op. 1, d. 47, ll. 33–34.
[66] Dzh. Bredli (Joseph Bradley), "Dobrovolnye obshchestva v Sovetskoi rossii, 1917–1932," *Vestnik Moskovskogo universiteta*, ser. 8 (Istoriia), 1994, no. 4, 34–44.
[67] Christopher Read, *Culture and Power in Revolutionary Russia: The Intelligentsia and the Transition from Tsarism to Communism* (New York: St. Martin's Press, 1990); Katerina Clark, "The 'Quiet Revolution' in Soviet Intellectual Life," in Fitzpatrick et al., *Russia in the Era of NEP*, 210–230; Hugh D. Hudson Jr., *Blueprints and Blood: The Stalinization of Soviet Architecture, 1917–1937* (Princeton: Princeton University Press, 1994).
[68] Jürgen Habermas, "Further Reflections on the Public Sphere," in *Habermas and the Public Sphere*, ed. Craig Calhoun (Cambridge: MIT Press, 1992), 453.

civil society, which was vulnerable to swift alteration from above when it entered an economic and political crisis at the end of the decade.

The creation of the League, with its explicitly ideological mandate, confirmed the regime's long-term radical agenda and suggested the limited scope of NEP social liberalism. Through the League, the Party continued to project its radical agenda onto society, even if it was cloaked in nominal moderation. Its moderation may have been due as much to circumstance as to design. Debates concerning the League highlighted the absence of sufficient numbers of qualified cadres to achieve Bolshevik aims directly. Cadres were perceived as crucial transmitters and, to the regret of the Party's leadership, transmuters of its agenda. Indeed, the debate on voluntary societies can be seen as a meditation on the need to extend the reach of the regime's limited base of cadres. To a great extent, the goals and structure of the antireligious effort and the overall campaign to remake society depended on and were even defined in terms of cadres.

Having brought a semblance of order to antireligion, the regime should have been in a position to promote its version of atheism broadly throughout society. To consider this image and how it was presented to the population, we turn in the next two chapters to the regime's propaganda.

3

Soviet Atheism?

Nonreligious man *in the pure state* is a comparatively rare phenomenon, even in the most desacralized of modern societies. The majority of the "irreligious" still behave religiously, even though they are not aware of the fact. . . . The modern man who feels and claims that he is nonreligious still retains a large stock of camouflaged myths and degenerated rituals.

—Mircea Eliade, *The Sacred and the Profane*

Despite the disagreements within the regime over how best to pursue secularization, authoritative Party organs decreed the deployment of a widespread antireligious propaganda campaign. During the 1920s and 1930s, millions upon millions of Soviet citizens were exposed to virulently atheistic propaganda on the streets, by the military, in the workplace, and throughout the public sphere. This campaign had many elements, ranging from the "hooliganism" of Komsomol activists rampaging in churches at the beginning and end of the decade to the "soft" intellectual atheism of Bolshevik "thick" journals in the mid-1920s. The League's contribution consisted of demonstrations, speeches, discussion "circles," lectures, "evenings," plays, "godless corners," and "wall newspapers" in public places. Councils orchestrated "public" meetings to demand the closure of churches, the prohibition of bell ringing, and the seizure of church bells for industrialization. Prosperous League councils might create an antireligious museum in a former church, or at least antireligious displays in the local history museum. The League's Central Council also sponsored radio broadcasts and administered a central antireligious museum in Moscow.

Despite the widely held realization that the Soviet Union was the first modern "propaganda state," there has been little systematic study of this propaganda in the regime's critical early decades.[1] Even less attention has

---

[1] Peter Kenez, *The Birth of the Propaganda State* (Cambridge: Cambridge University Press, 1985), covers more the mechanics of Soviet propaganda than its content.

been accorded to specifically antireligious propaganda.[2] Dimitry Pospielovsky dismisses it as the demonstrably false propaganda of "contempt
and hate."[3] Richard Stites provides a more nuanced reading of antireligious propaganda, stressing the deep roots of the intelligentsia's conflict
with Orthodoxy and limning the state's multifaceted efforts to create a
modern, secular faith.[4] In this chapter and the next, I narrow the focus to
the printed propaganda designed for large audiences that promulgated the
regime's official view of atheism. This material offers insight into Bolshevik society in the making, and reveals how the regime defined itself (and its
perceived opponents) in continuously changing terms. It also provides a
benchmark against which to examine the "real story" of local League outposts.

Notwithstanding the regime's pretension of disseminating an objective
atheism, the antireligious propaganda of the 1920s and 1930s constituted
many, often conflicting atheisms—rural and urban, for the educated and
the illiterate, for the young and the elderly. Bolshevik antireligious propaganda also evolved dramatically, from the experiments of the Civil War
period and the early 1920s toward propaganda with a more or less set
agenda by the mid-1920s. By decade's end, League materials increasingly
reproduced the regime's general political and social agenda rather than
promoting atheism.

Justifying Propaganda in Soviet Russia

The founding of the Bolshevik regime coincided with developments in
communications technology and transport that permitted Western governments to mobilize, influence, and intervene in the lives of their populations
to a degree previously unknown. Beginning around the turn of the century,
these governments became able to produce and mobilize popular support for their policies. The need to do so itself reflected the emergence of
mass politics (if not quite yet popular democracies) in much of Western
society at the turn of the twentieth century.[5] The initial applications of

[2] The postwar period is covered in David E. Powell, *Antireligious Propaganda in the Soviet Union : A Study of Mass Persuasion* (Cambridge: MIT Press, 1975).

[3] Dimitry Pospielovsky, *A History of Marxist-Leninist Atheism and Soviet Antireligious Policies*, vol. 2 (New York: St. Martin's Press, 1988), 19–46.

[4] Richard Stites, *Revolutionary Dreams: Utopian Vision and Experimental Life in the Russian Revolution* (New York: Oxford University Press, 1989), 101–123.

[5] Eric Hobsbawm, "Mass-Producing Traditions: Europe, 1870–1914," in *The Invention of Tradition*, ed. Hobsbawm and Terence Ranger (Cambridge: Cambridge University Press, 1983), 267.

government-sponsored propaganda were particularly exuberant, and reached a feverish pitch during World War I.[6] Domestic propaganda agencies did not cease when the guns fell silent, and during the 1920s, the governments of Europe employed various forms of propaganda to pursue domestic agendas. They shared a conviction that the citizenry was malleable and ought to be directed in its views and passions by the government. Propaganda at that time carried little of the pejorative connotation that it has acquired over the course of the twentieth century, and in Russia it was natural for a revolutionary party coming to power with an ambitious agenda for social transformation to use it. The Bolsheviks' mass propaganda techniques differed little from the propaganda regimes introduced in Germany, Italy, and Mexico.

Practical considerations also contributed to the Bolsheviks' use of propaganda. Primary among them was the regime's need to consolidate its initially tenuous political support. Although this pressure was particularly acute during the Civil War, the need for propaganda increased greatly in the 1920s when the regime began pressing its cultural agenda. Its idea of leadership was informed by the broader, Leninist conception of the Communist Party's responsibility to direct the population, particularly the working class, toward the necessary consciousness.[7] Infused by revolutionary ideology and buoyed by the perceived rectitude of its cause, the Bolshevik leadership also equated propaganda with the dissemination of undeniable truths about a certain future—hence the self-conscious use of terms such as "propagandists" and "agitators." The dictatorship of the proletariat certainly would not shy from propaganda to achieve its goals. The regime's visionaries foresaw a rapid jump to modernity, a swift and comprehensive transformation along utopian lines; "education" in all its forms would be used to pry the population from the traditional culture. As with other points on the Bolshevik social agenda, however, the tremendous distance between the Bolshevik Party's vision of an atheistic modernity and the inherited Orthodox culture left ample room for and even demanded a program of extensive antireligious propaganda.[8] A cynical view of Bolshevik propaganda may seem appropriate from the perspective of the post-Soviet period, but the contemporary sincerity of the effort to forge a new *Homo soveticus* cannot be denied.

[6] In regard to England, see Muriel Grant, *Propaganda and the Role of the State in Inter-war Britain* (Oxford: Clarendon, 1994); Gary S. Messinger, *British Propaganda and the State in the First World War* (Manchester: Manchester University Press, 1992).
[7] On this notion, see Kenez, *Birth of the Propaganda State*, 5–7.
[8] The gap between Bolshevik plans and Soviet Russian reality is discussed in depth in Roger Pethybridge, *The Social Prelude to Stalinism* (New York: St. Martin's Press, 1974).

The Illiteracy Problem

Not withstanding the enthusiasm of Bolshevik planners, the high illiteracy that plagued Soviet Russia had two important consequences for the regime's propaganda campaigns.[9] First, the Bolsheviks extensively employed visual images in their effort to influence the population. Even during the Civil War, before the systematic propaganda campaign was launched, the regime produced large numbers of posters that took advantage of a presumed popular anticlericalism by grouping together the Whites, the clergy, and former landlords. Later, in addition to posters, the Bolsheviks widely employed banners, "corner" displays, museum exhibitions, wall newspapers, illustrated journals, and films. These means were vital to the regime's effort to inculcate its new culture in the illiterate and minimally literate.[10] Like the windows and murals in Catholic churches throughout premodern Europe, these sources told a story that could be understood by all, and they offered a simple, indeed miraculous, transition from the old world to the new.

Second, the same low level of literacy led the Bolsheviks to exploit the tendency in societies of limited literacy to view the printed word as sacred and a source of great power.[11] Until well into the nineteenth century outside government and urban circles, literacy still retained a religious connotation: in most communities, only priests could read, and the only books were Church-related. Words were thought to be central to achieving salvation, determining morality, and distinguishing between good and evil. Words were guides to behavior, and peasants read to be instructed in their daily lives.[12] According to one observer of the peasantry early in the century, "printed means it is true, printed means it is just."[13] The respect for written texts also helps explain the increasing popularity of the Western sects in late nineteenth-century Russia as literacy spread.[14]

[9] On the general problem of illiteracy in Soviet Russia, see ibid., 132–195.

[10] Victoria Bonnell, "The Representation of Women in Early Soviet Political Art," *Russian Review* 50 (1991): 267, 288. See also Stephen White, *The Bolshevik Poster* (New Haven: Yale University Press, 1988), 18–19. Many of the Bolsheviks' most notable early posters are gathered in White and in *The Soviet Political Poster, 1917–1980* (Harmondsworth: Penguin, 1985).

[11] See Steven Justice, *Writing and Rebellion: England in 1381* (Berkeley: University of California Press, 1994), 13–66; and Alan K. Bowman and Greg Woolf, eds. *Literacy and Power in the Ancient World* (Cambridge: Cambridge University Press, 1994).

[12] Jeffrey Brooks, *When Russia Learned to Read* (Princeton: Princeton University Press, 1985), 25–34.

[13] Ibid., 32–33.

[14] Ibid., 25–27. The same is true of Western Protestantism. See David Vincent, *Literacy and Popular Culture: England, 1750–1914* (Cambridge: Cambridge University Press, 1989), 5–7.

The rapid pace of change in Russia did not allow the printed word to lose its sacred nature, as it had done in Western Europe, where this process occurred over centuries.[15] Modernization came to Russia in a matter of decades, bequeathing to the Soviet period the primitive power of literacy. The transformation of Lenin's words into a Bolshevik canon of sorts was but one manifestation of this orientation, but this sacralization was not without its problems for League leaders. In 1926, the League's deputy chairman, Anton Loginov, criticized a request from a *Bezbozhnik* reader for a list of short books that could quickly dispel one's belief in religion. This reader, Loginov charged, accepted atheism as facilely as he had accepted religion; he "believes in a book, believes in a book as in some kind of miracle-working talisman. . . . [The view of books as a] magical panacea . . . spreads the same religious prejudices, only inside out."[16] Loginov's criticism aside, the Bolsheviks in general, and certainly the League leadership, sought to make use of this faith in the printed word.

Print Propaganda

Printed materials formed the framework for the regime's propaganda efforts. Despite the difficulties of the Civil War period,[17] the Commissariat of Justice's "liquidation" department published a series of propaganda pamphlets,[18] and its irregularly published journal, *Revoliutsiia i tserkov'* (Revolution and Church, 1919–1924), also carried propaganda materials.[19] Initially the ODGB's and League's main responsibility was to distribute the newspaper *Bezbozhnik* and other printed matter, and not just because of their presumed ability to disseminate atheism. Given the importance attributed to publications in Bolshevik political culture, the visibility of antireligious periodicals was crucial to efforts to justify the

[15] See David F. Mitch, *The Rise of Popular Literacy in Victorian England* (Philadelphia: University of Pennsylvania Press, 1992).

[16] A. Loginov in *Bezbozhnik*, 13 June 1926.

[17] Kenez, *Birth of the Propaganda State*, 44–46.

[18] Among the titles in the department's Antireligioznaia Biblioteka were P. A. Krasikov, *Sovetskaia vlast' i tserkov'* (Moscow: Narodnyi Komissariat Iustitsii, 1920) and *Krest'ianstvo i religii* (Moscow: Narodnyi Komissariat Iustitsii, 1920); and I. Stepanov, *Pochemu padaet vera i narastaet bezverie?* (Moscow: Narodnyi Komissariat Iustitsii, 1920). These pamphlets ranged in size from 8 to 16 pages; the size of the print run was not indicated.

[19] *Revoliutsiia i tserkov'* came out as a journal of some 80 to 125 pages five times between 1919 and 1920, with a print run of 30,000–40,000. In 1921, five issues came out in newspaper form in runs from 30,000 to 50,000. From 1922 to 1924, one issue appeared each year, with print runs of 5,000 to 20,000.

League's existence and indicate its vitality in an arena in which resources were limited and publications often short-lived. And by issuing its own publications, the regime could control the presentation of antireligious propaganda when local cadres were of questionable quality. These centrally issued materials provided detailed instructions to local League councils and cells on how to organize and run a cell, how to construct a Godless corner, how to run an antireligious evening, and the content of antireligious lectures in the most minute detail. The most important propaganda organ was the weekly newspaper *Bezbozhnik* (1922–1934, 1938–1941). The League's Central Council also published several specialized journals: *Bezbozhnik* (1925–1941), initially for the peasantry and after 1927 for general audiences; *Antireligioznik* (1926–1941), a monthly thick historical-methodological journal for propagandists; and the monthly *Derevenskii bezbozhnik* (1928–1932) for the peasantry. The League also issued numerous journals in the minority languages of the Soviet Union.[20] Some larger local Party organizations intermittently published antireligious periodicals, of which the most significant was *Bezbozhnik u stanka* (1923–1931), issued by the Moscow Party Committee.[21] The League also produced mass-circulation textbooks for League activists and the general population. The *Krest'ianskii antireligioznyi uchebnik* (Peasant Antireligious Textbook), which consisted of detailed lecture and discussion outlines, was printed in many editions through the 1920s and into the early 1930s.[22]

[20] The weekly newspaper *Bezbozhnik* (1922–1934, 1938–1941) had a print run ranging from 210,000 in 1925 to 172,000 in early 1929 to over 500,000 in the early 1930s; it had between 4 and 16 pages. The journal *Bezbozhnik* alternated as a biweekly and monthly and its print run ranged from 35,000 to 60,000 copies. The Ukrainian-language newspaper *Voiovnicheii vezvirnik* supposedly printed 200,000 copies in 1931. Among the other non-Russian-language propaganda periodicals were *Allahsyz* (Baku, 1922–1933, in Azeri), *Anastvats* (Erevan, 1928–1934, in Armenian), *Bezvirnik* (Kiev, 1923–1924, in Ukrainian), *Der Apikoires* (Moscow, 1931–1935, in Yiddish), *Khudosilzar* (Tashkent, 1928–1933, in Uzbek), *Allakhyz* (Ufa, 1928–1935, in Bashkir), *Bezvirnik* (Kharkov, 1925–1935, in Ukrainian), *Bezboznik wojuiacy* (Moscow, 1929–1935, in Polish), *Mebrdzoli ateisti* (Tbilisi, 1937–1941, in Georgian), *Sugyshan allasyz* (Moscow, 1925–1937, in Tatar), *Erdem ba Shazhan* (Verkhneudinsk, 1928–1934, in Buriat-Mongol), *Neuland* (Khar'kov, 1926–1934, in German), and *Religiis tsinaalmdeg* (Tbilisi, 1930–1931, in Georgian). This list is incomplete, and many of the journals changed titles during their existence, some of them frequently. See *Periodicheskaia pechat' SSSR, 1917–1949* (Moscow: Izdatel'stvo Vsesoiuznoi Knizhnoi Palaty, 1958), vol. 1, pt. 1, 85–87. See also S. Oliutin, "Na knizhnom fronte," *Antireligioznik*, 1931, no. 6, 51–56. Print runs of pamphlets and brochures published by the League ranged from 2,000 to 50,000. Although such materials were not seen by everyone, they did represent a commitment by the central authorities to a broad propaganda campaign.

[21] *Bezbozhnik u stanka* was originally a monthly and then a biweekly. Its print run ranged from 35,000 to 70,000 in a format of 24 pages, some 4 to 8 usually in color.

[22] M. M. Sheinman, ed., *Krest'ianskii antireligioznyi uchebnik*, 6th ed. (Moscow: OGIZ/ Moskovskii Rabochii, 1931); 200,000 copies, with 274,000 of previous editions printed.

Two characteristics of these propaganda materials stand out.[23] First, they stressed the external aspects of religious belief (clergy, churches, rites, and so on) rather than belief per se. To some degree, this tactic was entirely reasonable in that it reflected the immediacy of the challenge posed by the Church as a nationwide institution, but it also reflected an underlying prejudice within Bolshevism's Marxist core, the wish to understand the subjective phenomenon of religion in coldly calculated, materialist terms. Second, the regime's antireligious propaganda evolved dramatically during the 1920s and into the 1930s, and these changes underscored the subjective nature of the enterprise and its sensitivity to specific political and social currents. Initially, *Bezbozhnik* and other propaganda materials ridiculed belief as the product of ignorance and superstition, and enthusiastically claimed that religion was dying out. The antireligious press bristled with reports of empty or closed churches, unemployed priests, and abandoned icons and religious holidays.[24] Although ridicule remained a constant theme of antireligious propaganda, this early approach was soon complemented by a comprehensive system of substitute values and rituals. The critique of religion in the mid-1920s also stressed economic reasoning, as it depicted the exploitation of the peasantry by the clergy or the loss to the national economy of religious holidays. By decade's end, antireligious strategy had shifted toward the explicit politicization of the secularization campaign. Where religious belief had earlier been treated as an obstacle to social development, by 1929 it was presented as a direct threat to Bolshevik rule from enemies within and abroad. Finally, throughout the 1930s, the League's so-called antireligious propaganda increasingly shifted away from the subjects of religion and atheism and moved toward the regime's general political agenda.

Anticlerical Propaganda

The focus on external manifestations of religion and the marked evolution in their treatment are clearly visible in the treatment of the clergy. This propaganda took advantage of the population's ambivalent attitude toward the local priest, who was seen as necessary for the performance of

[23] Most of the examples here are drawn from the main antireligious periodicals in the 1920s and early 1930s: the newspaper *Bezbozhnik*, the journal *Bezbozhnik*, and the journal *Bezbozhnik u stanka*.

[24] By their initial optimism, the Bolsheviks parted company, if only briefly, with their French predecessors, who immediately sought to replace Catholicism with a secular religion. See Mona Ozouf, *Festivals and the French Revolution* (Cambridge: Harvard University Press, 1988), 267–271.

rituals but was often resented for living off the villagers.[25] Although the terms of the clergy-parishioner relationship had changed dramatically as a result of the Revolution—parishioners now controlled the parish, and clergy in general were under siege—the regime brought its prerevolutionary attitudes and prejudices to the propaganda directed at the clergy. Propaganda organs in the 1920s provided an unending stream of verse, fiction, caricatures, and supposed news accounts ridiculing and attacking priests. Kostelovskaia's *Bezbozhnik u stanka* was particularly crude in its depiction of gluttonous and rapacious clergy.

Reflecting the regime's initial optimism, early anticlerical propaganda depicted priests rapidly losing their influence and giving up their pulpits. *Bezbozhnik* periodically published priests' supposed renunciations of their profession. In one account, a debate between a priest and a local Communist took an unexpected turn when the priest announced, "Yes, brothers, the Party secretary has spoken the truth. I admit I have deceived you. I preached from the pulpit without believing what I preached. . . . From now on, I am not a priest. I no longer want to deceive you; I want to expiate my sins before the toilers by working for Soviet power." To the reported cheers of the audience, the priest removed his cassock and submitted to having his hair shorn.[26] Such notices in *Bezbozhnik* often ran under the heading "The Disintegration of Religious Organizations," a view that emphasized the Bolsheviks' institutional view of religion.[27]

Regular attacks on priests as exploiters of the peasantry fitted easily into the paradigm of rural class warfare that eventually triumphed among the Bolshevik leadership in the 1920s. In a typically cautionary tale about economic exploitation, *Bezbozhnik* reported the case of one Father Sergei Tomilin, who supposedly demanded nearly 150 kilograms of grain and over 21 meters of linen for each marriage ceremony he performed. In just a few weeks, he had conducted thirty marriages, receiving as much as a teacher earned in ten years. "Peasants, think! Is it worth uselessly paying this tribute to a spider parasite?!"[28] Bolshevik propaganda conveniently

---

[25] Gregory L. Freeze, *The Parish Clergy in Nineteenth-Century Russia: Crisis, Reform, Counter-reform* (Princeton: Princeton University Press, 1983), and his "A Case of Stunted Anticlericalism: Clergy and Society in Imperial Russia," *European Studies Review* 13, no. 2 (1983): 177–200; L. I. Emel'iakh, *Krest'iane i tserkov' nakanune oktiabria* (Leningrad, 1976).

[26] *Bezbozhnik*, 20 May 1923.

[27] For example, see *Bezbozhnik*, 20 May and 11 November 1923, 10 January 1931; "Raspad tserkvi," ibid., 25 January 1925; "Begut s tonushchego korablia," ibid., 22 November 1925. Many former clergymen were compelled to make public declarations renouncing their professions to qualify for state employment and to avoid persecution.

[28] *Bezbozhnik*, 4 March 1923.

ignored the declining social conditions of the rural clergy in the postrevolutionary period, and instead exploited an inherited discourse that presented the clergy as living well off the peasantry's hard work.

The late 1920s brought a distinct change in the depiction of the clergy, who now were shown actively conspiring against Soviet power. The image of religious revival was integral to the League's own rhetoric, but it also was closely linked to developments in the general political arena. At the April 1929 Central Committee plenum, Stalin introduced his famous thesis that class tensions would increase as Soviet society approached socialism.[29] However convincing such rhetorical strategies may have been in other fields, the rising menace scenario ultimately made a mockery of the religious "threat," especially after the regime's decimation of organized religion beginning in the late 1920s. Nevertheless, the presentation of aggressive clergy and religious organizations continued into the 1930s. In 1931, for instance, *Pravda* introduced a review of antireligious propaganda by stating that "recent data indicate a revival in the activity of churchmen."[30] This type of indictment harked back to the discourse of the early Soviet and Civil War periods, with its rich imagery and nefarious associations. The real agenda, however, was contemporary, focusing on the regime's determination to transform society, particularly through collectivization. *Bezbozhnik u stanka* warned of "kulak-priestly terror . . . directed primarily against collective farmers and the bearers of Soviet policy," and the cover of an issue in 1929 depicted clergy of all denominations as vermin tunneling through the earth to undermine a Soviet village with its electrified garage, school, club, grain elevator, and apartment building.[31] In mass-produced brochures with titles such as "Religion at the Service of Capitalist Elements in the USSR," readers learned how kulaks and their clerical and sectarian supporters were working against the organization of collective farms.[32] *Pskovskii nabat* screamed "Terrorists in Cassocks," and enumerated the "crimes" committed by priests against collective farms.[33] The cultural concerns of earlier antireligious propaganda were all but cast aside.

The heightened attack on religion also brought a final end to the tense relationship between the regime and sectarians. The support for agriculturally progressive sectarian communes had ceased by mid-decade, and by the

---

[29] *Bol'shevik*, 1929, nos. 23–24; see also Moshe Lewin, *Russian Peasants and Soviet Power* (New York: Norton, 1975), 368–373.

[30] "V peredovuiu sherengu voinstvuiushchego bezbozhiia," *Pravda*, 15 January 1931.

[31] *Bezbozhnik u stanka*, 1929, no. 11, 3, and no. 19, 16.

[32] V. Shishakov, *Religiia na sluzhbe kapitalisticheskikh elementov v SSSR* (Moscow: Bezbozhnik, 1931).

[33] *Pskovskii nabat*, 24 December 1929.

A guided tour of the Central Antireligious Museum, in the former Strastnyi Monastery, Moscow, 1930. (Courtesy of the Russian State Archive of Cinema and Photographic Documents, no. 118149.)

late 1920s sects were lumped with all other religious groups and activists as direct enemies of socialist construction. Fedor M. Putintsev, the League's specialist on sects, wrote in 1929 that sects had not really suffered under tsarism and were in no way socialist. Even today, Putintsev charged, sectarian leaders were exploiting their followers in league with kulaks, and were allied with foreign enemies of socialism.[34]

Homo Soveticus

In contrast to the plotting clergy and deluded believers, Soviet antireligious propaganda posited the new Soviet man and woman. On a sym-

[34] Fedor Maksimovich Putintsev, *Politicheskaia rol' sektantstva* (Moscow: Aktsizdatel'skoe Obshchestvo Bezbozhnik, 1929).

bolic level, the battle for the hearts and minds of the Soviet population was transformed into a personnel campaign. The new Soviet man was tall and strong, an authority figure armed with secular knowledge. He might be an engineer or an agricultural specialist trained in modern farm methods. Mikhail Gorev wrote in *Bezbozhnik* in the early 1920s, for instance, that farmers in the United States and England were successful because they followed the advice of veterinarians and agronomists, whereas Russian peasants still relied on the priest's prayers for a good harvest.[35] A full-page drawing in the journal *Bezbozhnik* in 1925 depicted a forlorn male peasant sitting barefoot in tattered clothes looking to the heavens. In the background a stalwart peasant plows his fields on a tractor: "The peasant sits, doesn't sow, doesn't reap, doesn't worry, lives by the Gospels, counting on St. Nicholas. Perhaps a miracle on the unplowed and unsown field will make the grain grow. But clearly the peasant on the tractor has read about agronomy instead of the Gospels; he knows that 'he who doesn't work doesn't eat.'"[36] These messages reflected the regime's short-lived "face to the countryside" policy, with its message of self-improvement and greater productivity through education and technology.

Women occupied a particular niche on the regime's propaganda front, primarily because they were identified as the main bearers of religious belief in Russian society. According to a prominent antireligious journalist,

A woman is more religious than a man. It is not her fault . . . The conditions of life in bourgeois society are such that a worker spends productive time by a machine, interacting with older conscious comrades, participating in the class battle and generally in political life, but to the lot of mothers and female workers falls domestic work by the heater, by the pots and clothing, in the company of equally undeveloped girlfriends and neighbors. . . . The male peasant is also not as religious as the female peasant: he travels to town, and participates in village meetings. The female peasant knows only field and domestic work.[37]

As a consequence, women required specific ministrations to cut off the source of new believers. This propaganda depicted religious women as ignorant, exploited, weak, and often resistant to the Bolsheviks' self-styled "liberation" of women. The cover of one issue of the journal *Bezbozhnik*

---

[35] *Bezbozhnik*, 21 January 1923.
[36] *Bezbozhnik*, 1925, no. 4, 5.
[37] V. Sarab'ianov in *Bezbozhnik u stanka*, 1923, no. 8.

"Religion is poison. Protect your children": Moscow, 1930. (The Hoover Institution Archives, Poster Collection, RU/SU 650.)

in 1925 depicted a husband beating his wife as Jesus and angels looked on approvingly. The caption read: "A wife should fear her husband." Another full-page drawing in the same issue showed a priest shackling a women with her baby to the kitchen stove.[38] *Bezbozhnik u stanka* printed a full-page color drawing in 1925 titled "The Family Front," in which a red-clad worker and son and a red-kerchiefed daughter trap the children's mother in the icon corner; a small child in red approaches her carrying an issue of *Bezbozhnik u stanka* and saying, "Give up, Mommy."[39]

These women were contrasted to the new Soviet woman, who was free from exploitation and social isolation. Early in the decade, women were shown to be leaving religion in droves on their own initiative. In 1924 *Bezbozhnik* published a letter from fifty-six-year-old E. Stratsenkova, who said that she had recently become an atheist because God "gave me nothing." She asked the editors to print that many older women shared her conviction.[40] Although such depictions continued throughout the decade, more often than not women were seen to be liberated from religious servitude through the agency of the new regime. The *delegatki* movement seemed almost magical in its ability to free women from the perceived grip of religion.[41] *Bezbozhnik* reported the story of Agaf'ia Borshchova, married against her will to a drunk who beat her endlessly and sold all her possessions. Agaf'ia was broken physically and spiritually, and she sought salvation in church. But the priest told her to submit and not to complain. Then a miracle occurred: a *delegatki* meeting in the village chose Agaf'ia to be its representative. "Little by little she was drawn into social activity." When her husband left her, she worked the land with the help of the mutual aid committee and cooperatives. She was able to send her children to school, where her daughter became a Pioneer. *Bezbozhnik* reported that she was working in the village soviet, was a member of the regional executive committee, and was an active Party member. Having long forgotten the Church, she had organized a milk production artel and a children's playground. According to the correspondent, Agaf'ia now "feels like a human being"—an exhausted one, I should think, after all those achievements.[42] Extreme exaggeration in such stories was, of course, standard fare, and so was their message: political activism within the Soviet-Bolshevik

[38] *Bezbozhnik*, 1925, no. 5, 4.
[39] *Bezbozhnik u stanka*, 1925, no. 11, 21.
[40] *Bezbozhnik*, 24 August 1924.
[41] See L. Tiurina, "Zhenshchiny-bezbozhnitsy i bor'ba za novyi byt," in *Voinstvuiushchee bezbozhie za 15 let*, ed. M. Enisherlov (Moscow, 1932), 267–282. On the depiction of Soviet women in propaganda materials, see Victoria Bonnell, "The Representation of Women in Early Soviet Political Art," *Russian Review* 50, no. 3 (1991): 267–288; Elizabeth Waters, "The Female Form in Soviet Political Iconography," in *Russia's Women: Accommodation, Resistance, Transformation*, ed. Barbara Clements, Barbara Engel, and Christine Worobec (Berkeley: University of California Press, 1991), 225–242.
[42] Anna Blium, "Tserkovnaia svad'ba i semeinaia zhizn'," *Bezbozhnik*, 13 June 1926.

community held the key to personal transformation and liberation. Even after the *delegatki* movement faded in the late 1920s, heightened political activism remained an important aspect of the effort to secularize women. As one headline in *Bezbozhnik* declaimed, "We will free the toiling women from religious slavery." Below the headline were printed several speeches from the "First All-Union Conference of [Female] Godless and Cultural Warriors," which had met in December 1930.[43] This propaganda implied that political activism on its own satisfied the multifaceted personal needs formerly fulfilled by religious belief and practices. In general, however, League propaganda simply ignored those needs.

The regime also promised social services to end the perceived isolation and ignorance that kept women in the grip of religion. Those services always seemed to be in the near future, but they rarely were actually available. In 1925, for instance, Gorev wrote of the need for day nurseries, daycare centers, clubs, cafeterias—all of which would allow women free time for self-development and education. Beneath the article, a smiling woman pilot waved her hand as she flew across the page.[44] In such cases, the presentation was normative: how society ought to be. It was a tentative picture that relied more on criticism of contemporary social conditions than on enumeration of actual achievements. The poor Soviet regime was far from realizing these implied promises.

The special resolution of the "woman problem" also merits attention because of its ideological implications. An emphasis on communal living ran counter to the non-Marxist justification of antireligious propaganda in NEP Russia, which declared that attitudes could be changed without fundamental alteration in the relations of production. For women more than men, however, secularization seemed to require the restructuring of daily life. Lectures and printed propaganda would not be sufficient. Were men able to learn from a lecture while women were impervious to its message? There remained a tremendous condescension toward women in antireligious propaganda; in many cases they were treated as idiots. In one typical account, a husband wished to remove the icon from the apartment but his wife refused. One evening while everyone slept, he quietly disposed of it. Questioned the next morning by his wife, he responded, "It's very likely a miracle. It disappeared on its own, as if it never existed." That evening the wife and her daughter went to a public lecture and spoke no more of icons. "Thanks to *Bezbozhnik*."[45] Throughout the 1920s, Bolshevik

[43] *Bezbozhnik*, 5 January 1931.
[44] Mikh. Gorev, "My ne raby," *Bezbozhnik*, 1925, no. 5, 3.
[45] M. Vinogradov, *Bezbozhnik u stanka*, 1923, no. 4, 15.

graphic illustrations depicted women as subordinate to men—the woman peasant alongside the male factory worker.[46] Gender roles would remain largely unchanged; only the particular burden of women would be eased somewhat by more abundant social services.

Churches and New Public Spaces

Like Bolshevik anticlerical propaganda, attacks on churches occupied an extremely visible position in the regime's antireligious campaign. Though also seeking to discourage church attendance, this propaganda explicitly emphasized closing churches, apparently equating a locked church gate with atheism victorious. In tones characteristic of *Bezbozhnik*'s early enthusiasm, it often reported that attendance in many churches had dwindled so much that they were no longer used. According to *Bezbozhnik*, the Komsomol in Danilov (Iaroslavl' Province) requested that the authorities shut the town's cathedral because the local youth no longer needed it.[47] The attack on churches late in the decade reflected the regime's new priorities. *Bezbozhnik* reported that a fire in the village of Novo-Egor'evka, Rushchovskii District, revealed hundreds of kilograms of grain hidden by kulaks in the local church.[48] Church bells also came under attack in the late 1920s. Petitions and letters orchestrated by the regime demanded that the bells be melted down for the industrialization drive, or requested that bell tolling be prohibited because it disturbed workers and students.[49]

The League's role in the process was that of noisy rabble-rouser orchestrating "popular demand" for the closing of churches. Although the decision to close a church and the formal authority to do so came from the Party and State, respectively, the League had the public role of holding meetings and producing petitions. Other efforts were made to make church attendance as difficult as possible. The League quickly hailed the introduction of the continuous workweek in 1929 as a blow to church attendance, but enthusiasm for altering work schedules was sometimes misplaced. A small notice in *Bezbozhnik* in late 1929 announced that because of the introduction of the continuous workweek, Sunday classes at Moscow University (designed also to hinder church attendance) were to

---

[46] Bonnell, "Representation of Women," 277–283.
[47] *Bezbozhnik*, 29 July 1923.
[48] *Bezbozhnik*, 20 October 1929.
[49] For example, *Bezbozhnik u stanka*, 1929, no. 18, 18–19; *Bezbozhnik*, 30 September 1928 and 23 December 1929.

be shifted to Sunday evening until a permanent solution could be found.[50] As elsewhere, the regime's many propaganda campaigns and social programs worked at cross-purposes.

The famed seventeenth-century churches of Iaroslavl' were at the center of a furor in the early 1930s when a plan for the city's "socialist transformation" called for the destruction of many of them. Because of the churches' status as protected monuments, experts from the People's Commissariat of Enlightenment were asked to approve the plan. The three experts proposed instead that Iaroslavl' be designated an International Center of Historical Monuments. The Iaroslavl' media and League rose in righteous indignation. The headline of *Severnyi rabochii* screamed, "We vote for a city of complete Godlessness."[51] The initial stages of this conflict remain unclear, but by the late 1930s many of Iaroslavl''s churches had been closed and destroyed. Ironically, one of the churches slated for destruction, the Il'ia Prorok Church, on the city's Red Square, survived to house the local antireligious museum.

League propaganda posited many alternatives to the Church. As agronomists and *delegatki* offered alternative roles for individuals in the new Russia, so Bolshevik propaganda defined new public spaces and spatial relationships.[52] Given the dearth of usable enclosed space in many Russian communities, church buildings were often converted for other purposes. Throughout the 1920s and into the 1930s, *Bezbozhnik* recounted how churches were being closed to make way for schools, clubs, cafeterias, and storage facilities. In 1926 *Bezbozhnik* described the village of Novoe (New), where sixty poor and middle peasant households had organized a school in the church and a cooperative store in the sacristy, and had used another church building for sorting and cleaning grain. The peasants also had resolved to make a club out of the winter church and to use the summer church for a school.[53] In early 1928, the journal *Bezbozhnik* printed photos of two churches, one in the town of Kirillov that supposedly had been transformed into a power plant (though the photo gave no evidence of that usage) and a second church at the Kozhvinskii lumber mill that had

[50] *Bezbozhnik*, 20 October 1929.

[51] IaSA, f. 2410, op. 1, d. 9; *Severnyi rabochii*, no. 38, 18 February 1932, and no. 41, 22 February 1932. One of the experts, Petr Dmitrievich Baranovskii, was arrested in 1933 for his protests against the destruction of churches. Conference on Baranovskii, Iaroslavl', February 1992. See also *Zolotoe kol'tso* (Iaroslavl'), 18 February 1992.

[52] The French revolutionaries pursued similar goals. See Ozouf, *Festivals and the French Revolution*, 126–157. On the nature of religious and nonreligious space and time, see Mircea Eliade, *The Sacred and the Profane: The Nature of Religion* (New York: Harper & Row, 1959), 20–95.

[53] S. Dobrofeev in *Bezbozhnik*, 13 June 1926.

become a workers' club.[54] Ever mindful of the value of symbolism, Bolshevik antireligious propaganda suggested that factories were the proper substitutes for churches as places of community, faith, and purpose. Particularly in visual propaganda targeted at urban audiences, factories effectively became the churches of a socialist era: large, formidable enclosed spaces, often with a single piece of machinery at one end serving as an altar to the god Industry. *Bezbozhnik u stanka* regularly printed half- and full-page multicolor drawings of such factories. Panels of the small windowpanes typical of factories often contributed to the effect of a cathedral.[55]

Icons, New and Old

Icons played a uniquely important and personal role in the lives of the Russian Orthodox; they were present in the home of each believer and occupied a special corner of the peasant hut. Not surprisingly, they were the target of extensive antireligious propaganda. The specific charges made against icons varied over time. In 1924 *Bezbozhnik* claimed that an epidemic of syphilis in the countryside was being spread through the practice of kissing icons.[56] Five years later, during collectivization, grain caches were claimed to have been found under icons.[57] The resolution of the icon problem was straightforward: icons should be removed and destroyed. Early in the 1920s, the antireligious media reported that the population was turning away from icons. *Bezbozhnik u stanka* printed a pledge signed by thirty-eight workers at the Krasnaia Zvezda factory in Moscow, vowing that none had an icon and none practiced "icon worship."[58] The consequences of disposing of icons were potentially miraculous. *Bezbozhnik* reported that after the Novyi Put' (New Path) commune in Nizhnyi Novgorod Province threw out its icons in 1925, the commune began to prosper: "Without God, our affairs are much better. We obtained two tractors, a sophisticated thresher, and all the necessary equipment for working the land. . . ."[59] Later in the decade, more pointed activism was

---

[54] "Vmesto chernykh gnezd," *Bezbozhnik*, 1928, no. 3. Other representative examples can be found in the issues of 29 July 1923 and 4 December 1927. On workers' clubs as Bolshevik cultural sites, see John Hatch, "Hangouts and Hangovers: State, Class, and Culture in Moscow's Workers' Club Movement, 1925–1928," *Russian Review* 53, no. 1 (January 1994): 97–117.

[55] *Bezbozhnik u stanka*, 1923, no. 6, and 1926, no. 4.

[56] For example, *Bezbozhnik*, 8 June 1924.

[57] *Bezbozhnik*, 20 October 1929.

[58] *Bezbozhnik u stanka*, 1923, no. 7.

[59] *Bezbozhnik*, 24 February 1929.

deemed necessary. In both Iaroslavl' and Pskov, the local League councils held campaigns to collect icons from apartments and workers' dormitories.[60] The regime's success in removing icons from urban public places seems not to have been repeated in private apartments or in the countryside generally. The League's own propaganda provides indirect evidence of the continuing widespread presence of icons well into the 1930s.

The issue for the atheistic culture builders was not just the removal of icons, but their replacement. Whether reflecting a conscious strategy of substitution or perhaps simply adopting extant spatial associations in Russian culture, the Bolsheviks urged that icon corners be replaced with Godless or Lenin corners. Godless corners featured photos, small exhibits, brochures, and a wall newspaper. The Lenin corner usually included an array of pictures of Lenin at various stages of his life. In overall appearance the Godless corner was not markedly different from the icon corner it replaced, suggesting that the regime was harnessing traditional Russian attitudes rather than fundamentally altering them.[61] The absolute and transcendental qualities attributed to Lenin in Soviet propaganda could easily have applied to a prophet or deity. On the third anniversary of Lenin's death, *Bezbozhnik* printed the image of a thousand-foot-tall Lenin standing above the Kremlin in an iconesque pose, as lines of workers marched toward him with placards proclaiming revolution—an image that resembled popular religious processions with icons.[62] Lenin's writings became the Holy Scriptures for the new regime. While Lenin was still alive, the regime had sought to undermine belief by "disproving" the popular notion that saints' bodies did not decompose. Ironically, after Lenin's death, his embalmed body became a shrine on Red Square.

Religious and Secular Holidays

Religious holidays provided another arena in which the regime first attacked a manifestation of religion, then encouraged its substitution. Although antireligious events occurred year round, the League's public exposure was greatest during its annual anti-Christmas and anti-Easter campaigns. Articles appeared in local and national newspapers, lectures

[60] For example, a campaign mounted at the Krasnyi Perekop in Iaroslavl' is regularly noted in IaSA, f. 3363, op. 1, d. 7, ll. 5ff.
[61] See Nina Tumarkin, *Lenin Lives! The Lenin Cult in Soviet Russia* (Cambridge: Harvard University Press, 1983).
[62] See, for example, *Bezbozhnik*, 23 January 1927 and 22 January 1928.

were arranged, and demonstrations were held to conflict with religious observances, and not infrequently to disrupt them.[63] Particularly strong League organizations also mounted protests against local feast days (*prestol'nye prazdniki*). These efforts attacked holidays from several angles, and the balance shifted during the 1920s from a culturalist agenda to a more political approach. Early Bolshevik antireligious propaganda depicted the "pagan" roots of religious holidays in the hope of quickly and easily delegitimizing them. Christmas was linked to winter solstice rituals; Easter was explained in terms of Jewish Passover and other pre-Christian celebrations of spring. The Day of the Holy Trinity (fifty days after Easter) was assailed as a "remnant of an old vegetative pagan cult."[64] Fedor Putintsev ridiculed the overwhelming number of saints' days in the Russian Orthodox calendar, and the practice of venerating each saint for a particular cause that was often very pedestrian.[65] By the late 1920s and into the 1930s, religious holidays were cast more and more as direct political threats to socialism. After the war scare in 1927, the League's next anti-Christmas campaign stressed the military threat represented by Christmas. Articles appeared with titles such as "The Christmas Holiday and the Defense of the USSR."[66] The following Christmas, *Bezbozhnik* emphasized the hypocrisy of Christmas's "peace on earth" message while the West armed for an attack on the Soviet Union.[67]

The regime's initial answer to religious holidays was simply not to celebrate them. With its characteristic easy confidence, *Bezbozhnik* in its first years reported that many peasants and workers had just stopped observing holidays. In a typical account, the peasants of one village resolved not to celebrate Nerukotvornyi Obraz (August 29) in the usual "drunken" manner. They would work instead.[68] The reasoning behind such propaganda seemed to involve less an embrace of scientific atheism than a simple desire to sober up. As this strategy appeared to have little appeal, Soviet citizens were soon encouraged to celebrate the growing number of officially sanctioned revolutionary festivities that had been created or

---

[63] F. Popov, "Antipaskhal'naia kampaniia v Iaroslavle," *Antireligioznik*, 1931, no. 5, 95–96.

[64] For instance, F. Putintsev, "Prazdniki i sviatye," *Bezbozhnik*, 16 and 25 December 1923, and *Proiskhozhdenie religioznykh prazdnikov* (Moscow/Leningrad: Gosizdat, 1925), 79–93, 110–138; *Bezbozhnik*, 25 December 1924, 12 April and 8 June 1924.

[65] F. Putintsev, "Prazdniki i sviatye," *Bezbozhnik*, 16 December 1923. This article focuses on saints associated with childbirth and child raising.

[66] *Bezbozhnik*, 18 December 1927. For a later example, see S. Lozinskii, "Tserkovno-fashistskii agent," *Bezbozhnik*, 1931, no. 23 (December).

[67] *Bezbozhnik*, 8 April and 23 December 1928.

[68] *Bezbozhnik*, 27 September 1925. Other examples can be found in the issues of 16 March and 25 December 1924.

appropriated in the years after the October Revolution.[69] *Bezbozhnik* declared that "religious holidays are being squeezed out by revolutionary ones."[70] Harvest Day, for instance, was proclaimed by the League in 1926 for the purpose of "taking stock of all our agricultural achievements." The Iaroslavl' Okrug Council hailed the new celebration as an alternative to Pokrov (Feast of the Protection, 14 October), and claimed that autumn religious holidays disrupted the harvest and interfered with industrialization.[71] In Pskov, mass amusements were planned for 14 October, though it is not clear how they were to be reconciled with the goal of working through former religious holidays.[72] Once again, Soviet antireligious propaganda strategies worked at cross-purposes. By 1929, Harvest Day had become Harvest and Collectivization Day to emphasize the regime's new agenda for the Soviet countryside.[73] For the cities, the front page of *Bezbozhnik* on 6 August 1929 depicted a priest clenching his fists in anger as the calendar showed Preobrazhenie, the feast of the Transfiguration, crossed out and replaced by Industrialization Day.[74] In addition to transforming religious holidays, the League sought a role in the regime's general celebrations, such as October Revolution Day and Red Army Day.

The new holidays often closely followed the format of the old: slogan-rich demonstrations followed by lectures, and merrymaking replaced icon-rich processions concluding with a church service and celebration.[75] Instead of observing Easter, one model collective farm celebrated the Day of the First Furrowing, during which the peasants lined up on both sides of a tractor and followed its progress, thus adapting the format of the traditional religious procession.[76] That the regime found it necessary to substitute an equal or greater number of innocuous or explicitly politicized holidays for the numerous traditional celebrations suggests how deeply those traditions were rooted—so deeply that the regime was obliged to incorporate the popular taste for frequent ceremonies into its plans for socializa-

---

[69] On early Bolshevik celebrations, see James von Geldern, *Bolshevik Festivals, 1917–1920* (Berkeley: University of California Press, 1993). On their evolution, see Stites, *Revolutionary Dreams*, 79–100; and Christel Lane, *The Rites of Rulers: Ritual in Industrial Society—The Soviet Case* (Cambridge: Cambridge University Press, 1981), 153–181.

[70] *Bezbozhnik*, 28 November 1926.

[71] GARF, f. r-5407, op. 1, d. 13, l. 27– 27ob; IaSA, f. 3363, op. 1, d. 1, ll. 78–79; *Bezbozhnik*, 25 September 1927.

[72] *Pskovskii nabat'*, 9 October 1927.

[73] IaSA, f. 3362, op. 1, d. 15, ll. 29–31; *Bezbozhnik*, 1 September 1929.

[74] *Bezbozhnik*, 6 August 1929.

[75] In this regard, the Bolsheviks were unable or chose not to follow the French revolutionaries' rejection of Catholic spatial and ritual patterns. (See Ozouf, *Festivals and the French Revolution*, 126–157.)

[76] *Bezbozhnik*, 28 July 1929.

tion. The regime's slogans and sober rationalism could not substitute entirely for a culture rich in commemoration. The new revolutionary holidays created a facade of legitimacy and Durkheimian social harmony, but it was a highly stylized facade with the temporal rhythms of prerevolutionary culture. In any case, the attempt to introduce new holidays largely failed. As Helmut Altrichter has written, "the old holidays were deeply anchored in rural customs and. . . . they served a social function even if their religious origins were disappearing." Meanwhile, the new holidays "invoked collective interests of the state and the relationship between the city and the countryside. They appealed to reason and economic rationality. The authorities wanted the festivities to be organized by party cells, soviets, the Komsomol, teachers, and agronomists. . . . At bottom, they presupposed a society that had still to be created. The existing . . . village had very little in common with it."[77] The regime either failed to appreciate or simply was unable to achieve the "transfer of sacrality" to its rituals that also had been the goal of the French revolutionaries in their own festivals.[78]

Soviet efforts to introduce new calendar systems also met with widespread resistance.[79] Although the Gregorian calendar predated the League's arrival, its adoption in February 1918 was designed in part to challenge the Church's control over the rhythms of daily life.[80] The masthead of the newspaper *Bezbozhnik* counted the years from 1917, but it retained the Christian counting system in parentheses. Throughout the 1920s, the League's Central Council received frequent proposals to change the basic calendar, but the League as an institution remained officially silent on this point.[81] Perhaps sensing the difficulty of such a project, and recalling the experience of the French revolutionary calendar, the regime did not attempt to challenge popular culture on this point. Even

---

[77] Helmut Altrichter, "Insoluble Conflicts: Village Life between Revolution and Collectivization," in *Russia in the Era of NEP: Explorations in Soviet Society and Culture*, ed. Sheila Fitzpatrick, Alexander Rabinowitch, and Richard Stites (Bloomington: Indiana University Press, 1991), 200.

[78] Ozouf, *Festivals and the French Revolution*, 262–282.

[79] The creative adoption of revolutionary politics and rhetoric by French lay believers to defend their religious practices is discussed in Suzanne Desan, *Reclaiming the Sacred: Lay Religion and Popular Politics in Revolutionary France* (Ithaca: Cornell University Press, 1990).

[80] Edward E. Roslof, "Calendar Reform of 1918," *Modern Encyclopedia of Religion in Russia and the Soviet Union* 5 (1993): 51–53. For the French model, see Ozouf, *Festivals and the French Revolution*, 158–196.

[81] See, for example, the petition to change the calendar printed in *Bezbozhnik*, 25 December 1923, or S. Kedrovskii, "O kalendariakh," *Bezbozhnik*, 1929, no. 21, 10–11; see also *Bezbozhnik*, 10 March 1929, for a proposal that would have created a five-day week (Profday, Partday, Sovietday, Cultday, and Restday), with the new year beginning on 1 May.

the introduction of the continuous workweek was abandoned soon after its introduction in 1929. The Renovationist Church learned a similar lesson when it sought to apply the Gregorian calendar to Orthodox religious life.[82]

Orthodox Rites, Soviet Rituals

Attacks on Orthodox rites and rituals constituted another prominent part of the antireligious package. There were several reasons why this should have been the case. First, the Russian variant of Christianity relied more heavily than its Western cousins on the performance of rituals to reflect faith.[83] Second, given the multitude of rituals and the comparatively weak theological grounding for many of them, individual rituals could be assailed without the risk of challenging the entire Orthodox culture.

Initially, *Bezbozhnik* and other propaganda media attacked Christian rituals as being derived from pagan rites linked to the agricultural cycle,[84] and they reported that these rites were falling into disuse. G. V. Blokhin, a sixty-five-year-old man in Tver Province, supposedly walked into the local Party office and declared that he did not want a religious burial, despite pressure from his relatives.[85] In Mozhaisk, a former believer claimed that the traditional procession of a statuette of St. Nicholas had declined in popularity dramatically after the Revolution.[86]

The regime's leading propagandists soon realized, however, that it would be easier to persuade the population to abandon religious rites if other ceremonies, equally impressive and serving similar functions, were created and promoted. A League publicist explicitly likened religious rites to the new Soviet life-cycle rituals, in that both fulfilled the same basic need "to note the most important events in a person's life by some sort of mystical ceremony. . . . This constitutes a need of contemporary mankind,

[82] Gregory L. Freeze, "Counter-Reformation in Russian Orthodoxy: Popular Response to Religious Innovation, 1922–1925," *Slavic Review* 54, no. 2 (Summer 1995): 305–339.

[83] Timothy Ware, *The Orthodox Church* (Harmondsworth: Penguin, 1984), 122; Pierre Pascal, *The Religion of the Russian People* (Crestwood, N.Y.: St. Vladimir's Seminary Press, 1976), 16–24. Rites are used here to identify the major sacraments of Orthodox life, especially baptism and marriage. Rituals include the wide range of religiously oriented procedures common in popular religious expression in Russia, including those with pre- or non-Christian origins.

[84] *Bezbozhnik u stanka*, 1924, no. 1; *Bezbozhnik*, 16 December 1923. See also the pamphlet by F. Putintsev, *Proiskhozhdenie religioznykh prazdnikov* (Moscow/Leningrad: Gosizdat, 1925).

[85] *Bezbozhnik u stanka*, 1924, no. 9.

[86] Ibid., 1924, no. 1.

even the workers. Believers, many nonbelievers, and those undecided still consider it improper to experience these days in a humdrum manner, without rituals or even music."[87] These procedures constituted one facet of a broader process of ritual creation that characterized Soviet Russia in the 1920s. Although many of these rituals were presented as being deeply rooted in a proletarian tradition that long antedated the Revolution, so as not to appear completely contrived,[88] Soviet rites in fact allowed the regime to promote popular identification with the forms and goals of the new state, and to overcome, at least on a symbolic level, the tremendous gap between Bolshevik visions and Russian realities.[89] Iaroslavskii saw an added potential benefit in the appearance of Soviet secular rituals: well-designed rituals would provide a powerful antidote to the violent intervention that had become associated with early antireligious carnivals.[90]

The leading Soviet rites were, of course, modeled on the most important Orthodox ones (baptism, marriage, burial), and borrowed extensively from Orthodox forms and imagery. *Bezbozhnik* printed numerous stories about the "Octobering" naming ceremony, "red weddings," and "civilian funerals." League propaganda depicted these as joyous events and contrasted them with religious rites that required payment to the clergy.[91] According to one League publication, a red wedding also produced a longer-lasting marriage than the traditional ceremony. In the village of Razdol'e in Voronezh Province, three couples had been married a year earlier—two in a church and one in a red wedding. The two church-married couples had since separated amid great scandal; the red pair was still happily married.[92] Civilian burials were simple affairs but supposedly rich in emotion. *Bezbozhnik* reported the burial of the worker Nikolaev in Petrograd. While he was not active in social work, his labor had meant everything to

[87] *Bezbozhnik*, 24 October 1926. See also Stites, *Revolutionary Dreams*, 109–114.

[88] See P. G. Shiriaeva, "Iz istorii stanovleniia revoliutsionnykh proletarskikh traditsii," *Sovetskaia etnografiia*, 1970, no. 3, 17–27, and her "Iz istorii razvitiia nekotorykh revoliutsionnykh traditsii," *Sovetskaia etnografiia*, 1975, no. 6: 63–70. The indigenous roots of many utopian aspects of revolutionary culture, including the "Godless" tradition, is a major theme of Stites, *Revolutionary Dreams*.

[89] On the integral nature of rituals to successful politics, see David I. Kertzer, *Ritual, Politics, and Power* (New Haven: Yale University Press, 1988). See also Christopher A. P. Binns, "The Changing Face of Power: Revolution and Accommodation in the Development of the Soviet Ceremonial System," pt. 1, *Man* n.s. 14, no. 4 (December 1979): 588.

[90] Richard Stites, "Bolshevik Ritual Building in the 1920s," in *Russia in the Era of NEP*, 297.

[91] *Bezbozhnik*, 4 December 1927. In this piece, the promotion of Soviet rituals is one of the standards for judgment in a "best cell" competition run by the League. See also Stites, "Bolshevik Ritual Building," 299–302.

[92] *Bezbozhnik*, 1926, no. 9, 21.

him, the paper continued. His many friends but no priests gathered to bury him. "A close worker family and worker orchestra accompanied the body of the beloved comrade."[93] Less successfully, the League also promoted cremation as an alternative to burial. In 1926, *Bezbozhnik* extolled its virtues and described the refitting of the former Donskoi Monastery in Moscow into a crematorium. Two years later, *Bezbozhnik* again promoted cremation, narrated its spread abroad, and called for its introduction in Russia, but made no mention of the transformation of Donskoi Monastery. The author blamed the absence of cremation in Russia on the clergy, who did not wish to lose burial fees.[94]

An account in *Bezbozhnik* designed to promote Octobering revealed as well the difficulties of having Soviet rites adopted. In a fictionalized dialogue, a teacher used crude bribery to persuade a respected village elder to have his newborn daughter Octobered. The teacher knew that if this elder Octobered his daughter, the other villagers would follow his example. The teacher promised gifts and honors from the Komsomol, the Party, and the regional Soviet, and an article about him in the newspaper. The elder reluctantly agreed. One Sunday the entire village gathered in the flag-draped People's Home. The long ceremony concluded with a gift of cloth, groats, and sugar. That evening, the elder's wife complained that the neighbors had laughed at her for having gone through the *oktiabrina*. He shrugged her off, saying, "Would a priest give away money?"[95] While some incentives may have been necessary to promote the new rites, the possibly unintentional emphasis in this account was on material gain, not revolutionary consciousness.

Despite the regime's efforts, these secular rites did not fundamentally displace religious ones. Until the end of the Soviet period, many nominally nonreligious citizens still had their children baptized. Others went through the Octobering while also allowing the child to be quietly baptized, perhaps by an older relative or in another town. And although the civil wedding did ultimately become the norm in Soviet society, it was more a bureaucratic measure than a celebration of the life cycle.[96] The regime failed in its efforts to sacralize the secular rites in a way that would have made them more enduring or convincing.[97] Similarly, by the late 1920s, Soviet mass festivals no longer celebrated revolution and cultural transforma-

[93] *Bezbozhnik*, 7 October 1923; also 27 September 1925.
[94] V. S. Tsvetkova, "Ognennoe pogreblenie," *Bezbozhnik*, 1926, no. 6, 1; "Krematsiia v bor′be s religioznymi predrassudkami," *Bezbozhnik*, 1928, no. 9, 10–11.
[95] *Bezbozhnik*, 1 July 1928.
[96] Lane, *Rites of Rulers*, 3, 67–88.
[97] Ibid., 35–36; see also Ozouf, *Festivals and French Revolution*, 262–282.

tion, but hierarchy and order.[98] Moreover, the regime's adoption of numerous rituals in the personal and political realm ran counter to the general antiritualistic orientation of most nineteenth-century European intellectual trends, including Marxism, and counter to the general processes of modernization characteristic of Western development in the twentieth century.[99]

Communist Theology

Oddly enough, faith was one issue that Bolshevik antireligious propaganda dealt with infrequently and usually derivatively. Faith, whether in Christ or in local water spirits, was treated with scorn and dismissed as the product of ignorance. Nonetheless, the regime's antireligious propaganda served to some extent to fill the void of faith that the attack on religion would presumably create. Western scholars and Russian émigrés have long debated whether the culture of Soviet Russia amounted to a new religion.[100] Did communism represent a new faith? As critics have long noted, atheism itself is less a coherent system of beliefs than a negation of existing beliefs; it is essentially hollow. Richard Stites characterized it as a religion with a "missing faith," despite the passions of the Civil War period and the attempts to sacralize Lenin.[101] Bolshevik propagandists seemed to acknowledge this, not offering atheism per se as a substitute faith, but promoting instead a vague and ever-changing "scientific materialism," the philosophical worldview of any proper Marxist-Leninist.

Depending on time and context, two particular tenets served as the core faith in this worldview. The first was a mix of rationalism and science that incorporated the intelligentsia's condescension toward the peasant culture, which rational Soviet culture could be expected to supersede. Iaroslavskii's *Bible for Believers and Nonbelievers*, serialized in *Bezbozhnik* and then

[98] Binns, "Changing Face of Power."

[99] Maurice Agulhon, "Politics, Images, and Symbols in Post-Revolutionary France," in *Rites of Power: Symbolism, Ritual, and Politics since the Middle Ages*, ed. Sean Wilentz (Philadelphia: University of Pennsylvania Press, 1985), 194; Binns, "Changing Face of Power," 585; Lane, *Rites of Rulers*, 253–254. An alternative view arguing for an expanded use of social and national traditions from 1870 to 1914 has been championed by Eric Hobsbawm in *Invention of Tradition*, esp. 5–14, 263–307.

[100] Stites, *Revolutionary Dreams*; René Fülöp-Miller, *The Mind and Face of Bolshevism* (New York: Harper & Row, 1965); Nikolai Berdiaev, *The Origin of Russian Communism* (Ann Arbor: University of Michigan Press, 1960); Andrei Siniavsky, *Soviet Civilization: A Cultural History* (New York: Arcade, 1990).

[101] Stites, *Revolutionary Dreams*, 119–123.

printed separately in ten editions through the 1920s and 1930s, was intended as a rational demystification of religion. Here and elsewhere, Iaroslavskii regularly pointed out contradictions in the Bible in an attempt to undermine its legitimacy. Assuming a widespread modern sensibility among his readers, Iaroslavskii ridiculed Bible stories, such as the claim that Joshua stopped the sun, as ludicrous and scientifically impossible.[102]

Bolshevik propaganda projected the intelligentsia's belief that science and technology amounted to a universal panacea that would swiftly undermine religious beliefs and lead to the creation of a modern and prosperous society. It evidenced little regard for what the peasants, the supposed beneficiaries, wanted.[103] Iaroslavskii stated clearly that science was the answer: overcoming religion required "a clear understanding of man's relation to nature."[104] Despite its more political overtones, *Bezbozhnik u stanka* was equally clear in its message. An early issue was devoted entirely to modern medicine and health practices; it pitted a befuddled God the Father against the enthusiastic, young, skilled Soviet medical worker.[105] In response to a letter from Petrograd asking why the regime was destroying religion without offering a substitute, *Bezbozhnik u stanka* answered: "Religion is nothing, a deception. Can you really fill a hole with emptiness? . . . Destroying religion, we say: study science. Science instead of religion. You need to know how nature and human society function. Only in these conditions is it possible to give meaning to your existence."[106] This rational approach to religion patently ignored the fact that reason was not the basis of religious belief. Nevertheless, the antireligious media through the 1920s regularly printed articles on astronomy, the planets, evolution, biology, and the technology of agriculture. In this religion, for instance, the barometer was a particularly powerful talisman, far more effective for predicting rain than the local priest or the prophet Il'ia. Electricity enjoyed the same power: in 1925, *Bezbozhnik* printed a letter from a formerly devout peasant: "I've become a complete *bezbozhnik*; electricity totally destroyed [my] belief in God."[107]

[102] E. Iaroslavskii, "Zadachi i metody antireligioznoi propagandy," in *Voprosy propagandy v derevne* (Moscow/Leningrad: Gosizdat, 1926), 5–6, a revised speech delivered to Moscow teachers in August 1924. See also the reference in E. Iaroslavskii, *Bibliia dlia veruiushchikh i neveriushchikh*, 10th ed. (Moscow: OGIZ/GAIZ, 1938), 293.

[103] Moshe Lewin, *The Making of the Soviet System: Essays in the Social History of Interwar Russia* (London: Methuen, 1985), 276.

[104] *Bezbozhnik*, 24 August 1924.

[105] *Bezbozhnik u stanka*, 1924, no. 6.

[106] Ibid., 1923, no. 3. That this journal would have readers and correspondents in Petrograd at such an early date is suspicious, but the intention of the editors in regard to science is quite clear, whether or not the letter was genuine.

[107] *Bezbozhnik*, 2 August 1925.

The promise of science and technology was not limited to the antireligious realm. The Bolshevik leadership perceived them to be central to the overall success of the Revolution. In Lenin's famous formulation, communism equaled Soviet power and electrification of the country. Technology would allow Russia to catch up with the West and achieve a communist utopia.[108] Ever since the Enlightenment, technology had served as a secular talisman for European modernizers, particularly against the perceived superstition and ignorance associated with popular piety. The Russian case was distinctive in offering an extreme, government-backed technological vision aimed at rooting out religion. Caught up in the promise of technology, Bolshevik planners were unaware of or ignored the fact that despite the loud debates about science and religion in the previous century,[109] the spread of technology and science had had little direct impact on secularization.

During the course of the decade, a second tenet—a highly politicized socialist morality—emerged to overshadow even science. Where science offered a cold neutrality in regard to morality, the religion of communism was explicit in creating its own moral code, "its own understanding of good and evil, of good and bad, of what is permitted and what is forbidden."[110] The origins and dictates of this morality remained vague and highly subjective. Soviet discussions of morality usually cited Lenin's statement at the Third All-Union Congress of the Komsomol in 1920 that "our morality is subordinated fully to the interests of the class battle of the proletariat."[111] Another short definition of morality was generated bureaucratically by a plenum of the Party's Central Control Commission when it declared that "all that facilitates the unification of the working class and assists the accumulation of revolutionary strength is moral and ethical."[112] In a more detailed assertion, an antireligious propagandist wrote in 1930 that "for the working class and poor peasantry, moral is everything that strengthens the dictatorship of the proletariat, promotes victory over capitalism, advances and promotes the construction of socialism. . . . All that assists in the victory of socialism, all that helps the work of the Party and the working class in socialist construction—all of this is good, moral, and

---

[108] On technological utopian thought in the 1920s, see Stites, *Revolutionary Dreams*, 145–164.

[109] Owen Chadwick, *The Secularization of the European Mind in the Nineteenth Century* (Cambridge: Cambridge University Press, 1975), 161–188.

[110] M. Sheinman, *Nravstvennost' religioznaia i nravstvennost' proletarskaia*, 2d rev. ed. (Moscow/Leningrad: Gosizdat, 1930), 29.

[111] Ibid., 32.

[112] A. Stratonitskii, *Voprosy byta v Komsomole* (Leningrad: Priboi, 1926), 11.

all that hinders the construction of socialism—all of that is immoral and deserves contempt."[113]

Several obvious problems arose from these formulations. First, such morality was predicated on the process of constructing socialism. But what would be the source of morality after socialism was constructed, a goal that would be reached sooner or later on this earth? Second, these creeds were so profoundly subjective and arbitrary as to be nearly meaningless. After pages and pages of attacks on Western "bourgeois" and clerical morality, a pamphlet on the subject written by a prominent atheist offered only a few examples of proletarian morality. Factory workers trying to resist efforts to raise productivity were acting immorally. Similarly, strikes in Soviet factories were immoral; those in capitalist factories were justified.[114]

The presence of a moral code, however crudely fashioned, and the other aspects of a substitute culture suggested at least the nominal presence of a secular religion. Although explicitly denying what might be considered crucial for any Western religion—a coming to terms with the supernatural or transcendent—Soviet atheism had the look of a secular religion celebrating humankind in the fashion of Feuerbach. At the same time, the regime's propagandists denied that they were creating a secular religion modeled on Orthodox culture. A two-page color illustration in *Bezbozhnik u stanka* in 1928 headed "Priestly spirit in Soviet life" portrays a family busily decorating a fir tree (*elka*) with Soviet symbols while Lenin beams from the corner. God is in the other corner laughing, "the old tune in a new setting."[115] Although similar criticisms of mechanical substitution were aired through the 1920s and into the 1930s, the antireligious media contributed their share to the officially sanctioned atheistic culture that emerged in the 1920s. Albeit contrived, this atheistic culture had its own mythology, heroes, spaces, rites, morality, and language in which to play out the gamut of life experiences in a secular context.[116] As propaganda, of course, these models more often than not were models for a future culture rather than models of an existing one.[117] The regime remained far too poor to fulfill its many promises. Despite these difficulties, Soviet atheistic culture was in some ways an impressive effort testifying to the exuberance of the first decade of revolutionary rule.

---

[113] Sheinman, *Nravstvennost' religioznaia*, 31.

[114] Ibid., 29–30.

[115] *Bezbozhnik u stanka*, 1928, no. 12.

[116] See Alasdair MacIntyre, *Secularization and Moral Change* (London: Oxford University Press, 1967).

[117] See Clifford Geertz, "Religion as a Cultural System," in *The Interpretation of Cultures* (New York: Basic Books, 1973), 93–94.

In comparison with the richness of Orthodox culture, however, this substitute offering was mechanical and bloodless, and in that regard all too modern. It was a pale imitation of the culture it was to replace, and was overwhelmingly negative as it relentlessly pursued the destruction of its competitor.[118] Befitting Bolshevism's materialistic roots and the limitations of its activists, Soviet antireligious propaganda focused on what was tangible and visible: the clergy, sectarian leaders, religious holidays, and rituals. The personal or emotional sides of religious belief were addressed much less frequently. As Helmut Altrichter indicates, the regime's propaganda "missed the central point of popular faith. Pointing out that popular religiosity was 'only of a formal nature' . . . [it] ignored the deep roots of the beliefs upon which these 'forms,' rites and customs were based."[119] The substitute offered in the regime's antireligious propaganda was less a coherent worldview than the outward trappings of official Soviet culture in general. Like the regime's broader official culture, Bolshevik antireligious propaganda acknowledged no dividing line between the public and private spheres. An expression of religious belief was tantamount to an open statement of political hostility toward the regime, and the League's "counter-world" came cloaked in similarly political justifications. Soviet rituals were less individual affirmations of belief in the new system than public statements of loyalty and integration into the political community. In this community, simply being nonreligious was not enough: members needed to adopt the most extreme position of public, militant atheism to legitimate the regime's attacks on religion.

Defined as radical cultural transformation, Soviet atheism was a stunning failure, even beyond the unremarkable performance of the League as an organization. Creation of an alternative worldview so clearly a substitute religion was almost an open acknowledgment that genuine cultural revolution—altering the habits, the rhythms, the symbolic systems and associations of the people—would be an impossible task. The League could only harness the predispositions of the population, rather than fundamentally reshape popular culture. As Moshe Lewin has written,

> the more the Stalinist system rushed ahead . . . the deeper it sank into the
> quite traditional values of authority, hierarchy, and conservatism. . . . The
> whole spiritual climate of the system showed signs of succumbing to some

---

[118] French revolutionary culture also had the scent of a negative religion in which most of the practices amounted to a rejection of the old as much as an articulation of the new. See Ozouf, *Festivals and the French Revolution*, 269–270.

[119] Altrichter, "Insoluble Conflicts," 205.

of the age-old currents of Russian Orthodox civilization. . . . The traditional devotion to and worship of icons, relics of saints, and processions
was apparently being replaced by a shallow imitation of iconlike imagery,
official mass liturgy, effigies, and especially processions and pilgrimages to
a mausoleum sheltering an embalmed atheist.[120]

Traditional popular culture exerted as much influence on the official culture as the government ideologists did, not just in regard to atheism but
throughout the social realm.[121] And by decade's end, the radical efforts at
genuine cultural creation characteristic of the regime's first ten years were
fading into the more limiting conservatism that would dominate the
1930s.[122] Of course, words have meaning and ideology counts, if only in
the context in which they are promoted. Even if Soviet atheism looked
much like Russian Orthodoxy and the broader Soviet culture retained the
scent of prerevolutionary Russia, Soviet culture still cannot simply be dismissed as Russian culture under a red gloss. It was a modernized Russian
culture (increasingly urban, industrial, and literate) offering a ritualized,
highly stylized, conflicted modernity that preserved forms that probably
would have faded in a less telescoped process of modernization. (One is
drawn to the parallel example of Stalinist architecture after the decline of
constructivism.)

However ineffective, this packet of cultural images constituted the
regime's "authoritative discourse" that was to be "accepted or rejected in
toto."[123] That indeed might have been the theory behind Soviet atheism,
but this "monologic" discourse looked markedly different by the time it
reached local audiences. Soviet atheism is less meaningful as a pure ideological construct than as a particular context. How distinct, even nonideological this context was will be uncovered in the next chapter, when we see
how the antireligious message was presented to the population and how
the process of transmission transformed Soviet atheism.

---

[120] Lewin, *Making of the Soviet System*, 274, 275.
[121] David L. Hoffmann, *Peasant Metropolis: Social Identities in Moscow, 1929–1941*
(Ithaca: Cornell University Press, 1994), 11, 177.
[122] Stites, *Revolutionary Dreams*, 225–241.
[123] Jeffrey Brooks borrows the term "authoritative discourse" from the Renaissance scholar
Mikhail Bakhtin, who was writing in this period. See Brooks, "Socialist Realism in *Pravda*:
Read All about It!" *Slavic Review* 53, no. 4 (Winter 1994): 975.

4

"The Battle against Religion Is the Battle for Socialism"

Russians will easily become atheists, more easily than anyone else in the world! And they will not just become atheists, but they will believe in atheism, as in a new faith, not realizing that they believe in nothing.

—Prince Myshkin in Fedor Dostoevsky, *The Idiot*

The League's propaganda was notable not only for outlining a secular religion but also for the way it presented that new faith. The League packaged its gospel in borrowed, awkward forms that limited its potential efficacy. Moreover, the League's propaganda maintained an essentially administrative and inward orientation, projecting antireligion into the public sphere as the official atheistic, albeit largely bureaucratic, facet of the regime's political culture. Finally, beginning in the late 1920s and throughout the 1930s, the League's messages became almost entirely political, designed to glorify the state, even to the point of avoiding discussion of religion or atheism. Thus the League's long-term purpose and viability were called into question by the very processes that had created it.

The Rhetoric and Reality of Campaignism

Although propaganda was central to the League's mandate, the League itself conducted surprisingly little propaganda. It encountered not only those obstacles common to all Soviet propaganda institutions in the 1920s (paper shortages, poor distribution), but also the reality that the League's propaganda seemed to be lost in the process of its production. First, "campaignism" (*kampaneishchina*), short, intense bursts of propaganda in quick succession, was a manifestation of this process. Throughout the Bolshevik propaganda world (and indeed, beyond to many other endeavors), "campaignism" became a dirty word denoting unsustained and ineffective operations. The regime was well aware of campaignism's causes—too many formally defined goals, to be pursued at the expense of all other tasks and pressed upon too few cadres—but it found no satisfactory resolution during the 1920s and 1930s. The usual Bolshevik response to campaignism was additional refinement of the system. When one participant at a meeting of propagandists in Pskov in 1926 commented that there were "too many campaigns" for the *politprosvet* authorities and the voluntary societies to handle, the other activists responded that only further revision of the campaigns was needed.[1]

This culture of campaigns found rich expression in a Bolshevik lexicon that suggested a mechanical and confident view of social transformation. Ten-dayers (*dekadniki*), two-weekers (*dvukh-nedel'niki*), monthers (*mesiachniki*), two-monthers (*dvukh-mesiachniki*),[2] among many others, denoted campaigns by the length of time necessary for their achievement. Socialist competition (*sotssorev*), an agreement between two organizations to achieve a list of goals in a specified time, was another popular format for the execution of tasks beginning in the late 1920s. League files in Iaroslavl' and Pskov are filled with competition agreements between various League councils and even cells.[3] In the late 1920s, brigades became another popular method of organizing Soviet labor to accomplish a wide variety of regular and ad hoc tasks. Later, shock brigades added a further element of melodrama to Bolshevik social transformation.[4] In both cases, the League—a would-be nationwide shock brigade—was directed to divide itself into these formations. The rhetorical heights were reached with the promotion of "Godless shock brigades" on collective farms and in factories.[5] By mid-1932, the League's Central Council claimed the existence of around 4,500 Godless brigades in industry alone.[6] A Soviet envelope from 1933 declared that "shock work and socialist competition" were

[1] *Pskovskii nabat*, 26 August 1926.

[2] These phrases sound as grating to the ear in Russian as they do in English.

[3] PSA, f. 247, op. 1, dd. 12, 13, 20. Socialist competition: *sotsialisticheskoe sorevnovanie*. Because of such an agreement between the Iaroslavl' and Pskov Leagues, the 1933 Iaroslavl' League City Council protocols are preserved in the Pskov archive.

[4] See Hiroaki Kuromiya, *Stalin's Industrial Revolution: Politics and Workers, 1928–1932* (Cambridge: Cambridge University Press, 1988), 319–323; Lewis Siegelbaum, *Stakhanovism and the Politics of Productivity in the USSR, 1935–1941* (Cambridge: Cambridge University Press, 1988), 40. As of March 1930, half of the Soviet industrial workforce claimed to be shock workers.

[5] A. Prokhorov, "Uchet pokazatelei raboty-dvigatelia bezbozhnykh udarnykh brigad," *Antireligioznik*, 1931, no. 6, 46–50.

[6] N. Lanin, "Bezbozhnoe udarnichestvo na proizvodstve," in *Voinstvuiushchee bezbozhnie v SSSR za 15 let*, ed. M. Enisherlov (Moscow, 1932), 182.

"the best weapons in the battle with religion: read and disseminate *Bezbozhnik*."[7]

Most of these structures were borrowed from the realm of Bolshevik economic and labor theory. That other organizations felt compelled to adopt these structures indicated both the preeminence of economic forms in Bolshevik political culture in this period and the pressure on all organizations to adopt uniform operating procedures. But the never-ending search for new tricks led to a succession of short-term strategies whose implementation proved disruptive in the workplace. Moshe Lewin has written elegantly of this "inherent 'split personality' of the state system, with one part trying to shake up the other that aimed at predictable and manageable working patterns."[8] Moreover, these strategies based on economic calculations were completely inappropriate for the subjective tasks facing the League. For instance, Stalin's promulgation in 1931 of his Six Conditions for structuring labor resulted in yet another internal review of League operations and reorganization along these lines, which were manifestly of little relevance to the League's work.[9]

Not surprisingly, such methods of organizing propaganda were ineffective. Although the large number of holy days and saints' days in the Church calendar meant that antireligious efforts would to some degree take the form of campaigns against particular holidays, campaignism for the League became the seemingly inescapable manner of operation. It was the rare League organization that was not accused of coming to life only at Christmas and Easter. One activist charged that Red Army cells were "active only during major antireligious campaigns (Christmas/Easter), claiming that it is impossible to link Godless work with the general plan of military political study, [and] that there are no cells capable of working year-round with undiminished energy."[10] The League itself was a reflection and victim of the greater campaignism within Bolshevik political culture, which produced a short attention span and limited material support for the many single-issue organizations. This style of operation was particularly inappropriate for tasks that could not be completed in a week or a month or could not be measured as easily as the production of cement.

[7] GARF, f. a-406 (Rabkrin RSFSR), op. 1, d. 1293, l. 133ob. My thanks to Golfo Alexopoulos for a photocopy of this envelope.

[8] Moshe Lewin, *Russia/USSR/Russia: The Drive and Drift of a Superstate* (New York: Free Press, 1995), 193.

[9] GARF, f. r-5407, op. 1, d. 75, ll. 1–2, and d. 100, l. 11; *Pskovskii kolkhoznik*, 12 December 1931, 4; "6 uslovii tov. Stalina—v osnovu raboty!" *Bezbozhnik*, 22 February 1932; A. Loginov, "Shest' ukazanii t. Stalina v prakticheskoi rabote SVB na proizvodstve," *Antireligioznik*, 1932, nos. 13–14, 23–25.

[10] *Antireligioznik*, 1932, nos. 15–16, 41.

Campaigns, ten-dayers, monthers, socialist competition, and shock brigades lent a certain rhetorical vitality to League reports, but they appear to have had little life beyond the bureaucratic. These were rituals of declaration, much more loudly declaimed than actually observed. Like other signs of League organization, they substituted for genuine propaganda work. For a local council to report that a brigade existed and that a socialist competition was under way was taken by higher authorities as evidence of a vibrant organization promoting atheism, although later investigation often found no activity whatsoever. Revolutionary discourse was running far ahead of revolutionary reality and was increasingly divorced from it. Not limited to the antireligious sphere, this phenomenon seemingly has been deeply embedded in modern revolutionary cultures.[11]

Ritualistic forms and even specific campaigns were often not the exclusive property of the League. Extensive overlap of competitions, monthers, and brigades allowed the League to claim accomplishments not its own. League reports regularly indicated the number of members who belonged to shock brigades, but did not state whether these brigades had been created by the League or what their purpose was, or account for their activity. This point was raised at the Central Council's plenum in June 1932 when one delegate asked, "What exactly are Godless shock brigades? How do they differ from Komsomol brigades, MOPR brigades, brigades in honor of the Ninth Trade Union Congress? Specifically, how are these shock brigades distinct?" In the very form of this question lies its answer: All institutions in Soviet society were under similar pressures to exhibit their participation in the regime's leading forms, however ephemeral. Another delegate at the same meeting wanted to know, "If a whole factory, section, or collective farm declares itself Godless, was it confirmed that they were indeed Godless at Christmas and the local holidays . . . or did they just declare themselves Godless and end the matter with a few antireligious slogans?"[12] Shock work, like brigades, was acknowledged at the highest levels to involve a large measure of fiction.[13]

The rigid rhetorical structure of antireligious propaganda extended to the Bolshevik depiction of organized religion. In addition to the unsurprising use of derogatory terms for the clergy and their activity, such as *popovshchina*,[14] the League usually couched religion's role in society in alarmist language. From the mid-1920s to the eve of World War II, all sub-

---

[11] See Lynn Hunt, *Politics, Culture, and Class in the French Revolution* (Berkeley: University of California Press, 1984), for an account of unbridled French revolutionary discourse.

[12] GARF, f. r-5407, op. 1, d. 95, ll. 23–24, 63.

[13] Ibid., d. 98, l. 20.

[14] A term suggesting degenerate and exploitative clergy. See chap. 2, n. 34.

stantial antireligious propaganda statements were prefaced by the assertion that churchmen and sectarians were intensifying their activities in an
unending spiral that threatened to overwhelm Soviet power. Among the
frequently used terms were "revival" (*ozhivlenie*) and "attack" (*nastuple-
nie*). As explicit statements and background formulations, these interpretations of Soviet reality both mirrored and furthered the general siege
mentality that characterized official Bolshevik political culture from its inception and throughout the 1930s.[15] In the religious sphere, the extensive
and repeated use of "religious threat" reflected less actual conditions, despite the apparent growth of sects in the 1920s, than the internal bureaucratic requirement to justify antireligious activities and organizations.

Internal Campaigns

Both the semantics and the content of the League's propaganda called into
question the organization's ability to be an effective agent of secularization. Much of the League's propaganda had little to do with the dissemination of atheism, and many of its campaigns looked inward to support
the League as an organization. What is striking is that League officials
treated these efforts as actual campaigns; they used the terminology and
methods of mass propaganda for internal, administrative matters, and
thereby diverted attention and resources from the League's purported
main responsibilities. The most prominent internal campaigns pressed for
subscriptions to antireligious periodicals and the payment of dues. Although the constant focus on subscriptions certainly was a legitimate part
of the League's propaganda agenda, it suggested a concern beyond just
getting the word out. In the Bolshevik political arena, the size of a journal's or newspaper's print run was a crucial consideration in the struggle
for Party-allocated resources—hence the League's frequent and high-
profile campaigns to expand the subscription base. In the summer of 1925,
the League announced the goal of doubling the print run of *Bezbozhnik* to
400,000 by autumn.[16] At the end of 1926, the League called for shock

---

[15] On ingrained Bolshevik paranoia, see Gabor Tamas Rittersporn, "The Omnipresent Conspiracy: On Soviet Imagery of Politics and Social Relations in the 1930s," in *Stalinism: Its
Nature and Aftermath*, ed. Rittersporn and Nick Lampert (Armonk, N.Y.: M. E. Sharpe,
1992), 101–120.

[16] By way of comparison, *Pravda*'s print run in 1925 was 504,000. *Izvestiia* in 1924 came
out in 350,000 copies. *Bednota* was printed in a run of nearly 750,000 early in the decade.
See Jeffrey Brooks, "The Breakdown in Production and Distribution of Printed Material,
1917–1927," in *Bolshevik Culture*, ed. Abbott Gleason, Peter Kenez, and Richard Stites
(Bloomington: Indiana University Press, 1985), 167; I. V. Kuznetsov and E. M. Fingerit,

work in the new year to gather subscriptions.[17] The League's Central Council announced in early 1929 a three-monther of "strengthened promotion of the Godless press among the masses." Thus began what was a nearly continuous campaign over the next several years to increase subscriptions: the campaign featured numerous monthers, an "All-Union Community Review of work to promote the antireligious press among the masses," and a special subscription bulletin.[18] In Iaroslavl' and Pskov, the local League councils regularly announced subscription two-weekers and monthers, and throughout the early 1930s, local League organizations frequently held conferences (*soveshchanie*), appointed commissions, and formed shock brigades for this purpose.[19]

There is ample evidence that these campaigns were no more successful than the League's general organizational efforts. Either they failed outright or the resulting increases in subscriptions were short-lived. The Iaroslavl' City/District League fell well short of its own goal of having 4,000 subscribers to *Bezbozhnik* in 1933, registering only 1,538.[20] Given the low organizational level of local League branches and numerous complaints about the poor distribution and dissemination of antireligious materials, the loud and steady declarations from Moscow were unlikely to be more than whispers by the time they reached the Pskov countryside or even the mills of Iaroslavl'.

Subscription numbers were by no means an accurate reflection of a propaganda organ's popular reception. Most subscriptions were taken out for short periods, from three to six months. Although the League's propaganda often claimed that *Bezbozhnik* was read to tatters by villagers, it may also have been a welcome source of cigarette paper. Moreover, many subscriptions were arranged administratively. The Central Council often sought to have its publications included as inserts in other periodicals. In 1928 the Pskov League succeeded in having the *okrug* educational authority order the anti-Easter issues of all League periodicals for every reading hut in the region. A few months later, the Pskov League also persuaded the trade union leadership to order *Bezbozhnik* for all workers' clubs, though only for three months.[21] There were other problems on the literature

---

Gazetnyi mir Sovetskogo soiuza, 1917–1970, vol. 1 (Moscow: Moskovskii Gosudarstvennyi Universitet, 1972), 21, 60.

[17] GARF, f. r-5407, op. 1, d. 13, ll. 5–5ob.

[18] Ibid., d. 17, ll. 38, 178ob; IaSA, f. 3363, op. 1, d. 1, l. 42.

[19] IaSA, f. 3378, op. 1, d. 7, l. 24; f. 3362, op. 1, d. 13, l. 11, and d. 1, l. 1; PSA, f. 247, op. 1, d. 5, l. 24; *Pskovskii kolkhoznik*, 8 October 1930.

[20] As noted in, for example, IaPA, f. 1, op. 27, d. 2865, l. 34; f. 2410, op. 1, d. 13, l. 69, and elsewhere. PSA, f. 247, op. 1, d. 13, ll. 41–42.

[21] PSA, f. 247, op. 1, d. 1, ll. 6, 37.

front. *Bezbozhnik* was poorly distributed and perceived as too expensive for the general population.[22] In 1933, many Iaroslavl' subscribers did not receive their copies, and this was in an urban area close to Moscow![23] The subscription campaigns had less to do with disseminating atheism than with promoting the external, bureaucratic signs of that development. They usually failed, and even when they succeeded, they could not be linked to a popular movement away from religion.

The second prominent internal campaign was for the euphemistically titled "financial discipline" *(findistsiplina)*. The League defined the challenge in terms not of excessive expenditures—no one seemed to doubt the propriety of having an elaborate national network—but of gathering the funds owed to it. The League would thrive if every member paid dues. In theory, local League councils relied primarily on dues to cover their expenses, while higher League bodies relied on publication income in addition to a share of the dues. Dues, however, were rarely paid in full. In 1927, the Central Council received all of 1 ruble and 20 kopeks in dues from lower-level councils; the following year, it took in 523.39 rubles.[24] In 1931, at the height of its development, the League received only 13 percent of the dues owed to it.[25] Unable to collect dues, the League sought subsidies from central and local Party committees, government authorities, and trade unions. The Central Council regularly directed local councils to arrange for unions to have 3 percent of their budgeted "cultural funds" *(kul'tfundy)* turned over directly to the League, or at least dedicated to antireligious work. Not surprisingly, the local unions proved resistant, and League officials in Iaroslavl' and Pskov frequently requested the Party to compel unions to provide financial support for antireligious work.

These fund-raising efforts became particularly prominent after the League's growth into an unwieldy, nominally multimillion-member organization, but the change in the League's size did not facilitate fund-raising. In December 1931, the Central Council held a ten-dayer devoted to "strengthening general and financial discipline in League organizations."[26] Six months later, the Central Council formed an All-Union Central Headquarters for the Monther of Strengthened Organizational and Financial Discipline. *Antireligioznik* reported in September 1932, however, that this

---

[22] According to a 1925 provincial Party report (IaPA, f. 1, op. 27, d. 1733, l. 40, and elsewhere).

[23] PSA, f. 247, op. 1, d. 13, l. 42.

[24] *Chetyre gody raboty: Otchet vtoromu vsesiouznomu s'ezdu bezbozhnikov* (Moscow, 1929), 9–14.

[25] GARF, f. r-5407, op. 1, d. 95, l. 5.

[26] Ibid., d. 93, l. 4.

monther had failed. Most councils did not fulfill their assigned tasks, and many did not participate at all.[27] At the end of 1933, the Central Council acknowledged the "recent complete decline of financial discipline in League organizations."[28]

While all institutions compete for resources, the challenges facing the League were particularly severe. The Soviet social landscape in the 1920s and into the 1930s was a patchwork of numerous single- and multi-issue advocacy groups, all drawing from the same limited, overworked pools of dues, activists, and direct subsidies. As a consequence, such institutions, even with official mandates and promises of support, spent a disproportionate amount of time merely trying to survive. The high organizational expectations of the League and its competitors exacerbated the gap between resources and demands. The League's chronic financial difficulties were not remarkable, then, but their being understood and treated in the same terms as the League's propaganda tasks was. A healthy League was taken as a sign of atheism ascendant. Obsessive attempts to maintain the League's health ultimately undermined the achievement of an atheist society. This organizational introspection was not unique to the League. In various forms, it characterized many corners of the Bolshevik world in the 1920s and 1930s: the ever-present concern about bureaucracy, the frequent purge of cadres, the bourgeois specialists issue, the periodic revival of soviets to foster greater governmental efficiency, the fate of *rabkriny*, the elevation of self-criticism (*samokritika*) to Bolshevik dogma, the changing labor forms mentioned earlier, the Stakhanovite movement later in the 1930s, and so on.[29]

Hewing to the Party Line

Pressured from within, the League was also under siege from without by a regime whose political agenda changed constantly. In many ways, the single-issue advocacy organizations that appear in the 1920s found them-

[27] *Antireligioznik*, 1932, nos. 17–18 (September), 58; GARF, f. r-5407, op. 1, d. 100, l. 28.
[28] GARF, f. r-5407, op. 1, d. 101, l. 31.
[29] Daniel T. Orlovsky, "The Antibureaucratic Campaigns in the 1920s," in *Reform in Modern Russian History*, ed. Theodore Taranovski (Washington, D.C.: Woodrow Wilson Center Press, 1995), 290–310; Roger Pethybridge, *One Step Backwards, Two Steps Forward: Soviet Society and Politics in the New Economic Policy* (Oxford: Clarendon, 1990), 145–188, 289–331; Siegelbaum, *Stakhanovism*; E. A. Rees, *State Control in Soviet Russia: The Rise and Fall of the Workers' and Peasants' Inspectorate, 1920–1934* (New York: St. Martin's Press, 1987); J. Arch Getty, *The Origins of the Great Purges: The Soviet Communist Party Reconsidered, 1933–1938* (Cambridge: Cambridge University Press, 1985), 40–48; Sheila Fitzpatrick, *The Russian Revolution* (Oxford: Oxford University Press, 1982), 93–97; Moshe Lewin, *Lenin's Last Struggle* (New York: Monthly Review Press, 1968), 117–128.

selves from their very creation in contradictory positions. Each of these societies was established by the regime to pursue one cause, but it was also expected to be a general propagandist for the regime. For instance, as early as 1926, Iaroslavl''s Third District Party Committee banned the wall newspapers of the local voluntary societies because they "did not illuminate production life and agitated exclusively for their own societies."[30] In focusing on their own agendas, the societies ran afoul of the rules of the regime; in adhering to those rules, they compromised their own sense of purpose.

The pressure on the League to adopt a generalist mission became particularly severe in the late 1920s, when the concrete manifestations of popular religious expression (open churches, functioning parishes, pealing church bells, omnipresent icons) receded rapidly. The League's own propaganda, which increasingly cast the answer to religion in terms of social transformation rather than direct antireligious work, left it with a dilemma. What role would the League play in the supposedly postreligious world? An obvious answer, that the League would simply dissolve itself when its mission was completed, was unacceptable to the League's bureaucrats and ran counter to the regime's preference for concrete manifestations of its successes. So League propaganda throughout the 1930s claimed that "religious remnants" continued to exist in Soviet Russia and required the League's ministrations. While there was some theoretical basis for such a conclusion, this view served mostly as a rationalization for the League's continued existence. It was a limited, weak mandate, however, and the majority of the League's energies in the early 1930s shifted from the religion/atheism axis to promotion of the general socialist culture. The few social organizations such as the League that lasted into the 1930s lost their identities in this transformation.

The League's alternative political character had many facets, but perhaps most revealing were those related to the foreign affairs and defense-related activities of the Soviet Union that looked outward and away from the League's difficult position at home. After several years of improvement in the mid-1920s, Anglo-Soviet relations soured in 1927, and the Soviet media warned of an impending attack by the Western powers.[31] Although historians have dismissed the war scare in part as a move by Stalin in his campaign against Trotsky, the issue permeated every corner of the Soviet propaganda world. Exemplifying this spirit, *Bezbozhnik* reported in early

---

[30] IaPA, f. 1, op. 27, d. 2234, l. 32.
[31] Gabriel Gorodetsky, *The Precarious Truce: Anglo-Soviet Relations, 1924–1927* (New York: Cambridge University Press, 1977), 231–240; Adam Ulam, *Expansion and Coexistence: The History of Soviet Foreign Policy, 1917–1967* (New York: Praeger, 1968), 164–167.

1928 that the Voskresenskii Church in Kostroma had reopened as a defense museum. Instead of a cross atop a cupola, a model aircraft flanked by two tanks perched atop the church. Here was a new type of trinity.[32] Nearly every 1928 issue of the journal focused on religious repression in foreign hot spots. Over the next few years, the regime's publications increasingly turned their attentions abroad.[33]

In addition to adopting a more martial tone, the League initiated several programs to ensure itself a place (and resources) in an increasingly militarized society. The first project was the collection of funds for an aircraft, aptly named *Bezbozhnik*. In announcing the project in the summer of 1927, Iaroslavskii wrote that "all the toilers' enemies around the world are arming themselves 'to the teeth' to attack the world's first soviet government."[34] The Pskov Provincial Council opened its local aircraft campaign with the statement that "all imperialistic wars have always been supported by the clergy in all governments."[35] The Central Council also launched a campaign for a tank, also to be named *Bezbozhnik*. Both of these campaigns suffered from the usual ailments associated with the League. In Iaroslavl', the League's leader complained that the local district councils did not participate in the plane collection,[36] while in Moscow the Central Council scolded its network for "unsatisfactory" attention to the tank collection. Apparently many councils "did not even know about this campaign."[37]

The League's greatest military endeavor began in early 1931, when it started gathering funds for a submarine to be named *Voinstvuiushchii Bezbozhnik* (Militant Godless).[38] The lack of response by local councils to this campaign led the Central Council to declare December 1931 and January 1932 "storm monthers" for the submarine collection.[39] In Iaroslavl',

---

[32] *Bezbozhnik*, 22 January 1928.

[33] For example, M. Zoeva, *Imperializm i religiia v koloniiakh* (Moscow: Bezbozhnik, 1930); Boris Kandidov, *Iaponskaia interventsiia v sibir' i tserkov'* (Moscow: OGIZ/GAIZ, 1932); V. G. Tan-Bogoraz, *Tekhnizatsii tserkvi v Amerike v nashi dni* (Moscow, 1931). The exhibition at the Iaroslavl' Antireligious Museum in 1931 was "Imperialist War and Religion" (*Antireligioznik*, 1931, no. 6, 73).

[34] *Antireligioznik*, 1927, no. 8, 3, 82.

[35] PSA, f. 247, op. 1, d. 1, l. 32.

[36] IaSA, f. 3516, op. 1, d. 1, l. 92.

[37] GARF, f. r-5407, op. 1, d. 19, l. 48.

[38] Iaroslavskii had written to the Soviet Fleet Command asking that a ship of the Baltic Fleet be renamed *Bezbozhnik*. On 31 December 1930, the navy's deputy commander responded that it would be preferable for the League to take up a collection to finance the construction of a submarine (ibid., d. 75, l. 101).

[39] According to a draft resolution before the Central Council (ibid., d. 76, l. 50ob); see also "V kratchaishii srok postroim podvodnuiu lodku Voinstvuiushchego Bezbozhnika," *Bezbozhnik*, 15 July 1931.

the League organized a *subbotnik*—a "voluntary" work project on Saturdays—in May 1932 to dismantle the walls of the former Kazan' convent to raise funds for the submarine.[40] The Pskov League planned a "shock ten-dayer" collection of funds for the submarine that September.[41] Beyond making a nominal contribution to the Soviet Union's defense and allowing the League to stay abreast of current concerns, these collections permitted the League to claim, if only symbolically, some of the militance that clearly was lacking in its "domestic" operations.

Not all of the League's foreign-oriented campaigns were irrelevant to its direct mission. In early February 1930, Pope Pius XI issued a statement condemning the persecution of religion in Soviet Russia. The response from the Soviet side was swift. Within a week, Metropolitan Sergei had delivered an interview to Western correspondents in which he denied any persecution of religion by the State,[42] and the League strained to have its voice heard in the regime's loud and vitriolic denunciations of the pontiff.[43] The League's specific response included a collection of funds for a tank, "Our Answer to the Pope in Rome."[44] The Central Council also used the occasion to launch another campaign for subscriptions to *Bezbozhnik* and other League periodicals.[45] However legitimate such campaigns may have appeared to be, they served a more immediate need to buttress the League financially and politically.

Foreign Diversions

Another one of the League's important foreign activities that might have contributed to its relevance at home was its involvement in the International of Proletarian Freethinkers (IPF), but here, too, form (in the guise of

[40] *Severnyi rabochii*, 23 May 1932. *Subbotniki* were initiated early in the Soviet era and continued throughout the Soviet period as a means for the State to get unpaid labor.

[41] PSA, f. 247, op. 1, d. 9, l. 31.

[42] "O polozhenii pravoslavnoi tserkvi v SSSR," *Pravda*, 16 February 1930.

[43] "Krestovyi pokhod kapitala i tserkvi," *Antireligioznik*, 1930, no. 3, 3–5; R. Novitskii, "Sviateishie molitvy," *Antireligioznik*, 1930, no. 3, 13–20; S. V. Mokin, *Internatsional'naia solidarnost' trudiashchikhsia* (Moscow: Moskovskii Gosudarstvennyi Universitet, 1976), 69–98. The Iaroslavl' League held a meeting to protest the pope's declaration (IaSA, f. 3362, op. 1, d. 1, l. 2).

[44] IaSA, f. 3363, op. 1, d. 7, l. 42. There is no further information on this effort. On the general response, see League publications from early 1930; for example, "Belogvardeiskie svideteli o religioznykh goneniiakh pod krylyshkom Piia XI," *Bezbozhnik*, 1930, no. 6 (March), 4–6; M. Shein, "Nas ne zapugaesh," *Bezbozhnik*, 1930, no. 5 (March), 1.

[45] GARF, f. r-5407, op. 1, d. 17, ll. 114–114ob.

Comintern politics) was privileged over function. In 1925 in Teplitz-Schönau (Czechoslovakia) the socialist free-thought groups of Europe had formed the IPF to counter the "bourgeois" Union of Freethinkers founded in Brussels in 1880.[46] The League joined this organization in 1926, and hosted IPF groups visiting the Soviet Union in 1926 and 1927. After a delegation headed by Aleksandr Lukachevskii, the League's deputy chairman, attended the group's Third Congress in Cologne in January 1928, the League began playing a greater, largely destructive role in the IPF. The previous month, in December 1927, at the Party's Fifteenth Congress, the Bolshevik leadership had announced a sharp radicalization of its policies. This announcement meant an end to cooperation with Social Democratic forces in Western Europe, a position that was canonized at the Sixth Congress of the Comintern, which convened in Moscow in July 1928. Accordingly, the League spent the next two years publicly vilifying the so-called social fascist leadership of the IPF—especially its chairman, Theodor Hartwig, and Max Sievers, head of the largest German freethinker organization—for its appeasement of European religious authorities, and for suppressing those IPF constituent organizations with communist sympathies.[47] At the group's Fourth Congress, in November 1930 in Bodenbach (Czechoslovakia), the Soviet and allied delegations staged a walkout, reconstituting themselves in the nearby town of Tetschen as a new IPF from which the former leadership was excluded.[48] With this task accomplished, the Central Council's International Department steadily fed League publications accounts of individual persecutions by religious authorities in the West, linkage of ecclesiastical and governmental bodies, and the role of Western churches in suppressing the working class. As open manifestations of religion disappeared from Soviet Russia, more and more space in League propaganda media was given over to the foreign landscape, creating a distant villain against which the Soviet Union must remain vigilant. The League projected onto Western Europe a battle that was nearing its end, at least officially, in Russia. During this transition, the League's discourse also was exported, so Western freethinkers were called Godless in

[46] Jochen-Christoph Kaiser, "Organisierte Religionskritik im 19. und 20. Jahrhundert," *Zeitschrift für Religions- und Geistesgeschichte* 37, no. 2 (1985): 205.
[47] E. Iaroslavskii, *Ocherednye zadachi antireligioznoi propagandy* (Moscow, 1930), 34–37; "V IPF," *Antireligioznik*, 1930, no. 1, 108.
[48] Jochen-Christoph Kaiser, *Arbeiterbewegung und organisierte Religionskritik: Proletarische Freidenkerverbände in Kaiserreich und der Weimarer Republik* (Stuttgart: Klett-Cotta, 1981), 205–215. See also A. T. Lukachevskii, *Za revoliutsionnoe edinstvo v Mezhdunarodnom bezbozhnom dvizhenii* (Moscow: Bezbozhnik, 1931); M. Sheinman, "Mezhdunarodnoe znachenie ateisticheskogo dvizheniia," in *Voinstvuiushchee bezbozhie v SSSR za 15 let*, ed. M. Enisherlov (Moscow, 1932), 506–529.

League publications, though the Western and Russian terms had very different meanings.[49] The League's involvement in the IPF, however legitimate, was a venture into the arenas of Soviet foreign affairs and Comintern politics, where, once again, it could at best play only a supporting role.

Collectivization

Like the regime's foreign policy concerns, its agricultural and industrial priorities became increasingly central to League propaganda after 1929. The League regularly exhorted its activists to promote collectivization, spring planting, and fall harvest.[50] In 1929, the Iaroslavl' Provincial Council issued instructions for the League's participation in the upcoming planting campaign, and stressed the need to counter the clergy's efforts to obtain seed and promote prayer.[51] According to *Pskovskii kolkhoznik* in 1931, the Pskov Godless should be leaders of collectivization.[52] Among the League's specific contributions was yet another campaign, this time for tractors. The Central Council planned to present twenty-four tractors to a collective farm in Rossoshanskii Okrug, in the central Black Earth region, on May Day 1930.[53] Emulating the mobilization of workers to transform the countryside—the "25,000ers"—the League formed its own brigades, the "150ers." The League's battalions overlapped with rather than extended the mobilization of workers, and their explicit mission was to engage in general political enlightenment work, not just antireligious propaganda.[54]

To a certain degree, of course, the League was entirely justified in its acclaim of collectivization. In practical terms, collectivization of a village usually meant the forced closing of its church. Collectivization also appealed on a primitive ideological level as a putatively more Marxist approach to the undermining of religion, by transforming production relations. The question raised here is not the relevance of collectivization to

[49] A. Lukachevskii, "Mirovoi kongress bezbozhnikov," *Bezbozhnik*, 1928, no. 6 (March), 2–3.

[50] For instance, A. L., "Bol'shevistskii vesenii sev," *Bezbozhnik*, 5 January 1931.

[51] IaSA, f. 3362, op. 1, d. 15, l. 6.

[52] *Pskovskii kolkhoznik*, 8 January 1931.

[53] GARF, f. r-5407, op. 1, d. 28, l. 62.

[54] Ibid., d. 17, ll. 21a (unnumbered sheet between 21 and 22), 103ob. Other than a few scattered references to the 150ers, I have found very little information. The project may not have gotten past the planning stage. On the 25,000ers, see Lynn Viola, *The Best Sons of the Fatherland: Workers in the Vanguard of Soviet Collectivization* (New York: Oxford University Press, 1987).

the antireligious effort but the matter of agency: the League as a self-declared vital participant in this process. For instance, instructions issued in 1929 by the Iaroslavl' League read in part: "Carefully disinfect storage facilities and the barn, destroying the nests of rats and mice." Similarly detailed directions on this and other farm-related procedures were printed regularly in *Bezbozhnik* and in the League's other mass propaganda materials.[55] While such information may have been useful to the rural population, it underscored the League's distance from its original mandate, as well as the tremendous pressures on it to conform to the regime's broader agenda even at the expense of its own identity. The League had no direct role to play in collectivization, and if its local leaders participated actively in collectivizing peasants, they did so not primarily or even secondarily as League cadres.

Industrialization

The question of agency can also be raised about the League's participation in the Soviet industrialization drive. The wonders, majesty, and promise of Soviet industrialization projects were loudly trumpeted in League materials.[56] In the early 1930s, the League formulated its propaganda in terms of the "518/1,040"—the 518 largest Soviet industrial projects and 1,040 machine tractor stations that were the centerpiece of Bolshevik economic rhetoric in the early 1930s. Clergy and sectarians were depicted as opposing these projects, and religious holidays were attacked for interfering with their construction and production schedules.

The League's participation in the industrialization drive, unlike its propaganda for the rural population, did not include dissemination of detailed information about the processes involved. This time it took more indirect forms, such as promoting the "industrial-financial plan" (*promfinplan*) and "socialist construction." At a meeting of the League's Central Council in 1929, Iaroslavskii stated that the League should not limit itself to antireligious measures, but should participate in the economic and cultural agenda of the Party and State.[57] The League's projects were to be integrated into "the five-year plan of socialist construction . . . particularly in regard to the specific current issues of socialist reconstruction of industry and agriculture."[58] (As might have been expected, the League adopted its

---

[55] IaSA, f. 3362, op. 1, d. 15, l. 11.

[56] For example, "Bezbozhnyi donbass," *Bezbozhnik*, 1930, no. 2, 2, with photos.

[57] GARF, f. r-5407, op. 1, d. 26, l. 50ob.

[58] IaPA, f. 229, op. 9, d. 2, l. 12.

"Religion is the enemy of industrialization": Moscow, 1930s. (The Hoover Institution Archives, Poster Collection, RU/SU 1916a.)

own five-year plans, one in 1930 and another in 1932. Neither was well publicized and both appear to have been produced for internal consumption.)[59]

Beyond its slogans, the League supported industrialization by selling the government bonds that supposedly financed it. With little or no linkage to religion and atheism, League propaganda aggressively promoted these loans. The Central Council announced its goal in 1930 of having all League members subscribe to the bond designated "The Five-Year Plan in Four Years,"[60] and in 1931 *Bezbozhnik* declared that the League's purpose was to bring the loan campaigns to "its" realm, the countryside.[61] The following year, the Central Council declared that "in the name of its five million members, the League, as usual occupying a forward post in the battle for socialism, has offered, with other voluntary societies, its help to the government's loan 'The Final Year of the Five-Year Plan.'" The League's specific goal was 14 million rubles, and the Central Council established a "Headquarters for the Realization of the Loan" which issued instructions to local councils.[62] The Iaroslavl' League planned to counter St. John's Day in 1931 by calling for 100 percent subscription to the loan "The Third, Decisive Year of the Five-Year Plan." The Pskov League approved a plan in 1934 for subscription to the bond "The Second Year of the Second Five-Year Plan." The goal was apparently achieved well ahead of schedule, on the second day of the month dedicated to it.[63] The League's role in this achievement, if any, remains unclear, but it willingly claimed a share of the laurels.

The League's propaganda on these and other tangential themes in the early 1930s reflected the tension surrounding its ideological function. Indeed, such tension had accompanied the League from its creation. While orthodox Marxism held that religion was a reflection of a particular mode of production, the Bolshevik justification for antireligious propaganda in the 1920s challenged this causality by suggesting that attitudes could be transformed independently of production relations. At the League's Congress in 1929, the commissar of enlightenment, Anatolii Lunacharskii, acknowledged that only the achievement of socialism would fully destroy religion, but, he continued, "This does not mean that we should say that, as long as we have not changed the economic conditions from which religion in-

[59] V. A. Alekseev, "Byla li v SSSR 'Bezbozhnaia piatiletka'?" *Disput*, 1992, no. 2, 12–23.
[60] GARF, f. r-5407, op. 1, d. 28, l. 49.
[61] "Prodvinem zaem v derevniu," *Bezbozhnik*, 15 July 1931.
[62] IaSA, f. 2410, op. 1, d. 6, l. 9; *Antireligioznik*, 1932, nos. 11–12, 40.
[63] IaSA, f. 2410, op. 1, d. 4, l. 61; PSA, f. 247, op. 1, d. 10, l. 12.

evitably grows, there is nothing for us to say about methods of cultural influence. . . . Sometimes [consciousness] outpaces [*operezhaet*] things."[64]

This ideological voluntarism contradicted other shibboleths in Bolshevik political culture. An individual could not change his or her class status—once a bourgeois, always a bourgeois, no matter what his or her current labor orientation—yet an individual's religious status could be changed, almost overnight if we accept Soviet images of peasant women. The notion that enlightenment could transform an individual underpinned Soviet propaganda efforts, but with a significant qualification: the right person was necessary, ideally an ill-educated peasant or semiliterate worker. By implication, antireligious propaganda would have little effect on an educated, bourgeois believer.

With a tenuous ideological basis, the League and many other single-issue advocacy groups in the 1920s were left unmoored, floating in the "superstructure" as NEP-era cultural experiments, and subject to the rapidly changing priorities of the regime. The re-creation of production relations in the 1930s introduced new contradictions. To continue emphasizing antireligious propaganda was to reject the optimistic and mechanical Bolshevik view of social transformation of the First Five-Year Plan and the Cultural Revolution. Despite the statements by Lenin, Trotsky, and Iaroslavskii in quieter moments acknowledging that the formation of an atheistic socialist culture would take decades, during the Cultural Revolution faith in immediate social transformation was rampant and, in any case, politically imperative.[65] Thus the League was left with little choice but to confront religion on the margins as a superfluous general propagandist for the regime.

Against this charge, the bureaucratic construct of antireligion offered by the League was fragile and far from convincing, even when it directly addressed religion in the 1920s. By the 1930s there was, in effect, little that was atheistic in Soviet antireligion. A Moscow-based activist commented at a meeting of the Central Council that the 1933 anti-Easter campaign under discussion had "nothing anti-Easter [in it]; it was all general political."[66] This shift accomplished, however, the League remained a poor vehicle for such propaganda. The League was hampered by the same rhetorical structure that had limited its efficacy against religion. Organizationally the League was as weak as ever, if not more so, for having lost its

[64] *Stenograficheskii otchet vtorogo vsesoiuznogo s'ezda Soiuza voinstvuiushchikh bezbozhnikov* (Moscow, 1930), 25.

[65] See Sheila Fitzpatrick, ed., *Cultural Revolution in Russia, 1928–1931* (Bloomington: Indiana University Press, 1978).

[66] GARF, f. r-5407, op. 1, d. 96, l. 38.

raison d'être, and there simply were too many campaigns for it to handle effectively. The nominal nonreligious responsibilities of League cells in Iaroslavl' in early 1931 were both overwhelming and distant from its original mandate: (1) spring planting; (2) the thirteenth anniversary of the Red Army and the fiftieth birthday of its leader, Kliment Voroshilov (23 February); (3) International Women's Day (8 March); (4) the Day of Overturning the Autocracy (12 March); and (5) Paris Commune Day (18 March). The League was also expected to arrange lectures on the role of religion in the suppression of the French Revolution, to note the speech of Pius XI and his crusade against the USSR, and finally to discuss the trial of the Industrial Party and "its links to religious organizations."[67] The League was simply incapable of meeting these expectations.

That the regime would want to define a substitute culture and might even need an extensive bureaucracy to promote that culture is not in doubt. The question is the process by which it sought to do so, a process to which the League contributed little, championing Soviet culture as poorly as it had promoted atheism. The League's propaganda was constrained by inappropriate and ineffective presentations, as well as by its internal orientation. At the same time, the League's presence was integral to the very notion of a successful campaign against religion: it was an organized, bureaucratized manifestation of a sentiment hailed by the Bolshevik leadership.

The campaign against religion offers yet another example of what Lewin called the "statization" of Soviet society. In the case of antireligious propaganda, the bureaucracy had assumed proportions that blurred the line between ends and means. Whereas the regime's leaders hoped that their efforts would raise the population to the desired ideological level, they instead found themselves promoting the State, not atheism, as a resolution to the regime's many difficulties. The result of this "idolatry of state" (Lewin's words again) paralleled the outcome in other fields such as the rural economy, where the State's distrust of the peasantry and even the new, higher Soviet forms created for it—the collective farms—resulted in a "peculiar socialism without the peasant."[68] In the League's case, the

[67] IaSA, f. 2410, op. 1, d. 4, ll. 5–6. On the last point, the League produced a pamphlet casting the Industrial Party against a religious background. The author warned that although there were no priests among the indicted, "that in no way means that the Church was on the sidelines in wrecking and preparation for [foreign] intervention": Boris Kandidov, *Vreditel'stvo, interventsiia i tserkov'* (Moscow: Bezbozhnik, 1931) (30,000 copies).

[68] Moshe Lewin, *The Making of the Soviet System: Essays in the Social History of Interwar Russia* (London: Methuen, 1985), 260–261, 270–271, 274.

regime offered State-administered antireligion without atheism. Using part semantics and part realistic policy, the regime was able to ignore or smooth over its fundamental inability to bridge the gap between the demands of its motivating ideology and the realities of a still largely rural and inertia-bound Soviet Russia.

So far we have been considering the regime's secularization campaign from the perspective of its leaders; that is, by chronicling the official measures taken in regard to religion, the League's history up to 1926, and the League's centrally produced propaganda. Now we turn to the League's local operations to examine what antireligion looked like to its intended audience, and the extent to which the populace responded to the regime's antireligious propaganda and its calls to join the League of the Godless.

5

The League of the Godless in Iaroslavl' and Pskov, 1926–1933

The danger is not only and not so much in the old bureaucrats stuck in our institutions, but—and particularly—new bureaucrats, Soviet bureaucrats, among whom "Communist" bureaucrats play far from the smallest role. I have in mind those "Communists" who, through paper orders and "decrees" in whose strength they believe as in a fetish, try to substitute for the creative initiative and independence of the millions of masses of the working class and peasantry. The task is to smash bureaucracy in our institutions and organizations, liquidate bureaucratic "customs" and "habits," and clear the way for the use of the reserves of our system, for the deployment of the creative initiative and spontaneous action of the masses. This task is not easy. It won't be resolved in an instant. But it has to be resolved, whatever the difficulties, if we really want to transform our country on the basis of socialism.

—Stalin, *Voprosy Leninizma*

From the League's perspective, perhaps the most significant outcome of the Central Committee's conference on antireligious policy in 1926 was that it gave the League a green light to join the ranks of the so-called mass societies. According to its own figures, membership in the League rose from 100,000 in 1925 to 700,000 in 1929 to over 5 million in 1932.[1] In June 1929, the League held its well-publicized Second All-Union Congress in Moscow and, befitting an organization at the forefront of the Cultural Revolution, changed its name to the League of the Militant Godless (Soiuz Voinstvuiushchikh Bezbozhnikov). The League's rapid expansion and its prominence implied that this agency of social transformation had been successful, but like the regime's message of atheism, these figures and their suggestion of dramatic cultural change instead illuminate the Potemkin-like phenomenon of antireligion.

---

[1] V. N. Konovalov, "Soiuz voinstvuiushchikh bezbozhnikov," *Voprosy nauchnogo ateizma* 4 (1967): 69.

Rather than serving as an actual measure of atheism abundant, these numbers constituted an officially promoted discourse of social progress that revealed how Bolshevik planners (as well as later Soviet commentators) perceived the spread of atheism in institutional terms. The rapid rise in reported League membership was assumed to indicate that atheism was taking root in society.[2] Even Western accounts point anecdotally to growing League membership as evidence of the social revolution achieved under the Bolsheviks.[3] To some degree, it was, but these numbers were highly misleading. They served simultaneously as a model "of" and a model "for"—a description of social reality and a normative expression of the regime's goals.[4] Tracing the League organizations in Iaroslavl' and Pskov reveals how these two functions were often at cross-purposes.

The League's actual experience in Iaroslavl' and Pskov reveals neither continuous growth nor a smoothly running operation. Indeed, as the League rode the turbulent waves of the Cultural Revolution, its record was one of extreme instability; organizational surges were followed by periods of complete quietude during which cells and councils ceased activity, many of them disappearing entirely. Membership in the League often amounted to little more than a name on a list. League councils came to life only during major religious holidays, and usually in response to direct pressure from the Party and other institutions. The population had little genuine interest in the officially sanctioned manifestation of secularization. Examination of this Potemkin facade of membership, cells, and councils not only reveals the League's flimsy nature but highlights an important aspect of antireligion: Bolshevik political culture's resigned acceptance of seemingly hollow organizational achievements in place of substantive social change.

Once again a distinction needs to be made between the regime's effective and brutal suppression of external religious manifestations and the League as an agent of atheism. Of the former there is little doubt, as existing

---

[2] V. Kalinin, "Dinamika rosta i sotsialnogo sostava SVB," in *Voinstvuiushchee bezbozhie v SSSR*, ed. M. Enisherlov (Moscow, 1932), 345; Konovalov, "Soiuz voinstvuiushchikh bezbozhnikov," 69–70; G. V. Vorontsov, *Leninskaia programma ateisticheskogo vospitaniia v deistvii* (Leningrad: Leningradskii Gosudarstvennyi Universitet, 1973), 162. Vorontsov writes that "the growth of the League of the Godless cannot be automatically linked to the spread of atheism," but he does make that link.

[3] Richard Stites, *Revolutionary Dreams: Utopian Vision and Experimental Life in the Russian Revolution* (New York: Oxford University Press, 1989), 106; John Shelton Curtiss, *The Russian Church and the Soviet State* (Boston: Little, Brown, 1953), 206, 237.

[4] The idea of models "of" and "for" reality is borrowed, somewhat out of context, from Clifford Geertz, "Religion as a Cultural System," in *The Interpretation of Cultures* (New York: Basic Books, 1973), 93–94.

accounts document and research affirms. Beginning in the late 1920s, a new cataclysm visited the Orthodox Church. This process only superficially, however, resembled the version of secularization officially promoted at the highest levels in Moscow, whereby industrialization and careful propaganda work would lead to a genuine and indeed "natural" decline of religion. Instead, local authorities closed churches on a variety of pretexts, and the formal seizure of a church often amounted to a violent intervention resembling a pogrom and recalling the open conflict of the Civil War. Those clergy not arrested as counterrevolutionaries or kulaks were taxed out of their parishes. Despite its ominous-sounding name and numerical growth in these years, the League had only a nominal role in this process of destruction: that of promoting public demand to close churches. In fact, the League as an institution was often invisible in the process. Foreign journalists and clergymen who chronicled religion's demise rarely noted the League's contribution.[5] Similarly, as we will see, the records of church closings preserved in Russian archives only occasionally reveal the League's presence.

The League's inefficacy as an agent of atheism and its secondary role in actual suppression raises the question of relevance: if the League was not the regime's main weapon in its attacks on religion, did it have any significance at all? Why did the League, so weak internally, occupy such a prominent and even noisy position within the Bolshevik propaganda apparatus? The question is not how the regime persecuted Orthodoxy—a topic covered in numerous other accounts—but how it conceptualized, administered, and measured its ideological goals. From this viewpoint, the League opens a broad perspective onto Bolshevik political culture.

Early Efforts, Early Failures

Although there had been sporadic efforts to create ODGB and League cells in and around Iaroslavl' before 1926, the Iaroslavl' League's first real organizational surge followed the Central Committee's conference in April

---

[5] Among the journalists, see Maurice Hindus, *Humanity Uprooted*, rev. ed. (New York: Jonathan Cape & Harrison Smith, 1930), 3–47; and Hindus, *The Great Offensive* (New York: Harrison Smith & Robert Haas, 1933), 165–189. William Chamberlin merely mentions his visit to the League's Central Council office in 1929 and repeats the claims of a League spokesman about its growth. See William Henry Chamberlin, *Soviet Russia: A Living Record and a History*, rev. ed. (Boston: Little, Brown, 1933), 317–318. For an exception in the clerical memoir literature, see S. S. Samuilova and N. S. Samuilova, *Ottsovskii krest*, 2 vols. (St. Petersburg: Satis', 1996).

1926. During the next two months, League councils at all levels formed or were appointed from above. A conference at each level convened and formally elected a council whose membership was already approved by the local Party. This initial drive led to a provincial conference of the Godless in Iaroslavl' on 13 June.[6] After hearing the "Internationale," the sixty-two delegates listened to reports on antireligious propaganda by an education official, Ivan Alekseevich Shalygin, and on the provincial League council by its head, Aleksandr Egorov, a Party agitprop worker.[7] Egorov reported that as of 1 May 1926, the provincial organization encompassed thirty-one cells with 581 members. Growth continued during the year, and in December a published Party report indicated a total of eighty-eight cells in Iaroslavl' Province, seven *uezd* councils, and three district councils, with a total membership of 2,600.[8] By the end of 1926, the Iaroslavl' League appeared to have established a core network throughout the province.

The League in Pskov got off to a somewhat earlier start. In early 1925, an ODGB organization grew out of an antireligious training seminar arranged for its activists by the Provincial Party Committee.[9] This seminar appears to have stemmed from the arrest and trial in late 1924 of several Pskov clergymen, including Bishop Varlaam, for arranging "fraudulent" renovations of icons. This incident reflected the regime's continuing attack on the Orthodox Church and its leaders, but in the new political climate in which propaganda was encouraged as a necessary complement to administrative pressure, the Party found itself lacking sufficiently trained cadres. During the summer of 1925, a group calling itself the ODGB Board confirmed the establishment of new cells and organized a conference in June that was attended by thirty delegates representing ten cells.[10] The Pskov Party Committee reported in November that a League provincial council had been appointed, and that the League had seventy cells with 591 members in five *uezdy* (out of a total of eleven) and the town of Pskov. The council was officially "elected" at a conference of the Pskov Godless in January 1926. As in Iaroslavl', the Pskov League reacted to the Central Committee's conference in April 1926 by establishing additional cells and holding another conference in May.[11]

---

[6] IaSA, f. 3362, op. 1, d. 2; f. 3362, op. 1, d. 5, l. 9; f. 3362, op. 1, d. 7, ll. 5–21, 31; "Pervaia Iaroslavskaia gubernskaia konferentsiia SB," *Bezbozhnik*, 29 August 1926.

[7] Egorov and Shalygin are discussed in greater detail in Chapter 7.

[8] *Otchet Iaroslavskogo gubernskogo komiteta VKP(b) za period dekiabria 1925–dekiabria 1926 g.* (Iaroslavl', 1926), 58, 61.

[9] PPA, f. 1, op. 4, d. 155, and d. 161, ll. 2–5.

[10] PPA, f. 1, op. 4, d. 161, ll. 13, 15, 20–21, 70–72; *Bezbozhnik*, 24 May and 12 July 1925.

[11] PPA, f. 1, op. 4, d. 161, l. 101, and d. 257, l. 2; *Pskovskii nabat*, 22 January 1926.

The League's first organizational wave crested in the late spring and summer of 1926—a short-term result of the April 1926 conference in Moscow. By the time attention again turned to the Iaroslavl' League in early 1927, many earlier achievements had proved fleeting, and the Party essentially had to recreate the League. On 20 January of 1927, the agitprop department of the Provincial Party Committee passed a resolution titled "On Strengthening Antireligious Propaganda."[12] The following month, the Third District Party Committee (the town of Iaroslavl' was divided into three Party regions) recommended the appointment of permanent antireligious propagandists and discussion of antireligious work in all Party cells.[13] At the same time, the agitprop collegium of the First District Party directed local Party cells to strengthen existing cells and work toward the creation of new ones. Nonparty activists were to be recruited.[14] These efforts in 1927 were not generally successful, and officials in Iaroslavl''s First District reported that only a few cells were functioning.[15] Moreover, in several cases, as at the Free Labor Factory and the State Industrial Construction Authority's dormitory, the 1927 surge amounted to reestablishing cells founded a year earlier.[16] Despite the pattern of creation, inactivity, collapse, and re-creation of cells, the Iaroslavl' League claimed that total membership continued to climb. In November 1927, the Iaroslavl' Party indicated that there were 3,080 League members in 140 cells in the province.[17]

Even with its earlier start, Pskov's network proved less enduring than Iaroslavl''s; it did not survive the summer of 1926. Pskov's Second District League Council (the town of Pskov was divided into two districts) reported in November 1926 that its disarray was due "to the circumstance that the new district council inherited very little from the former one. . . . [We did not have] even a rough sense of the number of League members in the Second District." The decline had been steep; when a new district council took over in October 1926, the thirteen cells with 284 members that had flourished at the beginning of the year had dwindled to six. "Thus, during the course of the summer, the number of cells decreased 50 percent and membership declined by 40 percent." No work was under way in the six surviving cells, according to this account.[18] After the sum-

---

[12] IaPA, f. 1, op. 27, d. 2746, ll. 112–115.

[13] IaPA, f. 1, op. 27, d. 2746, l. 54.

[14] IaPA, f. 1, op. 27, d. 2746, ll. 41–43.

[15] IaSA, f. 3362, op. 1, d. 7, l. 37.

[16] IaSA, f. 3362, op. 1, d. 8, l. 64; f. 3362, op. 1, d. 10, ll. 7, 34.

[17] *Otchet Iaroslavskogo gubernskogo komiteta VKP(b) za period ianvaria—noiabria 1927* (Iaroslavl', 1927), 75.

[18] PPA, f. 6, op. 1, d. 133, l. 34.

mer's collapse, the Pskov City-Party Committee in early September directed Party cells to engage in antireligious propaganda and to arrange for the participation of Party members in the League.[19] As in Iaroslavl', the League found itself reestablishing cells created earlier. On 15 November 1926, the Second District Council announced the formation of "new" cells at the Metallist and Uritskii factories, the Land Management Office, and the Teachers' Union. All were being recreated, having previously been established in 1925.[20]

Despite the flurry of activity in the autumn of 1926, the Pskov League was no more successful in that effort to create a functioning network than in its earlier attempt. On 12 December 1926, the Second District Council's chairman reported that with few exceptions the existing cells did nothing, and that the Second District Council was still unable to make a full account of its membership.[21] Six months later, another district council meeting found little change. The report on the cell at the Land Management School observed that it had existed until 15 May and then had bit the dust.[22] The First Pskov District Council was in even worse condition. A meeting on 20 November 1927 noted that there had been only one previous gathering of the council since its election over a year earlier, and that had been an organizational meeting. No antireligious work was being conducted by the League.[23] The League's visibility declined so alarmingly that *Bezbozhnik* placed the Pskov organization on its black list in December 1927.[24] In its issue on the eve of Orthodox Christmas in January 1928, *Pskovskii nabat* ran a biting account of the League. Headed "The Forgotten Front," the article told

> a sad story of how the League's work collapsed in Pskov. Everyone knew that in Pskov . . . there were supposed to be two district councils and that there were 20 cells with 600 members. Many knew this, but when efforts were made to unite the councils into one city council, then there were [not only] no members and cells, but also no district councils. In December a

[19] PPA, f. 6, op. 1, d. 133, ll. 11–12. Pskov was initially divided into two districts, each with its own district party committee.

[20] PPA, f. 6, op. 1, d. 133, l. 35.

[21] PPA, f. 6, op. 1, d. 133, l. 37.

[22] The title of this protocol, "Meeting of the *Raikom* ODGB Activists of 1 July 1927," is notable for its use of the ODGB title, by then over two years out of date. See PPA, f. 6, op. 1, d. 202, l. 6.

[23] PSA, f. 247, op. 1, d. 1, l. 39. There is one indirect reference to a Second Pskov League Congress in August 1927 (ibid., d. 3, ll. 11).

[24] "Na chernuiu dosku," *Bezbozhnik*, 4 December 1927.

provisional council was somehow thrown together and the search began for cells, their members, and the *aktiv*.[25]

Such bleak assessments were the most constant feature of the League's coverage in local newspapers.

Established in these early years, the League's organizational pattern changed little through the rest of the 1920s and early 1930s; it simply expanded to a much larger scale. The next upsurge started in the middle of 1928 after another Central Committee antireligious conference in May; this round also benefited from the intensified atmosphere of cultural warfare stemming from the well-publicized trial of the Shakhty engineers the same month. The investigations that accompanied this revival provided further evidence of the League's short life cycle. An inquiry into the Iaroslavl' League in August 1928 found that the elections for district councils in 1927 did little to revitalize antireligious work, and that "in a variety of *uezdy* and *raiony*, organized cells collapse." It cited several cells in the Third District that "had collapsed by the time of the investigation." The report also discussed the Second District, "where League cells had only just been organized, and before that—that is, before the investigation—absolutely no work had been conducted." This account placed membership at 3,174 in 133 cells, only a marginal increase over the membership claimed the previous November.[26] While the League's presence outside Iaroslavl' was becoming more visible, the quality of these League outposts was questionable. A propagandist from Poshekhone-Volodar'e Uezd, in the far north of the province, wrote in October 1928 to the Provincial League that there were only seven cells in the *uezd* and that they had just recently been created. An investigation into antireligious work in the area the same month, however, did not mention the League at all.[27]

The Pskov League also experienced a recrudescence in 1928, including a congress at the *okrug* level in September. The forty-two delegates were greeted at the opening ceremonies by a message of support from the Pskov Union of Esperantists.[28] The new leader of the Pskov League, Ivan Nikitich Sigov, noted that as a provincial organization, the League had 4,000 members, but in the smaller *okrug*, there were about 1,500 members in sixty-six cells.[29] (The "high" figure of 4,000 contradicted the 5,000

[25] *Pskovskii nabat*, 5 January 1928.

[26] IaPA, f. 1, op. 27, d. 2865, ll. 183–187.

[27] IaSA, f. 3362, op. 1, d. 9, ll. 6, 87–89.

[28] The Pskov Esperantists had recently held their own conference. PSA, f. 247, op. 1, d. 2, l. 7.

[29] Ibid., d. 3, ll. 6–12. Sigov is discussed in Chapter 7. (In mid-1927, Pskov had been downgraded from an oblast to an *okrug* of about half its former size, as discussed in Chapter 6.)

members reported by the Provincial Council in October 1926, again suggesting that the League had no accurate sense of its membership.) Sigov's report implied that the Pskov League barely existed. He complained that not one district council had forwarded dues to the *okrug* level; letters and instructions went unanswered. In the absence of a League network, Sigov gathered membership and activity information and assigned tasks via his own connections as an education official.

The League's Great Turn

Through 1928 in Pskov as in Iaroslavl', there was little evidence that the League was having much impact at all on actual religiosity in the country. Beyond the publications it disseminated from Moscow and the occasional lecture or debate, the League remained a barely visible institution. Nevertheless, the volume of the regime's antireligious tirade began to grow during the year in sync with the Cultural Revolution. Cyclical waves aside, these years (1928–1932) brought a uniquely intensive campaign against religion as part of the *Velikii perelom*—the great transformation of Soviet society that was designed to resolve the cardinal questions left unanswered since 1917. Even if the Orthodox Church no longer constituted a political threat, religion was still perceived as a cultural obstacle and offered an excellent whipping boy for the regime. The efforts of the 1920s—selective repression combined with propaganda campaigns—had failed, as religion on a popular level appeared to flourish. More important, religion was caught up in the chaos as the regime resolved its troubled relationship with the countryside. The priest was lumped with the rhetorical kulak as a threat to the regime, and collectivization of agriculture usually meant the summary closure of the village church, which was often then used (against Soviet law) for grain storage. In the cities, the First Five-Year Plan of socialist construction brought destruction to thousands of churches that supposedly stood in the way of new boulevards and squares. Resolutions to close churches were added to the "mandates" presented to candidates in the local elections in early 1929. Other churches were closed because they were too close to factories or schools or troop garrisons, or for some other reason thought up by local officials. Predatory taxation forced religious communities—the "twenties"—to renounce the agreements with local authorities allowing them to use churches.

Although Metropolitan Sergei (Stragorodskii) had declared his loyalty to the Soviet regime in 1927, the Orthodox clergy found themselves again subject to arbitrary arrest, summary exile, and even execution. Ruinous taxation was applied by local officials to chase away those priests still at liberty. In one particularly articulate letter of complaint from a church council in the northern Caucasus, the petitioners wrote that "of course, there is no persecution of Orthodoxy in our country, but what does one call it when religious communities such as ours are literally suffocated by unbearable taxes? How is one to explain it . . . when rural clergy, most without farms and poor, are assessed monstrous taxes, not by their own declaration of income but according to the principle of 'squash the priests.'" The letter ended sarcastically: "Yes, of course there is no persecution of religion here, but all the same, what does one call [this situation]?"[30] Mikhail Kalinin, in his capacity as chairman of the All-Russian Central Executive Committee, acknowledged that "servers of cults are taxed from every direction and in such amounts so that they cannot fulfill the demands made of them. And then all of their property is seized, even what is necessary for their family, and then the family is exiled." P. G. Smidovich, the head of the newly created government committee to oversee religion, added that "local tax assessment of cult servers has turned into sheer taunting [*sploshnoe izdevatel'stvo*]."[31] These assessments often had no basis in law, but the new tax codes were draconian on their own: clergy were officially taxed at a rate of 75 percent of their income. Clergy also were evicted from their apartments, or presented with exorbitant rents, and prevented from receiving rationed food. On 27 December 1932, priests were officially forbidden to reside in cities.[32] Believers also found their legal rights sharply circumscribed. A new law promulgated on 8 April 1929, "On Religious Associations," strictly limited the activities of religious groups to performing divine worship. A few months later the RSFSR constitution was amended to remove the guaranteed right to engage in religious "propaganda."[33]

Although this period represented a return to the State's direct intervention in religious affairs after a nominal hiatus of several years, the nar-

---

[30] GARF, f. r-1235, op. 66, d. 426, l. 355–358.

[31] Mikhail Odintsov, *Gosudarstvo i tserkov': Istoriia vzaimootnoshenii, 1917–1938* (Moscow: Znanie, 1991), 49, 51. Smidovich chaired the Permanent Commission on Questions of Cults of the Presidium of the All-Russian Central Executive Committee, created in 1929.

[32] O. Iu. Vasilieva, "Russkaia pravoslavnaia tserkov' v 1927–1943 godakh," *Voprosy istorii*, 1994, no. 4, 38; Curtiss, *Russian Church and the Soviet State*, 230–232; Matthew Spinka, *Christianity Confronts Communism* (London: Religious Book Club, 1938), 102–104.

[33] Joshua Rothenberg, "The Legal Status of Religion in the USSR," in *Aspects of Religion in the Soviet Union, 1917–1967*, ed. Richard H. Marshall Jr. (Chicago: University of Chicago Press), 82, 438–445.

rower enterprise of antireligious propaganda received no small encouragement from these cataclysms. More virulent propaganda delivered by an in-
vigorated League with the explicit support of key institutions would now
complement rather than replace a strategy of direct intervention. The
League's marching orders came in a directive from the Communist Party's
Central Committee dated 24 January 1929 and titled "On Measures to
Strengthen Antireligious Work."[34] Citing a supposed religious revival that
was mobilizing counterrevolutionary forces, the Central Committee demanded heightened antireligious activity. The resolution hailed the League
of the Godless as the "sole antireligious organization in the country," but
noted that the League had not yet become a powerful "mass organization." The Komsomol followed suit in March 1929 with its own criticism
of current antireligious efforts, and specifically called for Komsomolers
and nonparty youth to become active members of the League. The same
month, at its Eighth Congress, the Central Trade Union Council issued its
own resolution on antireligious propaganda.[35]

This new siege of religion brought the League to its pinnacle of development. Local cells organized on a variety of occasions and pretexts. Many
were created in early 1929 (after the January Party directive) and in June
1929, after another Central Committee antireligious conference and the
League's well-publicized Second All-Union Congress. Mass enrollments in
the League also resulted from church closures, which tended to peak during the Easter and Christmas seasons. Some of the closing resolutions
called for collective enrollment in the League. The resolution to close a
church in Rossosh (Central Black Earth region) in January 1930, for example, also called for the 350 petitioners present "to join collectively the
League of the Militant Godless." Another resolution to close the same
church called for establishment of a League cell whose membership was to
consist of all office workers in the area.[36]

Sixty-five railroad workers joined one Northern Railroad cell in Iaroslavl'
on 1 March. League membership at the Iaroslavl' Provincial Soviet/Party
School grew from 53 on 1 September 1928 to 153 by mid-February 1929.[37]

---

[34] Approved by a Politbiuro meeting of 24 January 1929, attended by Bukharin, Voroshilov,
Kalinin, Kuibyshev, Molotov, Rudzutak, Rykov, Stalin, and Tomskii. Kaganovich, Krupskaia, Krinitskii, and Iaroslavskii also were present (RTsKhIDNI, f. 17, op. 3, d. 723, l. 1).
The Iaroslavl' Provincial Party Committee received a copy of the directive and with a cover
sheet dated March 2, 1929, passed it on to the *uezd* and district committees (IaSA, f. 3363,
op. 1, d. 1, ll. 12–16).
[35] *Izvestiia TsK VLKSM*, 1929, nos. 5–6 (31 March), 23; GARF, f. r-5451, op. 13, d. 470,
l. 28.
[36] GARF, f. r-1235, op. 66, d. 429, ll. 356, 366.
[37] IaSA, f. 3378, op. 1, d. 7, l. 33; f. 3362, op. 1, d. 1, l. 95.

To facilitate the task of creating new cells, the well-organized Third District Council in Iaroslavl' distributed the following form: "To the bureau of the Communist Party cell at _____: The Presidium of the Council of the League of the Godless, in accordance with a resolution of the District Council Plenum and a general meeting of the Godless, directs you to organize a Godless cell in your enterprise."[38] The council had only to fill in the name of the addressee and send it out. The size of cells in Iaroslavl' also began to increase sharply, from an average of around twenty to over eighty members per cell. In the scramble to increase numbers, it proved easier to add members to existing cells than to create new ones. As cells grew larger, however, so did the likelihood that the significance of membership declined.

Despite (or more likely because of) the coerciveness of all these events, League membership spiraled upward. By 10 April 1929, the Iaroslavl' Provincial League claimed 259 cells with 9,441 members, nearly a threefold increase in membership from less than a year earlier. League membership in 1930 in the eight districts of the newly formed Iaroslavl' Okrug (significantly smaller than the former province) was claimed to be 11,257 in 282 cells, up from around 9,100 in an area twice as large one year earlier. As of 1 October 1930, the head of the League organization for the city of Iaroslavl' and its surrounding suburbs reported 58 cells with 4,700 members. One year later, in October 1931, the City-District League had grown even more, to 210 cells with 14,271 members. In the summer of 1932, the Iaroslavl' Godless reported 285 cells with 23,056 members. The League's chairman placed 1933 membership of the City-District League at 27,000.[39] The reported population of Iaroslavl' in 1929 had been 134,407. Even when we allow for a substantial increase in population during the First Five-Year Plan, claimed League membership still constituted a significant percentage of the city's entire residents.[40] The League's growth followed the contours of Iaroslavl''s industrial development. The First Five-Year Plan had brought new factories to Iaroslavl', as well as the expansion of existing facilities. These included the sprawling Resin-

---

[38] IaSA, f. 3362, op. 1, d. 1, l. 290a.

[39] IaSA, f. 3362, op. 1, d. 14, l. 81 (membership information for 1929 excludes two *uezdy*); *Otchet o rabote Iaroslavskogo okruzhnogo komiteta partii za iiun'–mai mes, 1929–1930* (Iaroslavl', 1930), 38 (in 1929, the Iaroslavl' Okrug League Council became subordinate to the Ivanovo Industrial Oblast League Council; see Chapter 6); IaSA, f. 2410, op. 1, d. 11, l. 77, and f. 3378, op. 1, d. 4, ll. 71,124; PSA, f. 247, op. 1, d. 13, ll. 28–29. League organizations, especially those involved in "socialist competitions" with one another, often exchanged protocols of their meetings. This was the case with Iaroslavl' and Pskov in 1933. The protocols for the autumn 1933 meetings of the City-District Council survive in the Pskov State Archive but not in the Iaroslavl' archives.

[40] *Bol'shaia sovetskaia entsiklopediia*, vol. 65 (1931), 771.

Asbestos Kompleks (RAK) on the city's northern side, an artificial rubber plant (SK-1), and a large truck assembly plant.[41] The League extended its presence to all these new establishments.

The League also maintained its visibility through regular conferences of the Iaroslavl' Godless. Several district level gatherings met in March 1929, leading to a provincial congress on 6 April. At least four city-district conferences were convened between September 1930 and October 1931. Through 1932 Iaroslavl' was the scene of dozens of smaller conferences of Young Godless, readers and correspondents of *Bezbozhnik*, and cell secretaries, among others.[42] The League's exposure in Iaroslavl' was enhanced in April 1930 by the opening of an "antireligious museum," actually a wing of the oblast history museum in the former Il'ia Prorok Church in the city's center.[43]

As a relatively large urban outpost, the Iaroslavl' League benefited tremendously from those changes that fed the League's growth nationally. The League in rural distant Pskov expanded too, though to a lesser degree. Intermediate data are unavailable, but in May 1932 the Pskov City-District Council reported 8,453 members organized in 187 cells, as well as 2,679 Young Godless. These numbers contrasted with a membership of 539 for the fledgling city-district council in March 1928, or 1,500 members in September 1928 for the much larger Pskov Okrug. At a time when other League organizations, including the Central Council in Moscow, were waning with the passing of the Cultural Revolution, the Pskov League experienced a renaissance that continued through 1933. That year, the local council met an impressive twenty-one times and overall membership continued to grow. The Pskov League's activism was even noted in the national antireligious press, an exception to the League's malaise elsewhere.[44] The high point was reached in the middle of 1933, when the Pskov League claimed 203 cells (100 in Pskov itself) with 10,593 members (8,381 in the town of Pskov). Given Pskov's population of 55,000 in 1932, the League's representation, at least on paper, was substantial for a rural community with little of the industry that would supposedly provide many of the League's members.[45] The explanation for the Pskov League's dynamism in 1933, as I suggest in Chapter 7, lay not

---

[41] See *Iaroslavl' sotsialisticheskii: Ocherki po istorii goroda, oktiabr' 1917–1959* (Iaroslavl', 1960).

[42] IaSA, f. 2410, op. 1, d. 10, l. 29; d. 11, ll. 6–12, 46, 51, 53, 65–67, 91; d. 12; f. 3362, op. 1, d. 1, ll. 85–85ob; d. 15, l. 5; d. 14, l. 36.

[43] Ibid., f. 229, op. 9, d. 132, l. 233ob.

[44] *Bezbozhnik*, 31 January and 5 March 1933.

[45] PSA, f. 247, op. 1, d. 4, ll. 1–1ob; d. 9, l. 42; d. 10, l. 3; 1933 membership as of 1 July.

in the League's network or oversight from Moscow but in the energies of dedicated individual activists.

In rural Pskov, opportunities to expand the League came in the form of collective farms. In a dispatch published in *Bezbozhnik* in January 1933 the Pskov League claimed that fifty new rural collective farm cells were to be established before spring planting.[46] Also in the course of 1933, greater attention was paid by the League Council to the three explicitly "Godless" collective farms in Pskov District: Godless, Iaroslavskii, and Matorin.[47] As we have seen, the League went to great lengths to appear politically and socially relevant. While organizing cells at newly established collective farms in Pskov and industrial enterprises in Iaroslavl' represented a legitimate opportunity for expansion, this practice also served the purpose of allowing the League to claim that it was a vital participant in the leading institutions of the time.

Potemkin Secularization

While this period certainly represented a *Velikii perelom* for the League, was it one as well for Soviet atheism? Was the country in fact abandoning God in favor of "scientific materialism"? The hollowness of the League suggested not. And although Soviet newspapers reported a swelling tide of atheistic feeling resulting in overwhelming and in some cases unanimous popular support for church closings across the country, archival materials paint a drastically different picture. First of all, the number of churches closed in those years was smaller than is popularly imagined. Given the numerous administrative/territorial changes in this period (see Chapter 6), tracing the number of functioning churches in the areas traditionally considered to encompass Iaroslavl' and Pskov provinces is difficult, but when the focus shifts to smaller administrative entities, a clearer picture emerges, and we see that far more churches were closed in towns than in the countryside.[48] The rural areas of Iaroslavl' District had sixty-nine

---

[46] *Bezbozhnik*, 31 January 1933.

[47] Matorin headed the Leningrad Oblast League Council.

[48] Of the some 1,650 churches within the boundaries of Iaroslavl' Province in 1917, around 950 were still officially open and functioning on the eve of the Cultural Revolution. Many of the prerevolutionary churches had been attached to institutions—schools, hospitals, large government facilities—and as a result were closed soon after the Revolution. The same fate befell the smaller number of chapels in large private residences. Other churches were destroyed during the ill-fated anti-Bolshevik uprising in 1918. The decline in parish churches was therefore proportionately less during the first ten years of Bolshevik rule. See IaSA, f. 3517, op. 1, d. 1, l. 8.

churches before the Revolution. As of 1937, when a new wave of closings would begin, forty-one were still functioning. In Tutaev District, thirty-six of the fifty-six churches were still functioning. In Liubim, thirty of forty-two were still open. In the town of Iaroslavl', which had seventy-two churches before the Revolution, only two (serving four congregations) were operating in 1937. In Kostroma, thirty-seven of the town's forty-one churches were closed by 1937.[49] Less information is available for Pskov, but it indicates fifty operating churches in Pskov City-District in mid-1933, compared to only twenty closed ones.[50] More generally across the country, the end of the First Five-Year Plan left many churches in the Russian heartland open and functioning, even if under regular siege and subject to temporary closures. According to statistics prepared by the Commission on Cults of the All-Union Central Executive Committee in 1936, some 61.3 percent of prerevolutionary churches remained open in Ivanovo Oblast (to which Iaroslavl' was subordinated). The figures for Moscow Oblast were 53.4 percent and for the RSFSR as a whole, 35.6 percent.[51]

Moreover, many closings were purely administrative affairs without popular input: local officials presented the chairman of the church council and the priest with a closing decree as a fait accompli and demanded the keys to the church.[52] When efforts were made to garner actual public support for the closings, the results were far more mixed. The League's activist at RAK asked to be reassigned after the workers gave him a rude reception; another reported being beaten up at Krasnyi Perekop.[53] In the campaign to close the Spaso-Nagorodskaia Church in Iaroslavl', workers were asked to sign beside their printed names on prepared sheets. Many did not sign, however, leaving large gaps in the signature sheets.[54] The effort to close the Peter and Paul Church in the Zakotorosl' region of Iaroslavl', near the grounds of the sprawling Krasnyi Perekop textile factory, involved the gathering of thousands of workers' signatures. The protocols of meetings called for this purpose, however, suggest difficulties in achieving this goal. On 21 October 1928, in the presence of 812 factory

---

[49] GARF, f. r-5263, op. 1, d. 1798, ll. 2, 5.

[50] PSA, f. 247, op. 1, d. 10, l. 3ob.

[51] GARF, f. r-5263, op. 1, d. 32, ll. 3–4. Figures are based on incomplete information.

[52] Thousands of such cases were appealed to the All-Union Central Executive Committee, headed by Mikhail Kalinin, the arbiter of last resort in regard to church closings. Before 1929, these cases were decided by the secretariat, and after April 1929, by a special commission on "cults" (1929–1938) headed by Peter Germanovich Smidovich. After receiving an appeal from believers, the Central Executive Committee requested that all materials concerning the closing be sent to Moscow. They remained there, in GARF, f. r-1235.

[53] IaSA, f. 2410, op. 1, d. 10, ll. 64, 95.

[54] GARF, f. r-1235, op. 75, d. 1745, ll. 40–48. About one-third of the spaces were left blank.

Throwing the bell from the tower of the Cathedral of the Assumption, Iaroslavl', 1929. (Courtesy of IaSA, N4-1084.)

The destroyed bell from the Cathedral of the Assumption, Iaroslavl', 1929. (Courtesy of IaSA, N4-1221.)

workers, the church closure issue was the twenty-seventh point to be discussed; that is, it was buried deep on the official agenda. At a meeting on 16 October 1928, the protocol noted the presence of 510 workers, but added that "there should have been a thousand." In another case where

1,600 workers were expected, only 613 appeared. Attendance may have been lower than expected for any number of reasons, but in this context, it is suggestive of a worker boycott. The believers' petition to keep the Peter and Paul Church open bore 774 signatures. Nowhere in the file on this church closure did the League as such appear.[55] One senses in some cases that the League was being deliberately kept in the background in order not to offend the people. On one level, this was, of course, a perfectly rational strategy; on another, however, it contradicted the need for a manifestation of this sea-change in popular attitudes.

When the League was prominent in closure campaigns, its appearance often smacked of overt Potemkinism. In Noginsk (formerly Bogorodsk) in Moscow Province, according to the protocol of an "Evening of the Godless" on Christmas (6 January 1930), the 1,200 assembled requested the government to close all the churches in the town. Earlier that same day, a gathering of seven to eight thousand on Karl Marx Square "unanimously" asked the government to close all the churches.[56] At times the regime's goal seemed surreal and calculated to fail: to have the believers themselves go on record as supporting the church closure. This was the case at the Vladimir (Renovationist) Church at the Vspol'e Railway Station in Iaroslavl' in 1929. The authorities claimed that 671 "believers" were among the thousands of people clamoring for the church to be transformed into a workers' cooperative.[57] Other believers in the northern Caucasus expressed disbelief when they read in *Bezbozhnik* that the "toilers" themselves wished to close churches: "Is it possible that we believers would close our own church? . . . Will that really be a victory for the League of the Godless? That victory will be bought at the cost of perverting the party line to the delight of the USSR's enemies."[58] In an effort to avoid opposition to such resolutions, meetings were furtively arranged at which the religious community was not represented, and believers vociferously complained that such petitions should not be used to justify church closings.[59] In one instance believers in Sverdlovsk wrote that the closure vote took place at a meeting of the "unorganized" population in one of the town's regions to hear a report of the city council. The question of the

---

[55] Ibid., op. 74, d. 2724, ll. 4–6, 22–43. While the numerous other protocols held in f. r-1235 note the size of worker meetings in favor of closure, none of the several hundred that I examined included the expected size of the gathering.

[56] Ibid., op. 66, d. 443, ll. 186, 187.

[57] Ibid., op. 65, d. 307, ll. 133. One wonders whether the "believers" may have been frustrated anti-Renovationist adherents of the patriarchal Church.

[58] Ibid., op. 66, d. 426, l. 358.

[59] For example, ibid., op. 64, d. 450, l. 257.

church was not on the official agenda and was only raised by a "Godless" during discussion of the city council's mandate. The measure passed by a slim majority. It was not discussed at all at the dozens of other meetings held in the area served by the church.[60]

Believers also reported threats made against them during these meetings. Workers at the Kaslinskii factory in Sverdlov Okrug wrote that only a small percentage of the population attended the preelection meeting at which the church closing issue was raised. Moreover, local officials reminded them that "anyone who votes against the resolution will be an enemy of Soviet power, a kulak . . . and will be deprived of civil rights up to the point of exile from the Urals oblast." Most of those gathered simply did not vote, according to an account by believers, but the local authorities took abstention as consent. At a meeting of the elderly, the gathered pensioners were reportedly told that if they voted against the resolution, they would not receive their pensions and could let the church support them.[61]

In far too many cases, failure to achieve the regime's goal according to the official script led to extreme measures: Party officials in Baradinskii Okrug (Siberia) apparently waged a multiyear effort to close the church in the village of Kazakulia, but had repeatedly failed to garner a majority in favor of closing. The local authorities then decided to close the church on the basis of a secret meeting of Party and Komsomol members. Late one night, they broke the lock on the church door, entered, and began destroying icons and other church property. According to the local Orthodox, the invaders cut up precious chasubles to make stage curtains and painted over icons as signs.[62] Hundreds of such cases were appealed to Moscow by believers; thousands more went unappealed.

Some believers criticized the closings in 1929 and 1930 as a fleeting phenomenon, not to be considered a reflection of a genuine secularization of society. The petitioners who appealed the attempted closure of the Fedorov Church in Iaroslavl' wrote that the closure petition was "raised in a moment of antireligious enthusiasm among a section of the working masses. At that time, there were no churches in Iaroslavl' about which closure petitions had not been filed."[63] There was clearly some justice to this comment. At the same time, the troubled popular position of the Orthodox Church before 1917, the genuine enthusiasm for socialist construction among many segments of the urban and newly urbanized population

[60] Ibid., op. 66, d. 448, ll. 59–60.
[61] Ibid., d. 436, ll. 22–23.
[62] Ibid., d. 437, l. 125.
[63] Ibid., op. 75, d. 1746, l. 16.

during the First Five-Year Plan years, and the inherent iconoclasm of youth charged with leading the way to socialism make it impossible to dismiss all of the closures as without any public support.

What remains unresolved is the degree of these feelings. Although the newly available archival materials touch on these issues, they do not permit definite conclusions. While large sections of the population may not have cared very much about the fate of local churches and clergy, this lack of support did not necessarily translate into a desire to see every church closed or to become a card-carrying member of the League of the Godless. Yet the official political culture demanded statements of absolute loyalty on issues for which there were numerous intermediate, overlapping, and contradictory positions. The same ambiguity characterized other elements of socialist construction in that period when genuine enthusiasm was tempered by hesitancy, passivity, and disagreement over means. As David Hoffmann has demonstrated, the construction of socialism in Moscow advanced by fits and starts, suffered reversals, and required compromises with a citizenry of uncertain and changing sympathies.[64] John Barber has found that most of the working class was indifferent to the official political culture and its demands in the 1930s.[65] The issue is less resistance—though there was plenty of that, particularly in the countryside, as several studies have shown[66]—than the intermediate positions taken by vast sections of the population as they were swept along by and participated in the creation of a new society. Their story is only now emerging from behind the shadows of historical discourses dominated by perpetrators, victims, and resisters.[67]

Surviving "Success"

Clearly the surge of Soviet atheism was less than the regime claimed, but of more direct interest here is how the League weathered its unexpected bounty. Indeed, the League's efforts to adapt to its spectacular expansion

[64] David L. Hoffmann, *Peasant Metropolis: Social Identities in Moscow, 1929–1941* (Ithaca: Cornell University Press, 1994).

[65] John Barber, "Working-Class Culture and Political Culture in the 1930s," in *The Culture of the Stalin Period,* ed. Hans Guenther (London: Macmillan, 1990).

[66] Lynn Viola, *Peasant Rebels under Stalin: Collectivization and the Culture of Peasant Resistance* (New York: Oxford University Press, 1996); Hoffmann, *Peasant Metropolis*; Barber, "Working-Class Culture"; Jeff Rossman, "Worker Resistance under Stalin," paper presented to the AAASS conference, Boston, November 1996.

[67] Stephen Kotkin, *Magnetic Mountain: Stalinism as a Civilization* (Berkeley: University of California Press, 1995), takes up this great middle.

revealed even further the League's fundamental weakness and its lack of genuine popular support. One strategy sought to create model or base cells that would serve as minicouncils in leading economic and political institutions. Strongly "fortified," these cells would provide leadership for others in the immediate area. In the cities, this approach meant focusing on the large industrial complexes. From 1930 to 1933, base cells were established and reestablished at the Resin-Asbestos Kompleks, the Liapino energy plant (on the eastern side of the Volga, just south of Iaroslavl'), at the railroad yard, at the Workers' Victory chemical plant, the Auto-plant, the Krasnyi Perekop textile factory, and the Iaroslavl' electric station.[68] The Iaroslavl' League's experiment with base councils, however, was no more successful than its general pattern of organization. Its efforts to maintain a base council at RAK, for instance, failed repeatedly.[69]

The rural equivalents of the factory minicouncils fared little better. Just as the Communist Party sought to make the machine tractor stations (MTSs) outposts of political control in the countryside in the early 1930s, the League tried to make them the basis for a heightened rural presence. In early 1933 *Bezbozhnik* reported that the Pskov League had promised that two base cells would be established at the local MTSs, and a month later *Bezbozhnik* announced that a recently created cell at the second Karamyshevo MTS would soon become a model cell. In August the Pskov League claimed that both MTSs in the region had cells, offered antireligious courses, and were frequently visited by district council staff. According to another account six months later, however, a base cell at the Pskov MTS was only in the process of creation.[70] In six months, League MTS operations had dropped from two active cells to one in formation, and the MTS itself had declined from two to one. Whatever the explanation, it did not suggest any great success in turning the MTSs into League strongholds in the countryside. Nationally, the League's effort to create a network of rural outposts was similarly unsuccessful. At a meeting of the League Executive Bureau in Moscow in December 1933, Fedor Oleshchuk reported that despite favorable conditions during the preceding six months, there were only about 200 base cells among the 2,500 MTSs in the country—far short of the Central Council's goal announced in June to have a base cell at each MTS by September. How had this happened? Because, Oleshchuk charged, the League had dealt with this task in a bureaucratic manner, yielding only "paper leadership."[71]

---

[68] IaSA, f. 2410, op. 1, d. 10, l. 92.
[69] Ibid., ll. 6-g, 59; PSA, f. 247, op. 1, d. 13, ll. 30–31.
[70] *Bezbozhnik*, 31 January and 15 March 1933; PSA, f. 247, op. 1, d. 12, ll. 111–112, 140.
[71] GARF, f. r-5407, op. 1, d. 102, ll. 6–7.

An illuminating failure occurred near Iaroslavl' District. In May 1933, *Bezbozhnik* criticized the Ivanovo Oblast League for failing to arrange antireligious work at the thirty-six MTSs in the oblast. Having provided 14,000 rubles for tractors to the Gavrilo Posad MTS (100 kilometers from Iaroslavl') and given it the name Bezbozhnik, the council had exercised no further leadership. Two months later, *Bezbozhnik* carried an interview with the head of the political department of the MTS, Comrade G. Struchkov, in which the OGPU official revealed that he had only just learned that the MTS was supposed to bear the name Bezbozhnik. "If you judge by the antireligious work done in Gavrilo Posad District . . . ," he commented, "it's obvious that for the Ivanovo Oblast League Council, 1931 was a year of 'dizziness from success,' but from what successes no one knows. . . . You can announce anything you like, but . . . what was done to strengthen Godlessness, at least to some degree? Nothing." There was no cell and certainly no antireligious activity at the Gavrilo Posad MTS.[72] Discussion of such an astounding incident in the League's own national organ was not simply an example of Bolshevik self-criticism. These revelations maintained the tension used to justify the League's central administrative apparatus and its continuing organizational efforts. The goal of a base cell at every MTS went unquestioned, even if utterly unattainable or inappropriate. Because the MTSs were to serve as miniature Bolshevik political systems in the countryside, they had to replicate fully all the overlapping and bureaucracy-laden social organizations and forms of administration characteristic of the Soviet political system. Rather than concentrate resources on areas of religious activity, the League emphasized the organizational uniformity that was expected within Bolshevik political culture.

Seemingly unable to maintain a deep and broad network of genuine cells and committed activists, did the League exist in any meaningful way? At issue here is not whether antireligious lectures were delivered, religious services disrupted, or even churches closed, because these things occurred regularly, either through the League or independent of it. Rather, the issue is the League's visibility. Because the regime deliberately measured its ideological success in organizational terms, this visibility speaks to the self-defined "success" of atheism in Soviet society. Yet, League and Party files are replete with statements questioning the League's organizational integrity. Although rural cells were particularly subject to question, urban League organizations were not immune to such charges. In the fall of 1930, the chairman of the First District Council acknowledged that, "up

[72] *Bezbozhnik*, 17 May and 29 July 1933.

to the moment of its liquidation, the district council of Godless as such did not exist." Even the provincial council of a large industrial city was called into question. In August 1928, Shalygin's account of the Iaroslavl' League to the provincial party's agitation collegium prompted its chairman to respond, "In essence, the League Provincial Council conducted no work, and if considered formally, then in fact our League organization does not exist." Shalygin weakly rejected this charge.[73]

League councils may have existed on paper, but many of them were storefront operations for local Party agitprop departments. A 1928 investigation into the Second District Council in Iaroslavl' concluded that all its work was done "over the head" of the Council by the staff of the Party's agitprop department and the Stalin Workers' Club. The district council conducted no independent campaigns; everything was undertaken by the Party agitprop department.[74] The same was true of the Third District where there was "a complete fusion of the district council and the Party agitprop department. . . . All antireligious work in the district has been due to the efforts of the agitprop staff of the Third District Party Committee, who simultaneously serve as members of the League district council."[75] In the eyes of many believers, little distinction was to be made among the forces that intervened in their lives: they were all Godless, whether they had anything to do with the League or not.[76] Given the role of the Party in establishing the League, some degree of overlap was to be expected, but the League's inability to establish even a minimally nonparty base betrayed not only militant atheism's lack of wide appeal but also the League's vulnerability in an environment of rapidly shifting Party priorities and allocation of resources.

The League's frequent conferences and congresses constituted another questionable aspect of antireligion's superstructure. The meetings followed a standard format (similar to that of major Party gatherings): a report on the tasks and methods of antireligious propaganda, often delivered by a visiting high-level propagandist, was followed by an account of the local council's activity before the election of a previously chosen slate of candidates for the League council. These gatherings also elected delegates to the conference of the next higher League body, which usually followed several

---

[73] Respectively, IaPA, f. 1, op. 27, d. 3088, l. 10, and f. 3378, op. 1, d. 4, l. 1. The "liquidation" was the merging of Iaroslavl''s three councils into one City-District Council in the fall of 1930.

[74] IaSA, f. 3362, op. 1, d. 11, ll. 56–58.

[75] Ibid., l. 51.

[76] For example, GARF, f. a-396, op. 4, d. 24, l. 523; f. r-1235, op. 65, d. 332, l. 66; and d. 331, l. 449.

Children with antireligious placards gathered for an event at the employees' club of the People's Commissariat of Finance, Moscow, 1929. (Courtesy of the Russian State Archive of Cinema and Photographic Documents, no. 251270.)

weeks later. There is no evidence of fictional conferences per se, but meetings in Pskov and Iaroslavl' were repeatedly postponed or delayed for lack of delegates, preparation, or some other necessary element.[77] Even when

---

[77] For example, IaSA, f. 2410, op. 1, d. 1, l. 52.

conferences were held, their significance for the dissemination of atheism seems slight. Only a few of them were elaborate affairs stretching over many days. Most of them were simply large meetings. Conferences of the Young Godless were little more than after-school assemblies.

For many delegates, participation in the League amounted to no more than attendance at these meetings; they did not necessarily result in additional organizational work. For instance, the agitprop head of the Poshekone' Volodar'e Uezd Party, Konstantin Evlamplevich Karasev, reported in October 1928 that the seven League cells in the *uezd* had just been organized. Karasev, who had attended both the June 1926 and the January 1928 provincial League conferences—the only representative from that district to participate in either meeting—clearly had not rushed back to organize the League in his area,[78] and he was not exceptional in this regard. These meetings of the Godless were important more for what they represented than for what they actually achieved. Part of the League's visible superstructure, they gave the impression of dynamism and a self-sustaining organization. With little evidence of actual antireligious activity, however, these conferences demonstrated how the means supplanted the ends in the functioning of antireligion.

Case Studies: Krasnyi Perekop and the OGPU

Heretofore the Iaroslavl' and Pskov Leagues have been viewed at an aggregate level, but following the League's experience at specific institutions might provide a better sense of the League's local presence. The Krasnyi Perekop textile mill in Iaroslavl' dated from the early eighteenth century and was known as the Karzinkin factory or, more commonly, the Bol'shaia Manufaktura until 1922. Its workers struck in 1883 and 1890; a much-celebrated strike occurred in 1895. Before World War I the plant employed over 10,000 workers, by far the largest labor force in the area. Although this number was reduced to 3,739 as a result of the Civil War, by 1929 there were 12,173 workers and 844 Communists at the plant, and Krasnyi Perekop remained Iaroslavl''s flagship enterprise until the completion of RAK in 1932.[79] Given the importance of Krasnyi Perekop, the

---

[78] IaSA, f. 3362, op. 1, d. 9, l. 6; f. 3362, op. 1, d. 4, ll. 89–96, 169–174.

[79] The plant's role is discussed *passim* in *Ocherki istorii Iaroslavskoi organizatsii KPSS* (Iaroslavl': Verkhne-Volzhskoe Knizhnoe Izdatel'stvo, 1967); *Ocherki istorii Iaroslavskoi organizatsii KPSS, 1883–1917* (Iaroslavl': Verkhne-Volzhskoe Knizhnoe Izdatel'stvo, 1985); *Iaroslavl' Sotsialisticheskii: Ocherki po istorii goroda, oktiabr' 1917–1959*, 109; *Materialy k XXII Iaroslavskoi gubernskoi partiinoi konferentsii: Otchet gubernskogo komiteta VKP(b)* (Iaroslavl', 1929), 68.

local leaders of the Godless felt that the League must be particularly well represented there, regardless of the actual level of religious activity at the complex. On one hand, a large, urban industrial enterprise such as Krasnyi Perekop may have "needed" antireligious propaganda less than other segments of society did. On the other, a significant percentage of the complex's laborers were women who retained close contacts with the countryside and therefore were presumed to be religious. Until 1931, when at least one church was closed, two churches operated on the grounds of Krasnyi Perekop, and Soviet textile mills in general were centers of urban religiosity well into the late 1920s.[80] Whatever the nature of Krasnyi Perekop's workers, the plant's organizational appeal to the League was irresistible. If the League were to be significant in Iaroslavl', it had to be a force at Krasnyi Perekop.

The first effort to organize the local Godless occurred in November 1925, when a meeting of Party officials in the Second District voted to establish an "organizational troika" for a cell of the League of the Godless. Along with the rest of Iaroslavl', the Second District held its first conference of the Godless the following spring. Twenty-seven delegates from four cells, representing 112 members, met on 14 May 1926.[81] In December, the council's secretary reported that the council had met only once since being formed in May, and had only six cells with a total membership of 170. The Second District Council experienced no revival whatsoever in 1927, and as of mid-1928, the League network had slipped back to four cells and 118 members, just about the same level as two and a half years earlier, and a substantial drop from the level of late 1926.[82] In November 1928, the provincial council was told that the "old district council had vanished without a trace."[83] Little changed at Krasnyi Perekop during the following year, when the rest of the League nationally and locally took off. In April 1929, a delegate to the League's Provincial Congress stated that "Godless work at Perekop is in a desperately poor state, and when the provincial council began searching for the bureau created in 1925, it could not be found. The Perekop administration has a devil-may-care attitude toward Godless work, and when I asked permission to hold a reregistration of members, they told me, 'If it's necessary,

---

[80] Chris Ward, *Russia's Cotton Workers and the New Economic Policy: Shop-Floor Culture and State Policy, 1921–1929* (Cambridge: Cambridge University Press, 1990), 37, 118–123.
[81] IaSA, f. 3362, op. 1, d. 2, l. 1, 12. Iaroslavl''s Second District consisted of the textile plant and its surrounding neighborhood. For all intents and purposes, the League's Second District Council and the Party's Second Raikom were synonymous with Krasnyi Perekop.
[82] Ibid., ll. 97–98, 112; IaPA, f. 1, op. 27, d. 2865, l. 190.
[83] IaSA, f. 3362, op. 1, d. 4, ll. 204–205.

then go ahead and reregister, but don't come to us with these problems.'"[84]

Later in 1929, the same cycle of complaint, investigation, and reestablishment was repeated. An activist at Krasnyi Perekop, Iakov Shugaev, complained to the *okrug* council that the local Party committee was indifferent to the League's inactivity at the factory, and he asked the *okrug* council to replace the dormant leadership of the local council. Shugaev blamed the failure of a recent conference of the Godless on the local Party's unwillingness to provide people for the meeting.[85] (Apparently the Communist Party was expected not only to sanction the League's activities but also to arrange its affairs.) The Iaroslavl' Okrug Council recommended dissolution of the Second District Council for "inaction" at its plenum on 22 December 1929, and a League meeting at Krasnyi Perekop, attended by forty-nine members, formally dismissed the old council on 19 January 1930. At this meeting, the council's departing head blamed the lack of work on summer leaves! He added that the former district council staff was not "competent." A few months later, the council's new leader wrote that the new district council's task had been not to continue earlier work but to begin organizing cells anew, "because the old staff not only had no information on the state of the League [in the district] but also had lost the stamp and seal."[86] The new council, in which Shugaev had become increasingly involved, began work immediately and met regularly through the summer of 1930. As of April 1930, the council reported twenty-five cells with 1,300 members and four Young Godless cells with 832 members.[87]

The League's vibrancy at Krasnyi Perekop during 1930 proved temporary. At some point in late 1930 or early 1931, Krasnyi Perekop's most effective antireligious activist, Iakov Shugaev, was promoted to the City-District Council. His departure dealt a death blow to the League's work at Krasnyi Perekop. When the League reviewed antireligious work at Krasnyi Perekop in November 1931, it found none.[88] Although the Nikola Mel'nitsa Church on the plant's grounds was closed on 4 December— 16,000 signatures demanding the closure were produced—it appears doubtful that the League had any meaningful role in this campaign, even

[84] Ibid., d. 14, l. 41. See also *Severnyi rabochii*, 10 April 1929.
[85] IaSA, f. 3363, op. 1, d. 4, ll. 25–26; f. 3362, op. 1, d. 1, ll. 4–5, 33. He was probably referring to the Party's failure to provide a slate for a new district council and a meaningful turnout of interested individuals.
[86] Ibid., d. 7, ll. 3–4, 25.
[87] IaSA, f. 3362, op. 1, d. 1, ll. 2–37 *passim*; f. 3363, op. 1, d. 7, ll. 10–25.
[88] IaSA, f. 2410, op. 1, d. 10, l. 72.

though this was precisely the type of activity the League had been created to pursue. The appointment of a League factory council in 1932 to oversee propaganda at the complex brought little change. In the autumn, the League's representative at Krasnyi Perekop reported to the League City Council that "the enemy is attacking," especially around the remaining Donskaia Church, and that sectarians were active in the workers' dormitories and outlying districts. As for the Communists, the activist cited the statement by Comrade Grigor'eva that "I am only willing to work on the churchmen's side, because antireligious propaganda is just deception." In its resolution, the council noted the collapse of the League organization at Krasnyi Perekop and the absence of all antireligious work. As a corrective measure, the council assigned a brigade of activists to the plant.[89] We may reasonably speculate that this measure yielded little change.

The League's history at Krasnyi Perekop—a cycle of organization, collapse, investigation, and reestablishment—was typical of the League generally. Despite the periodic attention accorded to the League by the Party, the League's outpost at Krasnyi Perekop was nearly invisible to those on the ground. To suggest, however, that all League operations in all places and at all times were complete fiascoes would be as misleading as the official Soviet view. There were well-organized, active councils, as in Iaroslavl''s Third District in the late 1920s (whose activists were all OGPU members assigned to the Iaroslavl' railroad yard), and there were individual cells whose level of activity transcended the mere writing of names on a membership list. Nevertheless, review of perhaps the best organized cell in all of Iaroslavl' calls into question the role of even the League's best cells in the effort to transform Soviet society. After an organizational meeting on 2 August 1926, attended by fifty-seven employees, the League's cell at the Iaroslavl' OGPU office held a series of well-attended, well-documented meetings that lasted through the autumn of 1927. The cell represented ninety-two members of the OGPU office, its military force, and the Iaroslavl' OGPU prison staff.[90] The OGPU cell's size and activism belied its actual significance. The large OGPU cell satisfied the League's need for numbers and regular communications, but an active League within the OGPU amounted to preaching to the converted. Moreover, a secretive organization such as the OGPU provided little opportunity for the League to propagandize the general population. One doubts whether OGPU staff read League lectures to those unfortunates who passed through OGPU

---

[89] Ibid., d. 7, ll. 20–22; d. 10, ll. 93, 95.
[90] IaSA, f. 3362, op. 1, d. 10, ll. 26–27; d. 8, ll. 15–95 *passim*.

portals.[91] Moreover, after its promising beginning, the OGPU League cell quickly disappeared. Even the dedicated organ of state security could not sustain the symbolic activism of running a League cell.[92]

The League's difficulties at Krasnyi Perekop and its brief and pointless success among the OGPU, were ultimately two sides of the same coin. The League was well represented, but not necessarily where it was "needed"; in those places where there was a greater perceived demand, at Krasnyi Perekop and throughout the countryside generally, the League remained a barely visible, inconstant presence. In other ways as well, the League was strongest where it was least needed. Throughout the Iaroslavl' and Pskov regions, the overwhelming majority of League members were city and town dwellers, and an equal preponderance of members were male. In both cases, then, the League was bypassing the groups perceived to be most in need of atheistic ministrations. While an activist core of nonbelievers may reasonably have consisted of male urban Party and Komsomol members, the inability to reach beyond this base group rendered the League a prisoner of a political system with too few resources and too many claimants.

In Iaroslavl', in Pskov, and throughout the nation, local League organizations ultimately fell victim to the utter indifference to antireligious propaganda that overcame the Bolshevik propaganda apparatus in the mid-1930s. Depending on one's view of the mid-1930s, several explanations for the League's demise are available. On the one hand, socialism had been declared victorious at the Party's Seventeenth Congress in 1934; religion had been eliminated—at least in its most visible manifestations—and so the League (along with much of the rest of the Soviet apparatus charged with attending to the population's backwardness)[93] was no longer necessary. On the other hand, with the passing of the Cultural Revolution and the onset of the so-called Soviet Thermidor or Great Retreat, it seemed natural that the cultural radicalism nominally associated with the League would recede from view.[94] Finally, as we saw in Chapter 4, the early 1930s

---

[91] Evgeniia Ginzburg certainly made no mention of antireligious propaganda during her stay at the Iaroslavl' prison in the late 1930s. See her *Krutoi marshrut* (Riga: TsKKP Latvii, 1989).

[92] There is a file of protocols from 1929 and 1930 from a short-lived League cell at the Moscow headquarters of the NKVD, equally well attended and well documented (GARF, r-5407, op. 1, d. 34).

[93] In regard to nationalities policy, see, for example, Yuri Slezkine, "The USSR as a Communal Apartment, or How a Socialist State Promoted Ethnic Particularism," *Slavic Review* 53, no. 2 (Summer 1994): 442.

[94] Nicholas Timasheff, *The Great Retreat* (New York: Dutton, 1946); Leon Trotsky, *The Revolution Betrayed* (1937; New York: Pioneer Publishers, 1945).

brought a homogenization of propaganda activities that put pressure on single-issue advocacy groups such as the League. Whatever the reason, the League as an organization declined rapidly. The records of the All-Union League and its Central Council all but disappear from 1933 onward, and the League lost its national organ, the newspaper *Bezbozhnik* (ostensibly as a paper-conservation measure), in January 1935. Evidence of the Iaroslavl' League disappears at the end of 1933. Documentation of the Pskov League ceases in 1934, when the City-District Council reported forty-nine cells with 2,497 members, down from 10,593 a year earlier.[95] The League declined nationally to somewhere between 350,000 and 400,000, a drop of greater than 90 percent.[96] These figures speak eloquently to the lack of popular support for the League. Beyond a few central publishing activities, the League of the Militant Godless had become completely quiescent.

Paper Achievements and Bolshevik Political Culture

From the mid-1920s into the early 1930s, the activities of the League of the Militant Godless in Iaroslavl' and Pskov reflected an approach to planned social transformation that relied on the development of a comprehensive, uniform network of activists and councils. The League's experience in fulfilling these expectations varied greatly across the nation. Leningrad's League organization seemed to be among the most stable and active, judging from its communications with the Central Council. Somewhat surprisingly, the Moscow organization was often moribund, perhaps reflecting its place in the shadow of the Central Council, the Moscow Party Committee, which had no great love for the League, and other central institutions. The League's archives show other local councils coming alive briefly at various times, but there is no evidence to suggest that they operated under different assumptions. And where exceptions occurred, they were due to the presence of dedicated, competent individuals. Beyond the unsurprising generalization that the League was strongest in the cities and weaker in areas where religious and national minority groups were prevalent, the League presented a nearly uniform record of underachievement.

Bolshevik political culture measured the League's success—and consequently the spread of atheism—by how close it came to an expected norm of bureaucratic development. Reacting to periodic resolutions from higher powers (there were antireligious conferences in Moscow in 1926, 1928,

[95] PSA, f. 247, op. 1, d. 10, ll. 11, 14.
[96] RTsKhIDNI, f. 17, op. 114, d. 805, l. 29.

and 1929), local Party committees appointed League councils and mounted campaigns to enlist members. Conferences were regularly scheduled to confirm these developments. The Communist Party's repeated failure to establish a viable League, however, gave antireligion the appearance of organization for organization's sake. Whatever people's feelings about the Orthodox Church, the League exerted no strong attraction. Fulfillment of the regime's ideological agenda was manifested in highly bureaucratic, form-oriented structures bearing little relation to genuine social change. The activity of cells was less important than their nominal existence. The protest of one Iaroslavl' activist, Aleksandr Shalygin, who commented during a flurry of cell creation in 1926 that "we should concentrate not on the number of League cells but on their organizational strength and on the quality of their work," came as a plaintive cry in the wilderness.[97] While the nominal spread of the League's network did not preclude the possibility that belief among the population was eroding, it certainly cannot be used to support that contention. Indeed, the lack of genuine popular support for the League and the explicit efforts by the population to protect churches suggests the opposite. Whether the League's failure was due to atheism's bureaucratic packaging or to the basic unviability of the project remains a matter of speculation, but this bureaucratic legacy placed a heavy burden on those who would have radically transformed Russian society. Bolshevik political culture itself fundamentally limited the regime's ability to achieve its ideological goals.

The privileging of form over function was not limited to peripheral agendas represented by the League. The vitally important collectivization of agriculture also fell victim to an exhibitionist discourse of organizational success.[98] Arguing that Soviet achievements in atheism, agriculture, and elsewhere may have been hollow is beside the point; the point is that the Soviet approach to conceptualizing social change relied on external manifestations beyond, or unrelated to, more substantive evidence of such change. The League operated as part of Lewin's rapidly growing superstructure made up of "socialist" State, Party, trade union, and voluntary organizations that had always "run ahead" of the working class as both agent and reflection of social change, and as justification for the Revolution.[99]

---

[97] IaSA, f. 3362, op. 1, d. 7, l. 21.

[98] Sheila Fitzpatrick, *Stalin's Peasants: Resistance and Survival in the Russian Village after Collectivization* (New York: Oxford University Press, 1994), 16–17.

[99] In Lewin's account, the State is the main constituent of this superstructure, but the Komsomol, union, and other regime-supported bureaucracies can easily fit in this model. See Moshe Lewin, *The Making of the Soviet System: Essays in the Social History of Interwar Russia* (London: Methuen, 1985), 261, 264, 265.

These formalist tendencies were clearly present in an investigation of Dno District League Council (100 kilometers east of Pskov) by a visiting propagandist in 1931. His report is worth citing at length for the way it measures not what the League was but what it was not:

> The League District Council consists of nine individuals, but they are only listed on paper. The council is completely incompetent. For its entire existence, there was not one planned meeting to discuss antireligious propaganda in the district. No plans, no work by sectors, no attachment or live leadership. [The eleven previous cells] were only listed on paper and not one was active because of a lack of leadership by the district council. [Antireligious propaganda was limited to campaigns at Christmas and Easter.] There is no record of antireligious study groups. The district education authority has no antireligious inspector. . . . The district council's incompetence [is due] to the absence of a full-time worker. The district Party has taken no steps to arrange antireligious work and has not even discussed antireligious work. The district Komsomol undervalues antireligious work, and the secretary of the Komsomol committee declared that "we have conducted no work and there is no time for it."[100]

Although self-criticism (*samokritika*) was by this time de rigueur in Soviet public discourse, the form it took shaped expectations about how an organization like the League should operate. In the Dno District case, the investigator touched upon those categories of administrative development that were assumed to be vital for every level of the League's network: full-time Party staff and education inspectors, regular meetings and resolutions, copious support from other institutions, an elaborate internal structure, and so forth. This centralized perspective automatically transformed inquiries about secularization in Soviet Russia into the question: How is the League of the Godless faring? The question, however, was formulated as a negative: How far does the local League deviate from the (highly unrealistic) organizational standard? The result was an appraisal according to which bureaucracy was both the problem and the resolution. This was the dilemma at the heart of antireligion, and in general, of the Bolshevik approach to radical social transformation.

How are we to explain not only the League's repeated organizational failures but the expectations placed on it? And why was the League regularly

[100] PPA, f. 578, op. 1, d. 576, l. 16.

resurrected, despite its inability to sustain itself?   An examination of the Communist Party offers answers to these questions, and inspection of the relationship between the League and the Party (and other authoritative institutions) in the next chapter will illuminate not only the League's history but its significance within Bolshevik political culture.

6

The League of the Godless, the Communist Party, and Bolshevik Political Culture

As night turns into dawn
Every day I see:
Some to Main,
Some to Comm,
Some to Polit,
Some to Enlight,
People scattering into offices.
Drenched in a rain of paper files,
As soon as you enter the building,
Picking from the half-hundred—
the most important!—
Clerks scatter to meetings.

—V. Maiakovskii, "Prozasedavshimsia," 1922[1]

The League of the Godless was a creation and ward of the Party. Modeled directly on the Bolshevik Party, the League consciously embraced its organizational trappings. The League was organized in a pyramid of cells and councils/committees that communicated internally through regular and exhaustive reports (*otchety*), directives, investigations, and resolutions. Both the League and the Party marked time with conferences and congresses, engaged in endless administrative/territorial reorganizations, and employed a highly structured discourse that, more often than not, suggested that social and political problems could be resolved by further reorganizations and additional introspection. Nevertheless, the League was not simply an extension of the Party but rather a reflection of it in the areas that the Party was unable or unwilling to arrogate to itself directly. By establishing such agencies as the League in the 1920s as ostensibly autonomous organizations, the regime created a system of overlapping and

---

[1] My thanks to Nathaniel Knight for assistance in translating this poem.

150

competing institutions that closely resembled one another in their functioning and responsibilities. The resulting conflicts and the manner in which they were expressed constituted key elements of antireligion and Bolshevik political culture in the 1920s and 1930s.

This chapter examines the League's relationship with the Party (and to a lesser extent the Komsomol, trade unions, and education authorities) to illuminate Bolshevik agitprop practices, in particular the fickleness and ambiguity of the Party's support, the demands it made of cadres, institutional conflict, and a mania for reorganization. The resulting matrix of discursive and administrative relationships cast the regime's nominal propaganda agenda in grave doubt in the same way that the emerging bureaucracy compromised the regime's other ideological goals. While the rapid expansion of the Soviet bureaucracy in the first decades of Bolshevik rule is usually understood to have overwhelmed the "people" (peasants, workers, intellectuals, idealistic Party members), the purpose here is to consider how the relations *among* bureaucratic institutions favored process over product, thereby contributing to the edifice of antireligion.

Party Support

In Iaroslavl' and Pskov, as elsewhere, the Communist Party had created the League, but the Party was neither monolithic nor consistent in its patronage. Resolutions directing local Party committees to assist the League were followed by periods of indifference or neglect. This cyclic relationship also had an important spatial element. Most Party support for the League emanated from Moscow or from the provincial capital. Local Party committees, where the League's fate was really decided, only briefly heeded these directives before more pressing concerns and limited resources required them to shift their energies elsewhere. This inconstancy not only debilitated the League but also characterized the internal, institutional discourse of antireligion in which the Party occupied a central position.

The Party's short attention span in regard to the League and the League's ensuing cascade of incriminations were readily apparent in Iaroslavl'. At a meeting of the agitprop collegium of the Third District Party in August 1927, the League activist Nikolai Bakhvalov complained that the "relation of Party organizations to questions of antireligious propaganda is bad: [they] completely ignore League cells, and Party leadership is absent . . . [There] is almost no attention from agitprop commissions and Party cells." A few weeks later, Bakhvalov again cited the absence of Party leadership, noting the "insufficient attention—to put it mildly—from the district Party bureau." The Party's instructor had "a devil-may-care attitude toward questions of antireligious propaganda. . . . Why should we agitate here about religion? Our workers believe neither in God nor in the Devil."[2] The Party's attitude was not simply one of neglect; it also reflected uncertainty over its self-defined "leading role." When the League's leader in Iaroslavl''s First District asked for help from Party and trade union officials in March 1927, he was told that "the organization is voluntary and working in it is also voluntary."[3] This excuse was only somewhat disingenuous. The Communist Party had created the League as an "open," voluntary organization in order to attract the nonparty population. While the theory held that the Party would provide the League's leadership, making League membership mandatory for Party members would have rendered the League meaningless, just another facet of Party life. According to a writer for *Pskovskii nabat*, Communists and Komsomolers considered themselves atheists by virtue of their membership in those groups. To belong to the League was superfluous; to work for it would be even more so.[4] Given the League's failure to establish a significant nonparty presence, however, participation in the League and oversight of its activities became all but obligatory for agitprop officials during those brief moments when antireligious matters ranked high on the Party's list of priorities. At other times, the League was left to wither on the vine.

Higher-level Party bodies blamed lower-level ones for their failure to implement decrees. A printed account of the Iaroslavl' Provincial Party's activities for 1927 commented that although local Party cells created League units, the Party then provided no leadership, and League cells then collapsed.[5] Discussing the effort to close the Tolgskii Monastery, several kilometers northeast of Iaroslavl', in January 1929, the Iaroslavl' League invoked a higher Party level to criticize lower ones: "Despite a series of most important resolutions by the provincial Party's bureau and agitprop collegium on the strengthening and broadening of antireligious work by local Party organizations, the latter have done extremely little to execute these . . . directives. Appropriate help is not rendered to local League organizations, which work extremely poorly without the Party's assistance."[6] The

---

[2] IaSA, f. 3362, op. 1, d. 2, ll. 172; d. 9, l. 43.

[3] Ibid., d. 4, l. 180.

[4] *Pskvoskii nabat*, 5 January 1928.

[5] *Otchet Iaroslavskogo gubernskogo komiteta VKP(b) za period ianvaria–noiabria 1927* (Iaroslavl', 1927), 72.

[6] IaSA, f. 2410, op. 1, d. 14, l. 3. When the closing commission arrived, it was attacked and had to take refuge in a house; news of the closing reportedly had been leaked to the villagers, and they had gathered to protect the monastery (ibid., f. 3362, op. 1, d. 4, ll. 215–216; d. 13, l. 1).

Party in Pskov also blamed its lower-level organizations. In early 1927, the Pskov provincial Party complained that "despite repeated decisions and resolutions, . . . [*uezd* Party committees are] not providing sufficient leadership and assistance to the League's work."[7] Even the central Party apparatus added its voice to the chorus: a front-page editorial in *Pravda* on Christmas 1928 charged that "it does not occur to [some Party members] that antireligious propaganda is a Party obligation just like all other most important Party responsibilities."[8]

Each critique followed a recognizable pattern. The higher Party organization directed lower-level structures to engage in a wide range of propaganda activities. These resolutions were, as a rule, vague and provided no resources for the antireligious work. Given the absence of local cadres and funds, such resolutions were patently unrealizable from the moment they were issued. Nevertheless, the superordinate bodies had fulfilled their leadership responsibilities. By complaining that Party organizations high and low did not carry out centrally issued commands, the League also played its role, deferring to the decreeing authority of the Party and deflecting attention from itself. The rhetoric of assigning blame for the League's failures followed a narrowly scripted, closed circle of indictment that shifted attention from the League to the institutions presumed to support it.

The Second Congress of the Godless, June 1929

How this discourse of blame operated as a system can be seen clearly at the League's Second Congress, in 1929. The events of this congress have been discussed in Chapter 2; review of the way these conflicts were expressed illuminates the role of language in Bolshevik political culture. The meeting in 1929 revealed shared rhetorical conventions, especially the delegates' self-justification by invocations of Lenin (and later Stalin), their calls for centralization, and their method of criticizing individuals rather than institutions. All took place against the backdrop of a political rhetoric that served as an increasingly opaque medium of debate. Although objective differences between the opposing camps existed, the debates occurred in the context of a dominant political culture that accorded as much importance to certain words, phrases, and metaphors as to the ideas they articulated. The battle raged on a field—language—sought by both contenders.

[7] PPA, f. 1, op. 4, d. 257, l. 8.
[8] "Antireligioznaia propaganda—klassovaia bor'ba," *Pravda*, 25 December 1928.

Delegates to the Second All-Union Congress of the Godless during a break in the proceedings, Moscow, 1929. (Courtesy of the Russian State Archive of Cinema and Photographic Documents, no. 242694.)

Both the interventionists and the culturalists tried to justify their positions in light of the already crystallized source of transcendent truth in Soviet political debate: the corpus of Lenin's writings. By 1929, Lenin had become apotheosized as the font of Bolshevik wisdom and political culture, and thus both sides professed adherence to the true doctrine of Lenin and charged the other side with straying from this line. The breadth of Lenin's written legacy, however, allowed almost any position to be buttressed by a significant quotation. Iaroslavskii frequently referred to Lenin, and in his closing speech to the congress, an emotionally charged rebuttal of the interventionists' criticisms, he declared: "That's how Lenin understood [it]: organization and enlightenment of the proletariat will lead to the dying out of religion, but we should not throw ourselves into the venture of a political battle with religion." The interventionist Ivan Bukhartsev also justified his position by citing Lenin's supposed claim that "it would be foolish to think that in a society based on the endless oppression and coarseness of the working masses, it is possible to dispel religious prejudices through purely propagandist means."[9]

The efforts of the opposing camps to determine antireligious policy relied on carving a generally accepted position on religion out of the broad and vague official dogma. The Godless operated in an environment of absolute doctrines characteristic of Russian intellectual development, yet no particular ism explicitly directed them in the creation of an atheist society. While no well-trodden path existed, the political culture demanded that at each stage of social development there should be precise procedures and methods of social management, and so the participants of the antireligious debates acted as if a detailed plan existed. Their task was simply to have their own answer to "What do we do next?" accepted as that of Lenin and the Party. Real policy alternatives existed, but the notion of "better" and "worse" approaches receded behind the importance of having one's own method designated as Leninist, however useless this label may have been in terms of policy, but a priori the only correct strategy. The debates at the congress revealed the profound subjectivity of this process and the tension between a constrictive rhetorical framework and divergent policy proposals.

The theme of centralized organization complemented obeisance to Lenin in the speeches at the congress. In his opening comments, Iaroslavskii attributed the weakness of antireligious activity in large part to organizational shortcomings resulting from a lack of centralized leadership control, and presented administrative reform to strengthen the Central Council as a panacea for the League's many failings. Following Iaroslavskii's lead, delegates from around the country linked the weakness of their councils to the absence of a strong hand in Moscow: "We need centralization!" A call by a delegate from Uzbekistan for the strictest possible control drew applause from the hall, and his description of decentralization's evils all but suggested that the League would overcome the persistence of religion in Central Asia by putting local cells on a short tether anchored in Moscow.[10]

Reliance on centralization carried within it the possibility of invoking deviationism as a powerful rhetorical weapon. The interventionists apparently succeeded in putting the culturalists on the defensive by implying

---

[9] *Stenagraficheskii otchet vtorogo vsesoiuznogo s"ezda Soiuza Voinstvuiushchikh Bezbozhnikov* (Moscow, 1930), 153, 271.
[10] Ibid., 52, 196–197.

that they were following a deviationist line. The Komsomol official Rakhmanov warned that the Party line must be that of the League, and that the Komsomol would fight against any deviations from this line. This assertion was greeted by "stormy applause." Iaroslavskii, too, warned of the extreme dangers of factionalism.[11] Such labeling was spreading rapidly throughout the political arena. The Sixteenth Party Conference, in April 1929, had announced a general purge of the Party to remove anyone determined ever to have opposed its official position on any issue. Less than two months later, when the congress met, the press bristled with discussion of the purge, which had been expanded to include nonparty individuals working in Soviet bureaucracies. Closely following the Shakhty trial of "wreckers" in 1928, discussion of the new round of purging during the summer of 1929 gave a particular potency to such labels as "deviationist" and "appeaser." Because the rules for purging were so broad and subjective, these labels became powerful political weapons distinct from any real threat to the Soviet system.

Both sides frequently framed their criticism in terms of deviation by individuals from the correct institutional lines. We find the culturalists Stukov and Iaroslavskii trying to patch up relations with the Komsomol by arguing that Bukhartsev's position was not that of his organization, and focusing on another leading irritant, M. Galaktionov. Iaroslavskii charged that if Galaktionov were to renounce his anarchical phrases, antireligious work in Moscow would benefit. The League's specialist on sects, Fedor Putintsev, joined the fray by calling Galaktionov "illiterate" in his work, and continued to harangue him until cries from the floor interrupted him: "Enough about Galaktionov!"[12] From the other side, the Komsomol's Rakhmanov expressed the hope that the congress "will renounce any unhealthy attitudes held by individual delegates." It was only logical, he said, that errant activists were to be found in such a large organization as the League. He admitted that the Komsomol had such individuals, and the League, he claimed, should welcome the Komsomol's assistance in correcting the mistakes of its members.[13] This form of censure, part of the broader Bolshevik emphasis on self-criticism, suggested that institutions could never err; only individuals in those institutions (or even their leaders) could stray. This convention permitted the system to continue operating without criticism, while individuals were held responsible for institutional practices beyond their control.

[11] Ibid., 243, 245, 270.
[12] Ibid., 272, 295–296.
[13] Ibid., 241–245.

Overloaded Party Workers

Beyond the rhetoric of institutional and ideological conflict in evidence at the congress and throughout the League's daily experience, specific practices in Bolshevik political culture also impeded the League's operation. Perhaps most important, Communist agitprop personnel had little time and even less inclination for antireligious propaganda work. This was a constant refrain during discussions of the League, when already over-worked Communists were given yet another responsibility, the oversight of the League. The term used, *peregruzka* (overload), referred to the statutory responsibilities of Party members, their "Party load" (*partnagruzka*). League documents are replete with references to "overloadedness." The chairman of the Pskov Provincial Council wrote in 1926 that the "main failing of the provincial and *uezd* councils must be considered the over-loadedness of [their] workers."[14] The chairman of the Porkhov District Council (65 kilometers east of Pskov) complained in September 1928 that "individuals too overloaded with [other] work are selected to serve in *okrug* and district organizations."[15] A commentator in *Kommunistich-eskaia revoliutsiia* noted that "in small towns such as Velizh [200 kilometers southeast of Pskov], one rarely meets an activist who is not in five or more organizations. Such an *aktiv* accomplishes little."[16] *Peregruzka* was not limited to the admittedly sparse rural outposts in the Bolshevik network. In Iaroslavl', a League report in 1928 concluded that the

> selection of *uezd* and district councils is as a rule extremely unsuccessful. They are filled by comrades too overloaded by Party and social duties. They approve resolutions of the [agitprop department], acknowledge work to be weak, and reelect a new [council] staff. The new composition . . . does not bring a noticeable revitalization to the work because while overloaded staff have been removed, they are replaced by other staff even more overloaded with social responsibilities.[17]

Specific investigations into Iaroslavl''s Second and Third District councils in 1928 also found "comrades too overloaded with Party and social obligations."[18]

[14] PPA, f. 1, op. 4, d. 257, l. 2ob.
[15] PSA, f. 247, op. 1, d. 3, l. 7.
[16] "Ratsionalizatsiia dobrovol'noi obshchestvennosti stuchitsia k nam v dveri," *Kommunis-ticheskaia revoliutsiia*, 1929, no. 5, 92.
[17] IaPA, f. 1, op. 27, d. 2865, l. 186.
[18] IaSA, f. 3362, op. 1, d. 11, ll. 52, 57.

The central Party apparatus in Moscow was well aware of the overextension of its cadres, but there was little it could do beyond issuing vague declarations that opposed the practice but added to the stream of paper flowing from Moscow. A resolution of the 1926 antireligious conference stated that "active work in League organizations [should be considered equivalent] to Party work and should be counted toward [a Communist's] load."[19] Similar resolutions passed locally amounted to somewhat disingenuous critiques by local activists of their own practices. In 1927, the Leningrad Party (by then overseeing Pskov) declared that antireligious work should be considered in the calculation of a Communist's responsibilities and called for "relief [from other tasks] for League staff."[20]

These resolutions were, in fact, just words, yet they constituted an important facet in the Bolshevik discourse of administration. Although the phenomenon of overloaded cadres was real, the resolution to the problem in the form of endless directives spoke less to producing more cadres (or lowering the high expectations on organizations such as the League) than to the process by which offices within the bureaucratic chain of command shed responsibility for actual conditions by passing meaningless resolutions condemning them. Even if antireligious propaganda in general and participation in the League in particular had officially been included in Party mandates, it would have made little difference. The official roster of responsibilities was already so excessive that inclusion would not guarantee greater attention from Communists and would only have aggravated *peregruzka*. Propaganda work generally was held in low regard, especially when cadres were faced with other pressing demands.[21]

Spreading the Blame

Although the League depended primarily on the Party's patronage, other institutions also were tapped to support it. These efforts to spread the burden were far from successful, however. The Komsomol's usual indifference to the League was punctuated, as we have seen, by periods of outright hostility. Centrally and in Pskov and Iaroslavl', the Komsomol resisted cooperation with the League, perhaps disapproving of its nominally culturalist methods, perhaps resenting another claimant on the energies of youth, or likely both. Beyond the open conflict in 1926 and 1929 in

[19] RTsKhIDNI, f. 89, op. 4, d. 123, ll. 52, 69; *Antireligioznik*, 1926, no. 8, 69.
[20] GARF, f. r-5407, op. 1, d. 18, ll. 9–10.
[21] See William G. Rosenberg, "Smolensk in the 1920s: Party-Worker Relations and the 'Vanguard' Problem," *Russian Review* 36, no. 2 (April, 1977): 145ff.

Moscow, a steady stream of resolutions flowed from central and local League authorities attacking the Komsomol for its numerous failures on the antireligious front.[22] While the relationship between the Komsomol and the League was distinguished by a certain hostility, the trade unions behaved more like the Communist Party itself in that they responded to demands on their resources by passing anodynic, empty resolutions, and complaining about the inactivity of other groups. In 1928, for instance, the League Central Council protested that the Central Trade Union Council directive on antireligious propaganda issued the previous August remained on paper only.[23] Indeed, although plans approved by the cultural department of the Central Trade Union Council in early 1928 called for substantial anti-Easter and anti-Christmas campaigns, the Iaroslavl' Trade Union Council seemed to have little interest in antireligious work, according to a report filed several months later.[24]

Unlike the trade unions, the Commissariat of Enlightenment was not regularly asked to provide financial support for the League. Nevertheless, the League's central bureaucrats were in almost constant conflict with education officials in Moscow over the teaching of antireligious materials in the schools. In a bitter note sent to the Narkompros collegium in May 1926, Iaroslavskii commented that no representatives of Narkompros or Glavpolitprosvet had deigned to attend the April conference, to which they had been invited. He added that if Narkompros spent on antireligious work even half of what it spent in 1924–1926 on the restoration of churches and monasteries (churches preserved as historical or architectural monuments were subordinated to Narkompros), then the League would not find itself in the severe financial crisis then threatening it.[25] Until 1929, school curricula remained officially nonreligious rather than antireligious.[26] The irony was that in both Iaroslavl' and Pskov the local League organizations were inexorably intertwined with the education authorities on an administrative level. More generally, there was tremendous overlap in Soviet propaganda matters: the Party, the League, the Komsomol, the trade unions, the education authorities, and the Red Army were all nominally responsible for conducting at least some antireligious propaganda. Believers may have viewed them all as "Godless," but in theory

---

[22] The ongoing conflict between the Komsomol and the League is a central theme of V. A. Alekseev, *Shturm nebes otmeniaetsia?* (Moscow: Rossiia Molodaia, 1992).

[23] GARF, f. r-5407, op. 1, d. 14, ll. 120ob–121.

[24] GARF, f. r-5451, op. 12, d. 547, ll. 180–191.

[25] GARF, f. a-2306, op. 69, d. 747, ll. 4–5.

[26] Larry Holmes, "Fear No Evil: Schools and Religion in Soviet Russia, 1917–1941," in *Religious Policy in the Soviet Union*, ed. Sabrina Ramet (Cambridge: Cambridge University Press, 1993), 136–138.

each group had its own constituency, means, and propaganda outlets, even if in fact the result often was a replication of bureaucracies and infighting for resources. This outcome was not limited to the battle against religion: the Soviet and Bolshevik administrative realms were characterized throughout by substantial overlap and the subdivision of responsibilities.[27]

Administrative Frenzy

Several administrative practices that contributed to and reflected the bureaucratic orientation of Bolshevik political culture were particularly devastating to the League. The State's repeated administrative/territorial reorganizations destroyed existing councils and substituted for genuine solutions to operational shortcomings.[28] These changes began early in the Soviet period and were initially designed to rationalize the cumbersome Russian bureaucracy. The replacement of *volosti* and *uezdy* by *raiony* (*raionirovanie*) in the course of the 1920s may have simplified some matters, but the constant realignment of administrative divisions proved chaotic, not only for Soviet administrative practice but also for all groups that were obliged to reorganize to accommodate new boundaries.

In August 1927, Pskov Province was dissolved and its territory was divided into Pskov and Velikie Luki *okrugy*. The Pskov Provincial League Council went the way of the province and was replaced by an *okrug* council. In a letter to all district councils in February 1928, the Pskov League leader, Ivan Sigov, complained that the *okrug* apparatus had been unable to establish regular ties with the district councils, and charged that in many districts no councils existed.[29] At the *okrug* congress later that year, Sigov alluded to two previous organizational waves that had been occasioned by *raionirovanie* and the subsequent administrative transfer of cadres from the League's liquidated *uezd* and *volost'* centers. He claimed that there were councils currently in only five of eleven districts; in the

[27] See, for example, Don Karl Rowney, "The Scope, Authority, and Personnel of the New Industrial Commissariats in Historical Context," in *Social Dimensions of Soviet Industrialization*, ed. William G. Rosenberg and Lewis H. Siegelbaum (Bloomington: Indiana University Press, 1993), 124–125.

[28] Administrative territorial shifts were so frequent that entire books have been produced to follow them in each oblast: *Administrativno-territorial'noe delenie Pskovskoi oblasti (1917–1988 gg.): Spravochnik*, 2 vols. (Leningrad: Lenizdat, 1988), and *Iaroslavskaia oblast': Spravochnik po administrativno-territorial'nomu deleniiu, 1917–1967* (Iaroslavl', 1972).

[29] PSA, f. 247, op. 1, d. 1, l. 14; *Administrativno-territorial'noe delenie*, 1:11.

other six, no cells existed.[30] A review of the Pskov League by the Central Council in February 1929 noted that "*raionirovanie* had negatively affected the work of the League."[31] At the peak of the League's expansion, the Okrug Council again fell victim to more administrative/territorial tinkering when the Pskov Okrug was eliminated on 23 July 1930, necessitating the liquidation of the Pskov Okrug League Council. It was replaced by a city-district council subordinate to the League in distant Leningrad.[32]

Initiated somewhat later in Iaroslavl', *raionirovanie* was similarly disruptive there. On 14 January 1929, Iaroslavl' Province was dissolved. Encompassing much of the former province's territory, Iaroslavl' Okrug was divided into ten districts. At a meeting of the Okrug Council at the end of the year, attended by two representatives from the Central Council, Aleksandr Egorov blamed the decline of his organization on *raionirovanie*.[33] The Okrug Council's report of its activity from 1 June 1929 to 1 May 1930 also noted that the League organization had spent most of the time recovering from its downgrading.[34] On 23 July 1930, the Iaroslavl' Okrug itself was eliminated, leaving Iaroslavl' as a district center in Ivanovo Industrial Oblast. At the Okrug Council's "liquidation" plenum on 7 August, Egorov declared that "there was nothing more disgraceful than what happened to the Vladimir Okrug Council. The Oblast Council fussed over it like a child, and the result was shameful disintegration and desertion by the council's workers. The Iaroslavl' Okrug Council does not suffer from such attitudes," he declared hopefully. "There is not one worker in the Okrug Council who would even think of deserting the antireligious front after the *okrug*'s dissolution."[35] Following the Party's lead, in 1930 the League also abandoned its three-district structure in Iaroslavl' proper, forming instead a city-district council comprising the three separate Iaroslavl' city districts and eight rural communities around the city's perimeter.

The disruption stemming from *raionirovanie* characterized the League's network nationwide. Having decreed these measures in the belief that they would improve administrative practice, the regime ultimately bore the responsibility for the confusion they caused. The reorganizations once again illuminate how form was privileged at the expense of content in the

[30] PSA, f. 247, op. 1, d. 3, l. 6. By the time of the congress there were 18 districts in Pskov Okrug. There had been eleven *uezdy* in Pskov Province. The continued use of the old boundaries suggests that the process of *raionirovanie* for lower-level social organizations lagged well behind its official implementation.
[31] GARF, f. r-5407, op. 1, d. 30, ll. 30–30ob.
[32] *Administrativno-territorial'noe delenie*, 1:12.
[33] GARF, f. r-5407, op. 1, d. 37, l. 13 (meeting of 31 December 1929).
[34] IaPA, f. 229, op. 9, d. 132, l. 232.
[35] IaSA, f. 2410, op. 1, d. 11, l. 29.

regime's management of society. The white noise of reorganization provided justification for nonsubstantive activity, as the League (and all other organizations) spent time and resources not on their chosen calling but on reestablishing their networks. That the League and other nominally nonparty social organizations followed these boundaries exactly emphasized the supreme importance of administrative uniformity in Bolshevik political culture.

Membership in Flux

An additional hindrance to the League's organizational viability emerged from the social upheaval and demographic change that swept the Soviet Union in the late 1920s and early 1930s. Soviet Russia was in tremendous flux in this period, with huge population movements and a high level of job turnover. The resulting constant disruption in the institutional associations that bound individuals within Soviet society was made all the more severe by the Bolsheviks' preference for expressing social transformation in bureaucratic terms. The League was particularly hard hit because many of its cells were based in transitional organizations, such as schools, and in newly created workplaces. Even existing workplaces were subject to phenomenal labor turnover in those years.[36] The League was undermined by every graduating class and job transfer, by every new construction site and factory opening, and by the constant reorganization of collective farms. Under these conditions, the collapse and re-creation of cells became unavoidable and routine. The 1933 list of members at the Pskov Land Management School noted that the cell had been formed originally in February 1925. The current crop of students had joined the League in the years 1930–1933. Only the chairman of the cell had joined earlier, in 1928, at the age of fifteen, so he must have joined some other cell. Though the teaching staff may have represented some continuity, the regular turnover of students ensured a cyclical process of creation and decay. A "new" cell also was organized in 1933 at the Pskov Soviet Party School, which had had a cell at least as early as 1926.[37] By the early 1930s, a large portion of the League's overall membership came from educational institutions, thereby guaranteeing organizational instability when just the opposite was the measure of success in Bolshevik political culture.

---

[36] On the influx of new workers to the factories, see David L. Hoffmann, *Peasant Metropolis Social Identities in Moscow, 1929–1941* (Ithaca: Cornell University Press, 1994), 32–72; Hiroaki Kuromiya, *Stalin's Industrial Revolution* (Cambridge: Cambridge University Press, 1988), 87–99.

[37] PSA, f. 247, op. 1, d. 27, ll. 10, 18.

Membership turnover was not limited to school-based cells. Of the nineteen members at the Pskov cord plant in 1933, sixteen had joined in a three-day period around Easter 1933. A list of cell members at the Proletariat tannery in Pskov indicated that all eighteen of them had joined in 1933.[38] Both the Shpagat and Proletariat cells had existed much earlier, but given the rapid migration of factory labor in this period and the short life span of League cells generally, it is highly unlikely that the 1933 members were veterans of 1926. Such intense demographic upheaval was not the result of a natural calamity; it resulted from deliberate actions—forced collectivization and rapid industrialization—that unsettled an administrative order particularly reliant on stable bureaucratic structures. This policy may have met the immediate needs of the regime, but it conflicted with other aspects of its own political culture.

A final challenge to the maintenance of the League's network came from Russia's still basically agrarian economy. Although the Bolsheviks sought to maintain the trappings of an industrialized society, with institutions that functioned uniformly throughout the year, the social timetable of Russia through the late 1920s was still profoundly influenced by the agrarian cycle. Little of the League's work was achieved during the summer, when all hands were required in the fields. The regime's policy of providing its bureaucrats with generous paid vacations, usually taken during the summer and often spent working the family's land, also worked against the expectation of uniform bureaucratic development. At a plenum of the Iaroslavl' Provincial Council in January 1927, the council's chairman, Egorov, blamed summer conditions in part for the fact that this was only the second full meeting of the council in over six months. In March 1927, one Musatov attributed the First District Council's lack of activity since being organized the previous May to the intervening summer.[39] The Iaroslavl' League even issued a letter headed "Methodological directives about the forms of antireligious work in summer conditions," in which it "protest[ed] vigorously against the slacking off of antireligious work locally in connection with the coming summer season and also with the rooted habit of considering the summer a 'dead time' for the League."[40] Though this problem appears to have receded in later years, it did not disappear entirely; comments on summer slowdowns appeared regularly in League documents into the 1930s. The regime had unsuccessfully sought to apply the norms of an industrial society to one that was not prepared

[38] Ibid., ll. 24, 38.
[39] IaSA, f. 3362, op. 1, d. 4, ll. 120, 180.
[40] Ibid., d. 15, l. 10.

for it, and again we encounter the consequences of telescoped social change described by Lewin.[41]

Such organizational problems might have been expected as the League struggled in its first years. They remained, however, when the League became a visible "mass" society in 1929. Indeed, they became more severe. While the League achieved its greatest size and visibility between 1929 and 1932, the question remains whether this era also brought any change in its effectiveness. Despite the League's accomplishments, the archival evidence indicates that the League's institutional relationships remained largely unaltered and in fact, the greater intensity of social transformation placed new obstacles before the League. This intensity was precisely what the regime's shaky edifice of social bureaucracies could not handle.[42]

A Great Turn?

In theory, the Central Committee's January 1929 circular decreed a new attitude by the Party toward antireligious propaganda, and local Party committees adopted appropriate resolutions suggesting that League membership and activity would be more important for Communists. Even the Komsomol appeared on the verge of cooperation with the League. In its January 1929 decree, the Central Committee had ordered local Komsomol organizations "to arrange systematic leadership of antireligious propaganda immediately," including assistance to the League,[43] and in the aftermath of the League's Second All-Union Congress, in June 1929, the Komsomol Central Committee ordered an increase in Komsomol representation in local League cells and councils.[44] Later that year, the Komsomol Central Committee's bureau and the League's Central Council planned "an all-union antireligious campaign" and "assault" to coincide with the upcoming anti-Christmas campaign.[45] And after years of insisting on a nonreligious (rather than antireligious) curriculum, the Commissariat of Enlightenment promised in 1929 to begin promoting atheism.[46] The

---

[41] See Moshe Lewin, *The Making of the Soviet System: Essays in the Social History of Interwar Russia* (London: Methuen, 1985), 209–257.

[42] These tremors affected not only the League but also the mass of social and cultural institutions caught up in the maelstrom of industrialization and collectivization. See Hoffmann, *Peasant Metropolis*, 136–157; Kuromiya, *Stalin's Industrial Revolution*, 80–87, 228–235; E. A. Osokina, *Ierarkhiia potrebleniia: O zhizni liudei v usloviiakh Stalinskogo snabzheniia, 1928–1935 gg.* (Moscow: MGOU, 1993).

[43] IaSA, f. 3363, op. 1, d. 1, l. 16.

[44] TsKhDMO, f. 1, op. 3, d. 60, l. 1.

[45] Ibid., d. 62, l. 45; GARF, f. r-5407, op. 1, d. 27, ll. 27–29.

[46] Holmes, "Fear No Evil," 138–139.

Central Trade Union Council's assistance came in the form of a "circular letter" dated 1 March 1929 headed "On Strengthening Antireligious Propaganda," which called for "broad assistance to the League of the Godless in its work."[47]

Despite these explicit decrees, the old patterns of institutional behavior persisted. League councils continued to cite the irregularity of the Party's support. Even Iaroslavskii's effort to have the Politbiuro issue an authoritative resolution on the June 1929 antireligious conference and the League's Second All-Union Congress sounded more like a plea than a call to arms, and ultimately was unsuccessful. His draft resolution called it "impermissible that a significant number of Party and Komsomol members stand on the sidelines of the antireligious battle. . . . A neutral relationship to religion is often observed from the trade unions and the Soviet apparatus. Passivity in this context is a manifestation of right opportunism. . . . All [organizations] should assist in transforming the League into a multimillion[-member] mass organization."[48] That the Politbiuro never adopted a statement supporting the League at such a critical moment demonstrated the Communist Party's ultimate inconstancy in regard to the League.

Locally, little in the Party/League relationship appeared altered. Five members of the Tutaev District League Council (thirty-five kilometers northwest of Iaroslavl') complained in February 1930 that local Communists played no part in the League, and that large cells at the Tulma and Konstantinov factories had collapsed as a result. Their letter also charged that the district Party's resolutions were being ignored.[49] At the height of the State's attack on the Church, the Ivanovo Industrial Oblast Party charged that "the oblast Party's agitprop subdepartment has repeatedly pointed out the need to strengthen antireligious work. Despite these directives, however, many Party organizations and a significant portion of Party members do not do enough in leading antireligious work, leaving League organizations without assistance."[50] Here again, in a well-established pattern, superordinate bodies fulfilled their duties by passing resolutions and criticizing other groups for failing to implement them.

---

[47] GARF, f. r-5451, op. 13, d. 470, l. 28.

[48] At least nine Politbiuro meetings between June and September put off final consideration of the proposal, and no action was taken before 5 December 1929, when the Antireligious Commission was dissolved (RTsKhIDNI, f. 89, op. 4, d. 122, ll. 22–23; f. 17, op. 3, d. 745, d. 747 [pt. 12], d. 750 [pt. 11], d. 751 [pt. 11], d. 752 [pt. 12], d. 753 [pt. 12], d. 754 [pt. 18], d. 755 [pt. 11], d. 758 [pt. 45], d. 767 [pt. 60]).

[49] IaSA, f. 3363, op. 1, d. 4, l. 34.

[50] IaPA, f. 229, op. 9, d. 2, l. 12.

Despite the high-level resolutions of 1929, the Komsomol's visceral hostility toward the League also appeared unchanged. In Moscow this attitude was reflected in an open assault on the League's leadership at the Second Congress in June. Locally, Komsomol hostility took somewhat less virulent but still explicit forms. A Party commission in 1930 blamed the poor preparation of the anti-Easter campaign in Iaroslavl' on disagreements between the League and Komsomol, and a Komsomol official at the Iaroslavl' Auto Plant announced that the Komsomol would not attend the Godless circle: "They'll get by without you."[51] In its turn, the Iaroslavl' League cited the continuing religiousness of Komsomolers, particularly in regard to sects, and charged that the Komsomol conducted no antireligious propaganda among its members.[52] As for the Commissariat of Enlightenment, most of its promises also went unfulfilled, and a more traditional curriculum returned to the schools after the First Five-Year Plan.[53]

The heightened pace of social transformation during the First Five-Year Plan only aggravated the already acute problem of overloaded cadres. At the Central Council's plenum in March 1930, a delegate pointed out that the League cell secretary at the Mechanical Plant in Iaroslavl' was given eighteen social responsibilities; at another Iaroslavl' mill, the "Godless" responsibility was the sixth in line, and so forth. This delegate added the obvious: Party decrees declaring antireligious propaganda an official Party responsibility and releasing staff for full-time propaganda work were being ignored.[54] An investigation by the Iaroslavl' City-District Council in late 1930 found that the chairman of the League cell at the Iaroslavl' Electric Station, Comrade Sedyshev, who also was chairman of the factory's Party committee, was so overworked that he "gave the League cell no time."[55] An assessment of the City-District Council's members undertaken in September 1931 stated that "because of his overload and his transfer to work at RAK, [Chairman Egorov's] attendance and participation in the City Council's work were unsatisfactory."[56]

Perebroska (the administrative transfer of cadres) also posed difficulties for the League's operations, and they became more severe during the hectic years of the First Five-Year Plan. Speaking at the League's Second Plenum in March 1930, one delegate commented that at his factory, "there have been cases where as soon as we have prepared a Godless *aktiv*,

[51] IaSA, f. 3363, op. 1, d. 4, l. 44; GARF, f. r-5407, op. 1, d. 49, l. 9.
[52] IaSA, f. 2410, op. 1, d. 1, l. 32; f. 3362, op. 1, d. 14, l. 81.
[53] Holmes, "Fear No Evil," 139–143.
[54] GARF, f. r-5407, op. 1, d. 49, l. 9.
[55] IaSA, f. 2410, op. 1, d. 5, l. 151.
[56] Ibid., d. 10, l. 58.

it is taken away from us."[57] A delegate from the Orel organization also complained about the transfer of trained staff, including the chairman and secretary of the Orel League council. When this activist protested to the local Party official, he was told: "What is this Godlessness of yours? Lock up your office. This isn't the time; there's a campaign on now."[58] In June 1932, a high Moscow Oblast League official remonstrated to a "brigade" from the Party Central Committee that "our core staff is extraordinarily fluid. If a [Party] cell secretary is assigned antireligious work—a good guy, a good Godless—all the same, he won't be working for us long, no more than a month, and then he's removed, or more likely moved on to other work."[59]

Collectivization and Policy Shifts

Although the overall framework of League-Party relations remained stable after 1929, the ongoing political and social maelstrom did affect the League's fortunes. In June 1930, Iaroslavskii wrote in *Pravda* that "the [League's] gigantic growth, which we see began in the middle of 1929, is connected directly to the growth of collectivization of the countryside."[60] Yet, the collectivization of agriculture that benefited the League also rendered it vulnerable to frequent shifts in policy and, perhaps more important, to the highly charged political context in which collectivization occurred.[61] Collectivization came to be associated with the forced closing of churches—areas of all-out collectivization were often made all-out "Godless" by zealous local officials who arbitrarily closed churches, arrested clergy, destroyed icons, and committed other so-called excesses—and such behavior increased tension in an already precarious political situation in the countryside. Central Party officials responded with repeated decrees forbidding the administrative closure of churches, especially in areas of intensified collectivization. These measures sometimes were interpreted locally as signals to discontinue all antireligious work, and local League organizations withered.

---

[57] GARF, f. r-5407, op. 1, d. 47, l. 116.
[58] Ibid., d. 49, ll. 5–6, 13.
[59] Ibid., d. 95, ll. 59–60.
[60] "Vyravniat' antireligioznyi front," *Pravda*, 24 June 1930.
[61] To link changing antireligious approaches and the regime's evolving policy in regard to the countryside is not to dismiss the role played by religious resistance in promoting policy changes. Nicholas Timasheff eloquently argues this point in his *Religion in Soviet Russia* (New York: Sheed & Ward, 1942), 58–110.

The League was caught between conflicting signals emanating from the center that both encouraged attacks on religion as part of the Cultural Revolution and collectivization and simultaneously warning against church closures and other measures that might further alienate the rural population. These messages were couched in the highly charged political rhetoric of the day, employing the main metaphors of Bolshevik political discourse: leftist and "hurrah-atheists" versus rightists and liquidationist opportunists. All deviated from the ever-correct Party line. Given the swerving of the Party line itself, however, it is unclear what the "deviationist" label signified; it served only as a general political tag, well removed from actual issues.

Local activists had good cause to be confused by policy statements coming from Moscow. The numerous shifts of the early 1920s continued into the late 1920s and contributed to an already chaotic situation. In May 1929—five months after the regime renewed its assault on religion—the Antireligious Commission prohibited church closings in harvest areas where they were likely to cause tension. The following month, the Central Committee issued a letter headed "On a Tactful Approach to Closing Churches," again warning against excessive zeal in antireligious matters that fed anti-Soviet feelings and sympathy for the clergy.[62] Late 1929 brought more mixed signals when. at the last minute, the Central Committee canceled the planned League-Komsomol All-Union Assault on Religion. Instead of an "attack," the Central Committee Secretariat called for "serious preparatory work leading to antireligious propaganda during the Christmas holidays."[63]

As long as the regime openly encouraged the forceful suppression of religion in 1929, the cautionary warnings were ignored, and the League itself joined in the antireligious frenzy. The next year, however, brought an explicit and high-level reversal. A Central Committee resolution, "On the Struggle against Distortions of the Party Line in the Collective Farm Movement," printed in *Pravda* on 15 March 1930, spoke of "inadmissible distortions of the Party line in the battle against religious prejudices. . . . There can be no doubt that such practices [administrative closures and other excesses] carried out under the flag of the "leftists" provide grist for the mill of counterrevolutionaries and have nothing in common with the policy of our Party." The resolution ordered that henceforth no church was to be closed unless an overwhelming majority of the population genuinely agreed to it, and then only with the confirmation of the relevant

[62] RTsKhIDNI, f. 17, op. 113, d. 871, l. 33; f. 89, op. 4, d. 122, l. 23.
[63] Ibid., d. 801, l. 3.

oblast executive committee.[64] Following hard upon Stalin's "Dizziness from Success" article, calling for a break in the pace of collectivization, this statement served to dampen the League's growth and activities. When the Central Council met in plenary session in March, many provincial League activists complained that their work had been abruptly blocked by local officials who cited the political situation.[65] A participant in a meeting of trade union propagandists in July 1930 commented that that year's anti-Easter campaign had been greatly muted as a result of the regime's withdrawal on the collectivization front.[66] Petitioners were well aware of the relationship between collectivization and closed churches, and used it to their advantage when they appealed to Moscow. Letter writers repeatedly linked the closure of churches to the resistance to collectivization. One believer in Nizhnii Novgorod Krai commented that collectivization had been moving ahead until churches began to be closed and icons destroyed. At that point, the writer claimed, the peasants left the collective farms in droves, preferring to suffer "all possible deprivations and sufferings."[67] The sharp if brief decline in the number of collective farms in the spring of 1930 also brought an end to specifically Godless farms. For instance, the Bezbozhnik collective farm that had been formed near Pskov in early 1930, after a three-year effort, had collapsed by May.[68]

The ambiguity concerning antireligious propaganda continued at the Communist Party's Sixteenth Congress, held from 26 June to 13 July 1930. Two days before it opened, Iaroslavskii contributed an article to a forum in *Pravda* discussing the congress.[69] Attributing the League's difficulties in the countryside to collectivization, he wrote that the antireligious movement suffered from

> its own "dizziness from success." Under the influence of the tremendous, tangible successes of antireligious propaganda, people in some places have decided that they can create "districts of complete [*sploshnoe*] Godlessness," and that in districts of complete collectivization, one can close every church, and so forth. . . . A special type of "hurrah-atheists" have

---

[64] "O bor'be s iskrivleniiami partlinii v kolkhoznom dvizhenii," *Pravda*, 15 March 1930.
[65] GARF, f. r-5407, op. 1, d. 49, ll. 6.
[66] GARF, f. r-5451, op. 14, d. 565, ll. 1–2.
[67] GARF, f. r-1235, op. 65, d. 345, l. 104.
[68] PSA, f. 247, op. 1, d. 5, l. 24. See also R. W. Davies, *The Socialist Offensive: The Collectivization of Soviet Agriculture, 1929–1930* (Cambridge: Harvard University Press, 1980), 277–286.
[69] "Vyravniat' antireligioznyi front," *Pravda*, 24 June 1930.

appeared, who believe that religion can be liquidated in a snap, who set a deadline for the liquidation of religion and set out to achieve it, causing great harm, antagonizing the peasants in some places.

Iaroslavskii acknowledged that "leftist" errors were still occurring in some places, accompanied by "the no less dangerous liquidationist temper." In his conclusion, Iaroslavskii sought to steer a middle course between the two apparent extremes that threatened the League's position as a legitimate and necessary institution in the Bolshevik political arena. Despite Iaroslavskii's hope of preserving a political and rhetorical niche for the League in unsettled political times, the congress only limply acknowledged the need for antireligious propaganda: "The Party should consolidate and extend the significant successes achieved in the matter of liberating the masses from religion's reactionary influence."[70]

This acknowledgment was at best a weak affirmation of the League, and from 1930 on, it had to battle a rising tide of indifference. Although it was still occasionally critical of "left extremism," from 1930 on the League's Central Council much more frequently spoke out against the "right, liquidationist deviation." Even when the regime advocated antireligious propaganda, the League no longer occupied center stage. In August 1930, an article on antireligious propaganda in *Pravda* mentioned the League only in passing.[71] Local sources also suggested that the League was simply being ignored by Party authorities.[72]

In this swirl of conflicting signals and political cross-currents, made worse by the chronic problems of *peregruzka* and *perebroska*, the League was hobbled by the practices and the very nature of the regime that had created it. The local activist body had been rendered numb, buffeted by the brisk winds of unpredictable policy change. Such rapid and extreme shifts in policy have characterized much of modern Russian history. During the early Soviet period, the regime's cadres had to serve loyally in turn "War Communism," NEP, collectivization/industrialization, "neo-NEP" in the mid-1930s, the Great Purges, Stakhanovism, and a late 1930s retrenchment. After decades of attacking the Orthodox Church, the regime abruptly reversed course during World War II.[73] From Stolypin to Gor-

---

[70] *KPSS v rezoliutsiiakh i resheniiakh s"ezdov, konferentsii i plenumov TsK*, vol. 5 (1929–1932) (Moscow, 1984), 129.

[71] G. Budnyi, "Osvobozhdenie millionov: antireligioznaia propaganda i kul'tpokhod," *Pravda*, 14 August 1930.

[72] For example, GARF, f. r-5407, op. 1, d. 91, l. 98ob; IaSA, f. 2410, op. 1, d. 13, l. 138.

[73] M. I. Odintsov, *Religioznye organizatsii v SSSR nakanune i v gody Velikoi Otechestvennoi Voiny* (Moscow: Rossiiskaia Akademiia Gosudarstvennoi Sluzhby pri Prezidente RF, 1995).

bachev twentieth-century Russia has been anything but a stable context for local officials charged with implementing central policies.

Whether being prohibited as politically destabilizing or simply ignored, the League found its prominence slipping further and further from the level achieved in 1929. Yet even at its peak the League had failed to construct a stable network reaching into the non-Bolshevik population, and was unable to carve a niche for its rather narrow propagandistic agenda. Despite strenuous efforts, the League fell far short of convincing local agitators that it represented an organization distinct from the Party. Instead, it languished near the bottom of the long list of self-proclaimed responsibilities for Party cadres.[74] However uninterested the Party was in the League, the nonparty population was even less interested in it, and the absence of popular involvement in the League rendered it utterly dependent on overworked Party cadres. On its own, the League's failure was not particularly notable; it may be attributed to the understandable overextension of a propaganda network charged with extreme goals that even in the best of circumstances may have been unrealizable. What was remarkable is that the Communist Party turned to the League time and time again as the presumed barometer and instrument of social change. The Party's repeated resurrection of the League revealed both the poverty of its ideas about disseminating atheism and the rigidity of Bolshevik political culture in regard to achieving social transformation.

Having established the League explicitly to promote antireligious propaganda among the nonparty masses, the Communist Party was left in an awkward position. Was it to continue conducting its own antireligious propaganda? What was the appropriate relationship between Party and League? At times the Party placed the League at the center of the antireligious apparatus; more frequently it appeared ready to abandon the League. Most of the time the League occupied an uncertain position. A conference of Iaroslavl' agitprop officials in June 1927 took an ambivalent position, noting in its resolution that "in light of the League of the Godless's weakness, it is necessary to conduct antireligious propaganda directly through Party and Komsomol organizations, as well as through all forms of cultural-enlightenment work. . . . At the same time, it is necessary to render the utmost assistance to the growth and strengthening of the League of the Godless."[75] All the main factors were present: conflicting

---

[74] OSOAviaKhim suffered from similar problems. See William Odom, *The Soviet Volunteers: Modernization and Bureaucracy in a Public Mass Organization* (Princeton: Princeton University Press, 1973), 126–31.

[75] *Resheniia Iaroslavskogo gubernskogo agitpropsoveshchaniia (2–3 iiunia 1927)* (Iaroslavl', 1927), 25.

loyalties, overlapping responsibilities, divided resources. Even when the League attained greater prominence, the division of antireligious responsibilities remained unclear. In a front-page editorial in late 1928, *Pravda* offered its understanding of what the relation of the Party to the League should be:

> The League of the Godless is a voluntary society that was created to conduct antireligious propaganda. The League's existence should facilitate antireligious work among the nonparty masses by Party members. . . . But the League of the Godless can conduct its work productively *only* if it is supported by *all* Party members, *all* Komsomol members, *all* Soviet organizations created by the Party and Komsomol. As you see, according to Lenin, it is a general Party obligation, an obligation of every Party member. That is why it is completely incorrect to think that the League can [function] on its own, without the active support of the Party and Komsomol.[76]

Molotov had come to a similar conclusion during a high-level discussion of the League several weeks earlier: "I don't know whether we have achieved more pluses or minuses by creating this organization. We have to revitalize the League, but in such a way that antireligious matters are attended to not only by the League but also by Party and professional organizations."[77] Inherent in both of these views and the League's endless complaints was the assumption that once the elusive goal of Party support was attained and properly cultivated, the League would turn into a well-functioning operation. It did not question the basic structure of overlapping political and social bureaucracies competing in a frenzy for limited resources.

Most League activists also assumed this situation to be a normal framework of operation, and it was exceptional for an individual cadre to question it. At the League's plenum in March 1930, the leader of the Tula organization commented that League officials ought to stop complaining about the failure of trade unions and cooperatives to help the League; he challenged the League activists to "propose work so that you don't go to them, they come to you to offer [their participation]." The delegates' laughter, noted in the protocol, suggested that this outcome was unlikely.[78] In June 1931, a member of the League Central Council, after a long ses-

---

[76] "Antireligioznaia propaganda—klassovaia bor'ba," *Pravda*, 25 December 1928; emphasis in original.
[77] RTsKhIDNI, f. 17, op. 113, d. 683, l. 56.
[78] GARF, f. r-5407, op. 1, d. 48, l. 5.

sion of Party bashing, interjected that they should stop whining, as if "we're poor little children, orphans, and no one cares about us."[79] In a similar vein, in March 1932 Fedor Oleshchuk criticized the accepted litany of charges against the Komsomol: "We should ask the Komsomol for help, that's true, but if none comes, we should rely on our own resources. The point has been made here that the Komsomol hinders work. That is completely incorrect, and we cannot use it to justify our lack of work."[80] In his capacity as Central Council Executive Secretary, Oleshchuk had been a prolific Komsomol basher over the years. These statements were the exceptions that proved the rule of the League's reliance not only on help from these other institutions, but on attacking them. The League required a ready external object to blame as it came increasingly to express its functioning in negative terms: not what it was accomplishing but what other institutions were not doing.[81] The League's militancy derived not from battling religion but from competing with the Komsomol, unions, and local educational authorities for resources and attention. The result was a cacophonous discourse of directives, complaints, instructions, requests, and investigations through which institutions regularly blamed one another and were blamed for departing from the Party line. The League operated in a closed rhetorical circle of bureaucratic conflict among the institutions that were responsible for social transformation yet were hampered by limited resources and the need to display evergreater ideological zeal. Their interaction—usually a struggle—constituted an important facet of antireligion and in large part substituted for genuine social transformation.

As we have seen, the number and quality of cadres constituted a central element in the League's struggle. Now, to get a better understanding of the face it presented to the people, let us turn in Chapter 7 to an examination of the League's local personnel.

---

[79] Ibid., d. 51, l. 214.

[80] GARF, f. r-5407, op. 1, d. 97, ll. 52–52ob.

[81] For similar developments in Soviet academia, see Michael Fox, "Political Culture, Purges, and Proletarianization at the Institute of Red Professors, 1921–1929," *Russian Review* 52, no. 1 (January 1993): 41.

7

"Cadres Decide Everything"

The notorious slogan "Cadres decide everything" characterizes the nature of
Soviet society far more frankly than Stalin himself would wish.

—Leon Trotsky, 1936

Stalin's famous statement "Cadres decide everything" captured the very
essence of the League. Bolshevik organizational culture placed a premium
on the availability of qualified cadres, and their chronic dearth was identified early on by Party authorities as the primary obstacle to the establishment of a viable antireligious propaganda network. In its first decades the
new regime generally had difficulty finding capable individuals who could
be trusted to administer the burgeoning workers' state and even its vanguard party. For the Party, the issue was reflected in debates about its size,
inclusiveness, and supposed social origins. These concerns animated some
of the most dramatic moments in prewar Soviet history: the Lenin levy, the
25,000ers, the purges, and the Stakhanovite movement.

Scholarly treatments of the personnel problem have focused on various
aspects of the issue. Scholars seeking the roots of Stalinism in the Civil
War experience have suggested that the wartime brutalization of the
regime's initial activist core contributed to later authoritarian outcomes.[1]
Others have looked at how the process of modernization (in its "overnight" variant initiated by the Bolsheviks) required a vast increase in administrative positions for which the Bolsheviks were not prepared.[2] The

[1] Sheila Fitzpatrick, "The Legacy of the Civil War," in *Party, State, and Society in the Russian Civil War*, ed. Diane P. Koenker, William G. Rosenberg, and Ronald Grigor Suny
(Bloomington: Indiana University Press, 1985), 385–398; Robert Tucker, "Stalinism as Revolution from Above," in *Stalinism: Essays in Historical Interpretation*, ed. Tucker (New
York: Norton, 1977); Robert Service, *The Bolshevik Party in Revolution, 1917–1923: A
Study in Organizational Change* (New York: Barnes & Noble, 1979).
[2] Moshe Lewin, *The Making of the Soviet System: Essays in the Social History of Interwar
Russia* (London: Methuen, 1985), especially the essay "The Social Background of Stalinism"; Roger Pethybridge, *The Social Prelude to Stalinism* (New York: St. Martin's Press,
1974).

need for administrative and technical "specialists," whatever their social origin, has attracted the attention of other scholars.[3]

Rather than highlighting the logistical or experiential aspects of the cadres problem, the League's case shows how the regime's political challenges and their resolution were defined according to a highly structured rhetoric that turned on the availability of reliable cadres. Secularization in Russia would stem not only from urbanization and industrialization but from the efforts of a "propaganda state" to "modernize" the lives and attitudes of its population in just a few years. The League's cadres—those "missionaries of modernity"—would carry out the regime's ideological will through a nationwide network of activists. That was the theory. In fact, however, these expectations clashed with an utter dearth of individuals willing or able to fill the role. The background, training, and work experiences of the League's cadres made the successful delivery of the regime's message of atheism highly problematic. As a result, protracted discussion within both the Party and the League about the number and quality of cadres became a central theme of antireligion. Creation of the secular New Soviet Man in the guise of an activist became not only a goal but an all-consuming process for the Bolsheviks.

Armies in a Holy War

Internal Party and League reports and published propaganda regularly depicted the battle against religion as a matter of competing armies. A typical presentation of the 1920s would open with the number of "soldiers" the religious enemy could muster, and compare that always tremendous phalanx with the meager ranks of the Godless. In December 1928, Iaroslavskii drew the battle lines for the Central Committee's Orgbiuro: the opposition consisted of a 500,000-member core representing Church councils (the "twenties"), plus 350,000 agitators in the form of clergy (including sacristans). He added to this number 100,000 monks. This nearly million-strong opposition enjoyed free use of 50,000 churches and other buildings. In addition, there was the sectarian community numbering several million, with its own press and extensive financial support. Arrayed against these inherently counterrevolutionary forces was, according to the

---

[3] See the essays by R. W. Davies, Don Rowney, and Hiroaki Kuromiya in *Social Dimensions of Soviet Industrialization*, ed. William G. Rosenberg and Lewis H. Siegelbaum (Bloomington: Indiana University Press, 1993); Sheila Fitzpatrick, "The Bolsheviks' Dilemma: The Class Issue in Party Politics and Culture," in her *Cultural Front: Power and Culture in Revolutionary Russia* (Ithaca: Cornell University Press, 1992), 16–36.

script, the "insignificant" 300,000-member League, which had trouble arranging even the most minimal activities.[4] These numbers were all but drawn from thin air, and in fact made little sense, but they served the purpose of emphasizing the importance of cadres if the cause of atheism was to prevail.

The same manner of presentation was used by local officials. In 1928 the Iaroslavl' Provincial Party Committee enumerated the forces on the side of religion: 972 churches, 1,121 religious communities, 618,000 active laity, all led by 2,700 clergy trained in agitation. The Godless had only 133 cells with 3,174 members, and no more than seventy to eighty antireligious propagandists were available at the provincial and district levels. Moreover, the report noted, while the atheist camp was dormant, the clergy were active and wily.[5] An internal report on religion in Pskov Province in late 1924 spoke of a religious apparat (staff) of 528 churches, 930 priests, and many sectarian preachers. Six months later, the comparison was repeated in even more dramatic terms. Of a total population of 1.7 million in Pskov Province, 1.2 million were claimed to be active in religious societies. At the time, however, there were just fifteen ODGB circles with a total membership of only 1,500.[6]

This accounting was, to say the least, highly selective. Every believer and potential sympathizer was counted among the mobilized, conspiring opposition, while only the League represented the Bolshevik forces. The atheist contingent did not include Komsomol and Party members, all of whom were supposed to be convinced atheists, regardless of their membership in the League. The purpose behind these numbers was clear: to emphasize the need to increase the number of antireligious cadres, primarily through the League of the Godless. This numerical presentation also was indicative of the Bolsheviks' almost exclusive reliance on quantitative measures of social transformation. How many churches were open? How many clergy were at work? How many people had joined the League? More qualitative assessments of social transformation, particularly appropriate in the subjective realms of religion and atheism, were absent from these calculations. This firm belief in statistical representations of reality was evident throughout the Bolshevik realm, even where it manifestly had little relevance, and again emphasized the conceptual and administrative uniformity expected within Bolshevik political culture.[7]

---

[4] RTsKhIDNI, f. 17, op. 113, d. 683, ll. 22–23.
[5] IaPA, f. 1, op. 27, d. 2865, ll. 183–184.
[6] PPA, f. 1, op. 1, d. 386, ll. 57, 60–61, 119.
[7] See the comment of Moshe Lewin, "On Soviet Industrialization," in Rosenberg and Siegelbaum, *Social Dimensions of Soviet Industrialization*, 276.

And so the Iaroslavl' and Pskov Leagues regularly and persistently blamed their organizational shortcomings on the absence of cadres. In 1925, the single worst problem in the antireligious campaign, according to Party officials in Pskov, was the lack of staff. One cell secretary who attended the League's first congress in Iaroslavl' in June 1926 cited the need for trained cadres, "in light of the complete absence of such."[8] Because the antireligious propaganda network was only just forming in this period, such early complaints might seem reasonable. Even after the League gained a somewhat better footing, however, it continued to bemoan the lack of activists. At the district level, particularly in rural areas, staff remained in short supply. In February 1930, the Godless in Tutaev complained to the Party that "the Tutaev League District Council does not have a paid antireligion propagandist, while other districts have paid workers and even the OSOAviaKhim District Council has two paid staff members."[9] (The League regularly pointed to OSOAviaKhim as a more amply endowed voluntary organization.)[10] The Central Council reviewed the Ostrov League (forty kilometers south of Pskov) in February 1931, and found the absence of a full-time employee to be the council's greatest shortcoming.[11] This rhetoric of blame established a simple excuse for the League's inactivity, and a promise of improvement if only sufficient cadres were provided. The League's cadre problem was so severe that it permitted what Bolshevik ideology would otherwise have proscribed: the use of former clergy as antireligious activists.[12] Most of these men were experienced public speakers who were well versed in the Bible. More important, the many social restrictions placed on the disenfranchised made former clergy available when and where "Soviet" cadres were not.

Complaints about the number of antireligious activists were regularly accompanied by commentary on the low quality of the activists who were available. The problem of political literacy encountered early in the decade continued throughout the 1920s and, if anything, was only exacerbated by the expansion of the Party during that decade. In 1929, a review of rural Party cells in Iaroslavl' noted that "the political level of the rural Communist is extremely low. The majority do not know the basic tasks announced by the Party. . . . The incidence of baptism, receiving priests,

---

[8] PPA, f. 1, op. 1, d. 386, l. 64; IaSA, f. 3362, op. 1, d. 4, l. 84.
[9] IaSA, f. 3363, op. 1, d. 4, l. 34.
[10] For example, "Dob'emsia prava grazhdanstva dlia antireligioznykh rabotnikov," *Antireligioznik*, 1931, no. 4, 28.
[11] GARF, f. r-5407, op. 1, d. 76, l. 89ob.
[12] Daniel Peris, "Commissars in Red Cassocks: Former Priests in the League of the Godless," *Slavic Review* 54, no. 2 (Summer 1995): 640–664.

and observing religious holidays in the families of Communists is high."[13] In 1930, Communists (even in urban areas) were still regularly expelled from the Party for observing religious holidays and rites.[14] There were chronic difficulties with one popular form of propaganda that was particularly dependent on cadres—public debates between regime activists and representatives of the Church. These meetings featured clergy and activists facing each other on questions such as "Did Christ live?" In the mid-1920s, the Commissar of Enlightenment, Anatolii Lunacharskii, and the Renovationist leader, Aleksandr Vvedenskii, debated several times in highly publicized meetings.[15] These debates and the locally arranged clashes were popular throughout the 1920s. Unlike the more controlled lectures, these debates represented a genuine interaction between society and a regime determined to change it. Though they did everything possible to undermine the opposition—determining the order and length of presentations and controlling questions from the floor[16]—the promoters of atheism were not always able to carry the day. When these events went poorly for the atheists, the outcome was universally blamed on the "unpreparedness" of the Godless speaker. A Moscow activist reported in 1921 that "debates on religious themes were poorly organized everywhere, which often contributed to the triumph of the priests."[17] In June of that year, the head of the Iaroslavl' provincial lecture bureau complained that a local Communist had "all but ruined a . . . debate with his unpreparedness and inappropriate expressions."[18] The Pskov Party agitprop department reported that no serious antireligious debates were conducted in 1923–1924 before the arrival of experienced activists from Leningrad.[19]

The debates were such failures that the Moscow Party Committee forbade them in the province in early 1925,[20] and in 1926 the chairman of the Iaroslavl' Provincial Council, Aleksandr Egorov, stated that it was better to refuse to debate than to participate without solid preparation. That

---

[13] IaPA, f. 232, op. 4, d. 329, l. 4ob.

[14] *Otchet o rabote Iaroslavskoi okruzhnoi KK VKP–RKI k 2-i Iaroslavskoi okruzhnoi partkonferentsii za iiun' 1929–mai 1930 g.* (Iaroslavl', 1930), 8–9.

[15] A. V. Lunacharskii, *Ob ateizme i religii* (Moscow: Mysl', 1972), 218–258; A. V. Lunacharskii, *Khristianstvo ili kommunizm: Disput s mitropolitom A. Vvedenskim* (Leningrad: Gosizdat, 1926).These are the printed transcripts of debates of 20 and 21 September 1925 and 3 October 1927.

[16] There is a detailed account of League-arranged debate in S. S. Samuilova and N. S. Samuilova, *Ottsovskii krest* (St. Petersburg: Satis', 1996), 127–166.

[17] RTsKhIDNI, f. 17, op. 60, d. 114, l. 1.

[18] IaPA, f. 1, op. 27, d. 662, l. 110.

[19] PPA, f. 1, op. 1, d. 386, l. 64.

[20] RTsKhIDNI, f. 89, op. 4, d. 116, l. 4.

same year, the Pskov Provincial Party warned that local propagandists should "in no case conduct debates with sectarians if there is no challenger well versed in the Bible."[21] The Antireligious Commission voted in September 1928 to request that the Central Committee forbid "antireligious debates with the participation of priests or sectarian preachers." Lectures were recommended instead.[22] Despite these warnings, debates continued to be conducted in the countryside. In early 1929, *Pskovskii nabat* reported the victory of an evangelist over a local atheist in the village of Pavlovo.[23] Over a decade into Soviet power, many debates were still being lost, and the chronic difficulties with this intensive form of propaganda highlighted the regime's lack of competent cadres, both in fact and as a central trope in the League's rhetoric of self-criticism and competition for resources.

The League's answer to the shortcomings of its personnel was simple: to create and maintain a network of full-time employees. The reasoning behind this goal was clear. Only with an ample staff would the League withstand the fickleness of support by the Party, Komsomol, and trade unions and avoid the organizational "campaignism" that characterized its existence. According to a 1929 League publication, "the quality of the League's work depends to a significant degree on the presence in our organizations of specialized, paid workers." Success required a staff "fully occupied with this work, answering for everything, dedicated to it day and night."[24] These cadres would bring a long-sought organizational stability to the League's network, and, able to specialize, they could develop the necessary competence. So the League set out to create its own nationwide force of activists. This process involved, on one hand, persuading the Communist Party to divert some portion of its own propagandists and those attached to other institutions to atheistic work, and, on the other, training cadres to fill those positions. These processes came to dominate the League as it spent as much effort in becoming as in being.

Here, as elsewhere, the League projected the resolution to its problems beyond its own gates to those institutions that were supposed to support it. Every complaint about the absence of trained activists was accompanied by a call for material support from Party, trade unions, and educational organizations to engage full-time staff and to support lecturers. The

---

[21] IaSA, f. 3362, op. 1, d. 5, l. 3; PPA f. 1, op. 1, d. 385, l. 313.
[22] RTsKhIDNI, f. 17, op. 113, d. 871, ll. 22–23. There is no indication whether this request was approved by the Central Committee.
[23] *Pskovskii nabat*, 16 January 1929.
[24] *Chetyre goda raboty: Otchet vtoromu vsesiouznomu s'ezdu bezbozhnikov* (Moscow, 1929), 25–27.

League could only ask; it rarely had the means to hire employees unilaterally. The Communist Party had to provide the necessary funds or direct other organizations to do so.[25] While the Party was at least nominally sympathetic to the League's personnel needs, its response was limited to repeated and vague resolutions that were rarely fulfilled. In September 1926, the Pskov Provincial Party directed local Party committees to arrange for the training of antireligious cadres.[26] At the end of August 1928, the Iaroslavl' Party resolved that "*uezd* and district League councils should be guaranteed . . . staff, no fewer than two individuals freed from other Party obligations."[27] In January 1929, the Iaroslavl' Party adopted another measure that would have appointed one antireligious propagandist for each *uezd* Party committee at the expense of the provincial Party.[28] This resolution remained on paper; by the time it was passed, Iaroslavl' Province no longer formally existed, and, there is no evidence that in the ensuing chaos of *raionirovanie* any actions were taken to supply the League with antireligious personnel. On four occasions between February 1927 and July 1929, the Iaroslavl' Third District Party Committee adopted resolutions on the necessity of having antireligious cadres. The resolutions' vague formulation invited the nonfulfillment suggested by their repetition, and the head of the League organization in the neighboring First District, Fedor Veselov, stated in his final report in 1930 that "the numerous resolutions on the need for a paid staff worker came to nothing."[29]

Even directives for the appointment of antireligious cadres issued from the highest levels had little long-term impact. In 1928, a resolution of the Central Committee's agitprop department called for "the appointment of League workers verified in mass work and theoretically trained." The resolution also urged the creation of cadre training programs at all levels, and the inclusion of antireligious training programs in university curricula, Soviet/Party schools, literacy and retraining schools, and generally throughout the Communist Party's training system. Annual courses and conferences were to be held by the Central Council and Glavpolitprosvet. Trained antireligious lecturers were to be included in the full-time staff of provincial political enlightenment authorities and trade union coun-

---

[25] The League occupied an unusual position. Although it collected dues, it was more dependent than other social organizations on outside subsidies and grants. See *Kommunistich-eskaia revoliutsiia*, 1925, no. 24, 7.

[26] PPA, f. 6, op. 1, d. 133, ll. 11–12.

[27] IaPA, f. 1, op. 27, d. 3088, ll. 11–12.

[28] IaSA, f. 3363, op. 1, d. 2, l. 6.

[29] IaPA, f. 1, op. 27, d. 2746, l. 54, and d. 3088, ll. 147–148. IaSA, f. 3362, op. 1, d. 1, l. 213; d. 2, l. 171; f. 3378, op. 1, d. 4, l. 1.

cils.[30] Few of these provisions were ever realized. Such resolutions were passed, distributed to local Party committees, approved by them, and then filed away, with some aspects entering into fanciful plans for the upcoming year. The rhetoric of antireligion represented an internal, circular flow of words among political institutions, and though it had little bearing on the outside world, it seemingly substituted for actual social transformation. This culture equated a resolution calling for change as, in essence, social transformation achieved.

The various levels of activism prevalent at the time the League was making a genuine attempt to create a nationwide network of cadres complicate any assessment of its efforts. The League's cadres ranged from full-time employees to rank-and-file members. The most important of these was the salaried council worker, paid directly from local League coffers. Many staff members worked in the League but were on the Party's or trade union's payroll. Activists on the staff of the Party, union, or educational authorities whose explicit responsibilities included antireligious work through the League constituted a third category. There also were lecturers paid by the event. Finally, there were the rank and file, who often did little more than sign their names to a list. Given this range of involvement, it is virtually impossible to determine how many individuals worked for a local League organization at any one time; moreover, the League's general history suggests that few councils knew the precise number of their activists.

How did Pskov and Iaroslavl' fare in the battle for cadres? In the early years, from 1925 through 1928, there were no full-time staff below the *okrug* level, and few above it. Antireligious propagandists in this period were first and foremost propagandists for the Party, a union, or an educational authority whose portfolio included antireligious work. Only when the League entered its period of rapid expansion did full-time staff on *okrug* and provincial councils became more common. In 1929, the League's Central Council in Moscow listed about fifty staff at lower levels across the country, and announced the goal of having full-time workers in every *okrug*. At that time, the Iaroslavl' Okrug Council had one full-time instructor; by 1930, the Iaroslavl' League had added a second full-time employee. As a city council, the Iaroslavl' League had two full-time workers in 1931, and in the spring of 1933, at least two individuals received their ration coupons through the League's City Council.[31]

[30] "O rabote soiuza Bezbozhnikov," *Kommunisticheskaia revoliutsiia*, 1928, no. 14: 116–118, a resolution from the May 1928 conference.
[31] *Chetyre goda raboty*, 25–27; IaPA, f. 229, op. 9, d. 132, l. 232ob; IaSA, f. 3378, op. 1, d. 1, ll. 209–210; f. 2410, op. 1, d. 12, l. 251.

Somewhat surprisingly, Pskov fared better. In 1928, the Pskov Okrug Council succeeded in arranging a full-time worker, apparently an executive secretary who also served as a traveling lecturer. Interim information is unavailable, but in the early 1930s the Pskov League maintained several full-time staff. In 1932, the local council employed three activists: an executive secretary, a lecturer-instructor, and a clerical worker. The following year, the Pskov League was distinguished by a total of four full-time employees.[32] Pskov's success in 1933 appears to have been exceptional. Reports submitted to the League Central Council from councils in cities much larger than Pskov rarely indicated more than one or two full-time staff. Moreover, the Pskov League reached its apogee when other councils were falling into desuetude. The Pskov council's very success highlighted the League's overall failure to establish a uniform, deep network of paid staff throughout the country.

Training the Godless

In response to the challenges of both numbers and quality, the League and Party established numerous training programs for antireligious cadres. This effort was only part of the much larger effort launched by the Bolsheviks in the 1920s to teach its own to run the country. Such training was realized through the network of Soviet/Party schools in each province, and a variety of specialized institutes in the capitals, such as the Krupskaia Political Enlightenment Institute in Leningrad and the Sverdlov University in Moscow.[33] Antireligious training programs ranged from local circles, which also served general propaganda purposes, to seminars on the district and provincial levels for specialized cadres, to more structured courses at the provincial level or in the capitals. The content of these programs varied but usually began with basic astronomy, biology, chemistry, and physics. This introduction was followed first by coverage of mythology and the early history of Christianity and other religions, and then by an examination of the more recent history and political role of the Ortho-

[32] PSA, f. 247, op. 1, d. 3, l. 7; d. 14, l. 2; d. 9, l. 42.

[33] Larry Holmes, *The Kremlin and the Schoolhouse: Reforming Education in Soviet Russia, 1917–1931* (Bloomington: Indiana University Press, 1991); Peter Kenez, *The Birth of the Propaganda State* (Cambridge: Cambridge University Press, 1985), 123–128; Sheila Fitzpatrick, *Education and Social Mobility in the Soviet Union, 1921–1934* (Cambridge: Cambridge University Press, 1979) and *The Commissariat of Enlightenment: Soviet Organization of Education and the Arts under Lunacharskii, October 1917–1921* (Cambridge: Cambridge University Press, 1970), 243–255; T. A. Remizova, *Kul'turno-prosvetitel'naia rabota v RSFSR 1921–1925* (Moscow: Akademiia Nauk, 1962), 17–60.

dox Church and sectarian groups. The programs concluded on themes such as "socialist construction and religion."[34]

On paper, the network of antireligious training programs was impressive. The League Central Council, while still the ODGB, trained cadres through a series of seminars. The Antireligious Bureau of the Moscow Communist Party also conducted an antireligious "seminary" in the mid-1920s. In the autumn of 1924, the Krupskaia Institute began to offer its antireligious lecture cycle. In October 1925, the League Executive Bureau voted to establish a central "seminary" for antireligious activists, and during the summer of 1928, the Central Council arranged for lecturers traveling around the country to provide short-term summer courses for provincial activists. Two years later, the First Moscow University created an antireligious training division in its History and Philosophy Department. At the same time, Leningrad State University also offered an antireligious program. The Central Council continued to administer a variety of courses into the early 1930s.[35]

The "antireligious university," a series of weekly lectures of varying duration designed for large audiences, was the largest training program launched by the League, begun in the capitals in 1929. The format soon spread on the coattails of worker, evening, Sunday, and radio "universities." Graduates of the programs were to be used in district and *okrug* councils, and in 1931, 100,000 students were slated for study in the antireligious division of the Radio University. For the 1931–1932 school year, this division became an all-union radio antireligious university of four departments with training periods from eight months to two years. As of late 1931, the League claimed eighty-four local antireligious universities of various sorts throughout the country, and plans called for 1.25 million people to be enrolled in some form of training during the 1931–1932 school year.[36] Although these programs also served as general propaganda vehicles, their main thrust was to train the members of the sponsoring organizations, who, some fifteen years after the Revolution, still were not prepared to go out and proselytize for atheism.

Local training programs also were nominally extensive. In August 1926, the Iaroslavl' League approved plans for a two-week antireligious seminar

---

[34] See, for example, G. A. Gurev, *Antireligioznaia khrestomatiia: Posobie dlia propagandistov prepodavatelei i uchashchikhsia*, 4th exp. ed. (Moscow: Bezbozhnik, 1930) (20,070 copies, 727 pages).

[35] RTsKhIDNI, f. 89, op. 4, d. 116, ll. 3–5; d. 185, ll. 14–20; GARF, f. r-5407, op. 1, d. 2, l. 4; d. 17, ll. 102, 106ob; d. 19, ll. 93–94; d. 27, l. 93ob; d. 88, l. 117; d. 89, l. 6; d. 91, ll. 42ff.

[36] GARF, f. r-5407, op. 1, d. 26, l. 42ob; d. 91, ll. 64–65; d. 94b, l. 108; d. 92, ll. 82–83; d. 94b, ll. 5–6.

for thirty activists.[37] An agitprop conference in 1927 called for a seven-month biweekly antireligious seminar to be organized by *uezd* and district Party committees.[38] In the autumn of 1929, an antireligious division opened at the local workers' university (*rabfak*). The program consisted of three-hour meetings every other Sunday for eight months. In 1932, the Iaroslavl' City League created a citywide antireligious seminar, and the following year, four antireligious seminars were reported to be operating in Iaroslavl'. Iaroslavl' activists were also to benefit from the Antireligious Department of the Political Enlightenment Technical College (Politpros-vettekhnikhum) in the new oblast center of Ivanovo.[39]

Pskov moved relatively quickly to train antireligious cadres, offering a seminar as early as the autumn of 1924. The program was designed for thirty students, with up to thirty additional auditors. In February 1929, the Pskov Okrug Council reported that twenty-eight students had completed a recent two-week training course. A few months later, the Pskov District Council announced the organization of another antireligious seminar, and the following summer (1930), the district council declared its intention to organize an antireligious university. Rural activists who could not attend regularly would be accommodated in a special two-week seminar.[40] The Pskov League opened an antireligious university at the Industrial Cooperative in 1932, and the same year the "pedagogical" antireligious university graduated fifteen students. Fifty-two individuals in Pskov District were claimed to be enrolled in a correspondence course through the Central Antireligious Correspondence Institute in Leningrad in the spring of 1933. At the same time, advanced antireligious courses were to be offered twice monthly in Pskov by a visiting lecturer from Leningrad.[41]

While these programs were a substantial response to genuine difficulties, more often than not they fell victim to a lack of resources and overwhelming demands on cadres. Most were no more than plans conditional on political approval, financial support, and actual enrollments. Indeed, ample evidence suggests that the same obstacles encountered in other aspects of the League's operations hindered the League's training mechanisms. Receiving an inquiry from the Central Council in September 1927

[37] IaSA, f. 3362, op. 1, d. 5, l. 27.
[38] *Resheniia Iaroslavskogo gubernskogo agitpropsoveshchaniia, 2–3 iiunia 1927* (Iaroslavl', 1927), 34.
[39] IaSA, f. 3363, op. 1, d. 1, ll. 5, 52; f. 2410, op. 1, d. 7, l. 11. *Antireligioznik*, 1930, no. 4, 91, and 1931, no. 5, 39.
[40] PPA, f. 1, op. 4, d. 155; d. 137, ll. 67, 75–77; GARF, f. r-5407, op. 1, d. 30, l. 30; *Pskovskii nabat*, 23 August 1929; *Pskovskii kolkhoznik*, 16 July 1930.
[41] PSA, f. 247, op. 1, d. 10, ll. 2, 3, 9, 11; d. 14, l. 6; d. 15, l. 31; d. 29, l. 37.

about the state of antireligious programs, the Pskov League chairman scribbled on the note that "it is necessary to organize an antireligious seminar in Pskov paid for by the provincial Party. The Provincial Council does not have the funds for this goal."[42] After the Pskov League council had recruited fifty students for the Antireligious Correspondence Institute, the Leningrad organizers informed the Pskov activists that the program had been abandoned for lack of resources.[43] Here as elsewhere, financing had to be arranged from outside sources—a difficult task given the League's low standing in the Bolshevik hierarchy.

Funding was certainly not the only obstacle. Frequently, and to no great surprise, the other institutions on which the League relied were uninterested or unwilling to train antireligious activists. This reluctance was particularly characteristic of educational authorities.[44] When the League Central Council requested support in September 1929 for six-month antireligious courses, Glavpolitprosvet "categorically refused to participate." The Central Council noted in June 1931 that 240 antireligious education inspectors promised by the Commissariat of Enlightenment had never materialized, and in October of that year, the Central Council protested that all antireligious courses had been removed from the curricula of teachers' colleges, despite an agreement between the League and the RSFSR Commissariat of Enlightenment that 110 hours of antireligious instruction would be included.[45]

A variety of other predictable problems plagued local training programs. At least one planned course was never given for lack of teachers. The chairman of the Third District Council in Iaroslavl' admitted in 1927 that "the District Council tried to start a seminar for antireligious activists during the summer, but . . . [had to cancel the class] because of the nonappearance of [class] leaders."[46] Other courses suffered from a lack of students. When the Pskov Okrug Council announced that eighteen students had completed antireligious courses in the summer of 1930, it added that "districts most in need of antireligious activists, for some reason, did not send anyone to these courses."[47] All too frequently, training programs collapsed after several meetings. Like the League's cells themselves, the programs registered many people, but far fewer showed up. An assessment made in May 1925

---

[42] PPA, f. 1, op. 4, d. 257, l. 9.

[43] PSA, f. 247, op. 1, d. 15, l. 3; d. 29, l. 37.

[44] See Larry Holmes, "Fear No Evil: Schools and Religion in Soviet Russia, 1917–1941," in *Religious Policy in the Soviet Union*, ed. Sabrina Ramet (Cambridge: Cambridge University Press, 1993), 125–157.

[45] GARF, f. r-5407, op. 1, d. 26, l. 40; d. 51, l. 187; d. 94b, l. 141.

[46] IaSA, f. 3362, op. 1, d. 9, l. 44.

[47] *Pskovskii nabat,* 16 August 1930.

called the Pskov antireligious seminar held the previous winter a failure "because of mass nonattendance . . . and [students'] manifested passivity." Only eighteen of the original fifty participants finished the program with satisfactory marks.[48] The problem of student attendance was critical in an antireligious seminar organized in early 1927 by the Danilov Uezd Party (Iaroslavl' Province). Of the nine registered students, two did not attend even once, and only one attended all eleven sessions. Many of the missed classes were explained with the notation "on Party assignment" or "attending a Party meeting"; one student missed eight of the eleven sessions while on assignment.[49]

Participation in the antireligious universities was no better. Despite the presumably higher level of discipline and organization of the military, student attendance at the Red Army Antireligious Evening University in Iaroslavl' in 1932 quickly dropped from seventy to fifteen. At the Pskov Worker Antireligious University in early 1933, attendance averaged about 50 to 60 percent of registered students. The head of the program reported that the quality of the students was poor and that only five would be able to conduct antireligious propaganda upon graduation. The rest had difficulty reading and writing, and many were "on loan" from Party organizations that frequently sent them to the countryside.[50] The problem of attendance was clearly a national phenomenon: according to comments made at the League's 1931 plenum, antireligious universities were distinguished by attrition rates of up to 70 percent.[51]

Even when training courses were successfully completed, the graduates were not necessarily assigned to antireligious work. The Pskov District Council reported in July 1933 that of the 145 activists who had passed through courses there during the previous six months, no more than 10 and perhaps fewer were employed in antireligious work.[52] Even the Central Council in Moscow had difficulty retaining its graduates. In October 1931, it announced the graduation of thirty-six propagandists from its second series of six-month courses. All of the activists had promised, the League proclaimed, to work as antireligious propagandists until at least the end of the First Five-Year Plan—only fifteen months away. That seems a paltry return on a six-month investment.[53] Of course, not all League training programs were expected to produce full-time activists; many were

[48] PPA, f. 1, op. 1, d. 386, ll. 63–64.
[49] IaSA, f. 3517, op. 1, d. 1, ll. 10–11.
[50] IaSA, f. 2410, op. 1, d. 12, l. 85; PSA, f. 247, op. 1, d. 14, ll. 8–8ob.
[51] GARF, f. r-5407, op. 1, d. 94a, l. 42.
[52] PSA, f. 247, op. 1, d. 10, l. 3.
[53] GARF, f. r-5407, op. 1, d. 94b, l. 141.

part of the general education of would-be well-rounded Soviet citizens. Still, the League's main goal was to produce its own professionals.

The Communist Party was certainly aware of this misdirection of local staff, and passed resolutions accordingly. In August 1927, the Iaroslavl' Provincial Party ordered district and *uezd* Party committees to "take into account completed preparation in the field of antireligious propaganda at provincial-level retraining courses, using these propagandists to strengthen and develop antireligious propaganda."[54] This directive seems to have had little effect, because in 1930 the Central Council noted in despair that out of 150 cadres who had been trained in Iaroslavl' Okrug in the past three years, not one was engaged in antireligious work.[55] This failure to use graduates of antireligious courses in propaganda work was hardly surprising. Had all the graduates actually wished to use their skills full-time, they could never have been accommodated. This fact, however, was conveniently overlooked in the League's rhetoric, which emphasized the constant need for more cadres.

Assessing the success of the League's training programs is difficult. The League's own appraisals were usually highly negative. Although the results of the League's training programs were genuinely disappointing and the spirit of self-criticism (*samokritika*) guaranteed humility in official accounts, the League also had a vested interest in making the state of cadres' training appear as bad as possible to attract attention, and, it was supposed, greater assistance. Moreover, the Central Council had very little information on which to base its judgments. For example, in October 1931, the Central Council's cadre department "insistently" requested information on antireligious universities at local collective farms. Despite the "severe shortage of rural antireligious cadres" that made this form of training a priority, the Central Council had information on just two collective farm antireligious universities. An earlier request for information in August had not generated even one response.[56] Such complaints about a lack of local information were a regular feature of the Central Council's correspondence.

Missionaries of Modernity

Despite circumstances that so strongly militated against the establishment and maintenance of an effective antireligious bureaucracy, League and

---

[54] IaPA, f. 1, op. 27, d. 2597, l. 111ob.
[55] GARF, f. r-5407, op. 1, d. 70, l. 1. This complaint was not substantiated by any details, and one suspects that the number of cadres trained and their total misdirection may have been exaggerated.
[56] GARF, f. r-5407, op. 1, d. 93, l. 59.

Party records bring to light certain individuals who served as dedicated activists in the 1920s and 1930s. Their success came despite rather than because of the League's bureaucracy, and the reliance on individual activists represented a striking reversal of the League's stated goal—to produce a comprehensive and anonymous bureaucracy that was not dependent on the enthusiasm or sense of responsibility of isolated cadres. Antireligious propaganda and work in the League in particular carried so little weight in the agitprop hierarchy that little harm appears to have come to those who simply ignored their antireligious responsibilities. By the same measure, even less was gained by active involvement in the League. Indeed, those Party propagandists who took a particular interest in the League ran the risk of marginalization. In 1929 a central Godless activist approached Iaroslavskii and requested transfer to other work. According to Iaroslavskii, the activist believed that "if he worked just a few more years in an antireligious position, then others would stop taking him seriously and would say how odd he is, all the time working in the League of the Godless."[57] Given these conditions, those propagandists active over a long period of time (in the League's case, a year was forever) represented a largely self-selected group. Who, then, were these cadres and what did they bring to the League's work?

The League's activists in Iaroslavl' and Pskov can be divided into three categories.[58] The first were the leaders. The second group consisted of the League's full-time employees. The final and largest group represented those cadres active in League councils part-time who were "volunteers" or those fulfilling party obligations. The first group, the leaders, underscored both the opportunities for advancement created by the Revolution and the regime's difficulty finding qualified administrators. Iaroslavl''s most prominent Godless in the late 1920s, Aleksandr Grigor'evich Egorov, was born in 1897 and joined the Party in 1918 while serving in the Red Army. After the Civil War, Egorov worked in a variety of administrative and ag-

---

[57] RTsKhIDNI, f. 89, op. 4, d. 30, l. 1a.

[58] This section is based on materials from the Iaroslavl' and Pskov Party archives that were made available to me in 1992 and 1993. The Iaroslavl' Party archive provided biographical abstracts based on personnel files and with varying levels of detail for a total of thirty-five activists. As I had only partial information on some names, some of the reports ended up not being those of League activists. In other cases, the archive was unable to provide any information. In addition, I examined the Party's personnel files for five of the Iaroslavl' League's most prominent activists, including Egorov and Shalygin. In Pskov I saw twelve Party files, including that of the Pskov League's leader, Sigov. Other information about League personnel was gathered from standard archival and newspaper sources. For an exercise in prosopography, these sources are woefully limited, but they do provide an overview of the League's local cadres.

itprop positions in Sergiev Uezd, rising by 1925 to head the agitprop department of the *uezd* Party committee. In 1926 he was sent to Iaroslavl' as an antireligious instructor-lecturer, and from March 1926 he ran the provincial Party's agitation subdepartment. In January 1928 he was made director of the Iaroslavl' Workers' School [Rabfak]. In 1931 Egorov returned to head the provincial Party's organization department, but he left Iaroslavl' soon thereafter to work in Ivanovo. Egorov's involvement with the Iaroslavl' League started in early 1926 and continued until 1931, when he asked to be relieved of his duties because of other demands on his time. For most of this period, he was the League's chairman or deputy chairman, first of the Provincial Council, then of the Okrug Council, and finally of the city-district organization.[59]

While Egorov served as the head of the Iaroslavl' League, his deputy, Ivan Alekseevich Shalygin, was its "theoretician." At League conferences, he regularly gave the report on the "tasks and methods" of antireligious propaganda. Born in 1895, Shalygin worked before the war as a manual laborer and trader. He indicated in his Party file that he had been arrested and had served some time in prison, although there is no indication of his crime. Immediately before World War I, Shalygin was unloading grain barges at Rybinsk, on the Volga. Having resisted the draft in 1915, Shalygin was arrested in 1917 and forcibly sent to the front. After he escaped, Shalygin joined the Bolshevik Party on July 25 and was sent back to the army as a political agitator. After the Revolution, Shalygin "participated in the establishment of Soviet power" in Uglich, his home town. He then did Party work in Liubim Uezd, where he served as secretary of the local Cheka. After duty on the northern front, Shalygin returned to Uglich, where he continued his work against "counterrevolution." After a stint of agitprop service with the military, during which he participated in suppressing the revolt in Tobol'sk, Shalygin returned to Uglich, where he served in Party and administrative positions, including that of head of the local educational authority. From mid-1925 until early 1928, he directed the Iaroslavl' Workers' School. Much of the Iaroslavl' League's correspondence in its early years was written on the stationery of the provincial education department, which suggests that Shalygin handled the council's paperwork. The League's address was also that of the provincial education department. Shalygin served on the Iaroslavl' League's presidium from 1926 to 1929, first as Egorov's deputy and briefly as chairman. At the same time, he also attended First District Council meetings.[60]

---

[59] IaPA, f. 1, op. 17, d. 2102.
[60] Ibid., d. 7798.

Pskov's analog to Egorov and Shalygin was Ivan Nikitich Sigov, who led the Pskov Okrug Council during most of its existence from 1927 to 1930. The son of a petty merchant and small landowner, Sigov was born in 1890 and went off to St. Petersburg when his father proved unable to support the family. His brother already worked in St. Petersburg, and led Ivan into revolutionary activity. He joined the Communist Party in September 1917. Sigov held various Party and Soviet positions in 1918, including that of Cheka "special detachment" member in Siberia. In the early 1920s, he served as a police inspector in the town of Nevel' (Pskov Province), and then as head of the Nevel' Uezd Education Authority. In September 1926 he was called to Pskov to become an editor of the provincial newspaper, *Pskovskii nabat*. In December of that year, he was appointed a *polit-prosvet* instructor responsible for antireligious propaganda, and in October 1928 he was placed in charge of the Party-Union Political Enlightenment Office (*kabinet*). Sigov remained there until at least the following spring.[61]

Sigov claimed that he had joined the League as early as 1924 and had run the Nevel' Uezd Council, organized cells, led circles, and conducted antireligious talks. Having arrived in Pskov in 1926, Sigov was appointed chairman of the provincial League sometime in late 1927, and after the province's dissolution, he served as head of the Okrug Council. In Pskov he taught an antireligious course at a Soviet/Party school, and he reported participating in ten debates. In 1929 Sigov wrote to Lukachevskii, the deputy chairman of the League, inquiring about full-time employment opportunities with the League; he said he was not happy with his current position as head of the Party *kabinet*. His wishes may have been accommodated, because protocols of the Leningrad Oblast League Council in 1933 identify a Sigov as the head of rural work and deputy chairman.

These men were the most prominent figures in the League's network up to 1930, when Iaroslavl' and Pskov still represented provinces or *okrugy*. All three had served at one time or another in agitprop capacities and also as education officials. What is striking, therefore, is their relatively low level of formal education. Egorov, one-time director of the Iaroslavl' Workers' School, wrote in his Party autobiography that his family was too poor to send him to school. His parents also believed that Orthodoxy was not taught well in the schools, so his grandfather tutored him at home using old Church books. After two years of such training, Egorov knew Church Slavonic while remaining "technically" illiterate in Russian. He learned to read Russian only while serving in the Red Army. In 1920 he

[61] GARF, f. r-5407, op. 1, d. 32, ll. 60–63.

was sent to Sverdlov Communist University in Moscow for six months. Shalygin's higher education amounted to three years at a municipal middle school and six months of Party training. Sigov's formal education was also limited. He claimed to have taught himself to read while in St. Petersburg, and later attended a factory evening school. He also pursued self-education programs, such as "high school at home" (*gimnaziia na domu*). Sigov's specialized training amounted to two months at the Vitebsk Soviet/Party School in 1923. Here and throughout the Soviet realm, the placement of individuals with little formal education in positions where they were to train others in matters of ideology and administration was indicative of the personnel problems facing the Bolsheviks in the 1920s.

Service in the Red Army was another common experience for these League leaders, including, in Sigov's and Shalygin's cases, work of a political-military nature. Shalygin in particular had the pedigree of a battle-tested revolutionary with blood on his hands. Historians continue to debate the legacy of the Civil War period for later Soviet history, but in the case of these League leaders, there is little evidence to link that experience with radical social transformation in the late 1920s. Indeed, as high-ranking League officials, these men were often cast as moderates seeking to control unruly, lower-level Komsomol activists and Soviet officials. Perhaps the most significant qualification for their League work was administrative experience hard earned during the Civil War and early NEP periods. However relevant antireligious training was, administrative experience was even at more of a premium for a regime that embraced bureaucratic solutions to its challenges.

These leaders generally were not full-time League employees. When they began their involvement, local League organizations had no such staff, and even when they became available in the late 1920s, the council chairmen usually retained their employment elsewhere, leaving the full-time positions to deputy chairmen, executive secretaries, or instructors. Those full-time personnel, along with the active volunteers, constituted the heart of local League organizations, but they present a mottled picture. Fedor Konstantinovich Popov came to Iaroslavl' in 1927 at the age of twenty-seven to work in the Consumers' Cooperative. Earlier in the decade, he had been a "propagandist-Godless" in Moscow, and between 1928 and 1932, he appears to have worked full-time for the Iaroslavl' League. By 1929 Popov had become head of the council's agitprop department, and in late 1929 he replaced the departed Shalygin as the Iaroslavl' League's de facto second in command. In March 1930 Popov was made deputy chairman of the Okrug Council, and he replaced Egorov as chairman in late 1931. In an assessment at the time, he was characterized as an "energetic and active worker, contributing much to the organization," and many of his reports on antireligious activity in Iaroslavl' appeared in the League's methodological journal *Antireligioznik*. In early 1932, Popov abruptly left Iaroslavl' to study archival management in Moscow.[62]

The individual who replaced Popov as chairman of the Iaroslavl' League in early 1932 was Iakov Semenovich Shugaev. Shugaev arrived in Iaroslavl' in 1929 from Ivanovo Province, where he had been the administrative head of a rural county. From November 1929 to December 1930 he worked as a propagandist at Krasnyi Perekop. Shugaev's League involvement began soon after his arrival in Iaroslavl', and by 1930 he was an active member first of the Okrug Council and then of the City-District Council. In December 1930 Shugaev became an employee of the Iaroslavl' League, and by the autumn of 1931 he had become deputy chairman, a position he retained until March 1932, when he replaced Popov as chairman. We find the last evidence of his activity in Iaroslavl' in the spring of 1933, when, as executive secretary, he was on the League's list of employees receiving food coupons. In 1933 he returned to Ivanovo.[63]

Among the more dedicated minor figures in Iaroslavl', Fedor Nikolaevich Veselov had begun work in 1927 as a Party propagandist in Liubim County (110 kilometers from Iaroslavl') and then served as an antireligious instructor for the Iaroslavl' Provincial Party. His association with the Iaroslavl' League dated from 1926, when he was a member of the provincial council while still a student at the Soviet/Party school. Veselov served briefly as deputy chairman of the Iaroslavl' League in 1929.[64] Anton Pavlovich Dervoedov arrived in Iaroslavl' in 1930 and worked briefly at Krasnyi Perekop as a loader. With little apparent experience, Dervoedov was appointed executive secretary of the city League in November 1931 (to replace Popov), and he held that post until June 1932, when he was sent to the Resin-Asbestos Kompleks (RAK) as a trade union organizer. Among other activities, Dervoedov headed the Red Army Antireligious University organized (or at least reported to have been organized) in Iaroslavl' in 1932.[65] Finally, Vladimir Andreevich Nikiforovskii worked in the Iaroslavl' Automobile Factory from 1929 to 1932, first as an accountant, then in the trade union as an antireligious

[62] Biographical abstract, IaPA; IaSA, f. 2410, op. 1, d. 1, l. 116; f. 3363, op. 1, d. 3, l. 9. In the late 1930s, a Fedor Konstantinovich Popov worked as a traveling instructor for the League's Central Council.

[63] Biographical abstract, IaPA; IaSA, f. 2410, op. 1, d. 10, ll. 9–10, 59, 95; f. 3363, op. 1, d. 4, esp. ll. 25–26.

[64] Biographical abstract, IaPA; IaSA, f. 3362, op. 1, d. 14, l. 20.

[65] Biographical abstract, IaPA; IaSA, f. 2410, op. 1, d. 10, ll. 77, 84, 95; d. 11, l. 64; d. 12, l. 85.

instructor. He continued as an antireligious instructor at RAK from 1932 to 1934.[66]

Information is less plentiful on lower-level cadres in Pskov than on those in Iaroslavl'. The most steady worker in Pskov in the early 1930s was Stepan Dmitriev, who, because he was not a Party member, left only limited information about himself. Having joined the League in 1929, he attended its congress in Pskov in 1929, and in the early 1930s he was the District Council's executive secretary. Sometime in 1933, he succeeded to the posts of deputy chairman and then chairman.[67] Information is also available on two other activists of the early 1930s. Mikhail Arulin arrived in Pskov in November 1926 as agitprop leader for the Pskov Uezd Party, a position he held until March 1928, when he was sent out into the countryside to head the agitprop department of a rural Party committee. As of January 1928, Arulin was chairman of the Pskov Uezd League Council, and in the early 1930s he led the Pskov Workers' Antireligious University.[68] Moisei Rafaelovich Kopman, having joined the League in 1925, was elected to the Okrug Council at the 1928 conference and attended the 1929 Okrug Congress. In 1932 and 1933 he was one of the League's paid instructors, and with Arulin taught at the local Workers' Antireligious University.[69]

The third category of activists were those individuals who participated in the League part-time as volunteers or to fulfill one of their Party obligations. Prosopographical information about them, particularly if they were not Communists, is extremely limited, but from what is available on them and the other activists described above, certain patterns among the League's local cadres emerge. The first and most important shared characteristic was, as might have been expected, Party membership. With the exception of Pskov's Stepan Dmitriev, not one of the dozen or so most important League activists in Pskov and Iaroslavl' was a "civilian." In most cases, however, Party members were active in the League as one of many propaganda responsibilities. Only Egorov in 1926 and Veselov in 1928–1929 were employed by the Communist Party as full-time antireligious activists. The nonparty members on district councils were usually less active and the membership of some was entirely symbolic. This is far

[66] Biographical abstract, IaPA; IaSA, f. 2410, op. 1, d. 7, l. 14; PSA, f. 247, op. 1, d. 13, ll. 30–31.

[67] PSA, f. 247, op. 1, d. 10, ll. 1, 12; d. 14, l. 10; d. 23, l. 76. Whether Dmitriev retained his nonparty status as chairman is uncertain.

[68] PPA, f. 1, op. 6, d. 122; PSA, f. 247, op. 1, d. 30, l. 6.

[69] PSA, f. 247, op. 1, d. 5, l. 11, 24–25; d. 14, l. 27; d. 15, l. 25; d. 29, ll. 24–25; dd. 28, 30; *Pskovskii nabat*, 26 September 1929.

from surprising given the Party's leading role in the creation of the League, but, as we have seen, the League's failure to reach beyond its core of activists rendered it vulnerable to all the ills of the Party's network, which in turn were magnified by the League's own operations.

Lower-level cadres were, not surprisingly, no better educated than the League's leaders. Most had only a grammar school education supplemented by short-term training in the Soviet period. Shugaev's and Dervoedov's education consisted of rural primary school and subsequent "lecturer courses" and "political" training; Dmitriev in Pskov claimed to have attended only primary school. Veselov had also attended the Iaroslavl' Soviet/Party School for three years. Fedor Popov claimed to have received some "higher education" at an unspecified institution. A less central figure in the Iaroslavl' League, Anton Nikiforovskii, was exceptionally well educated for a regime activist (though not necessarily in this area): he had studied for five years before the Revolution at the Moscow Commercial Institute (in the Soviet period the Plekhanov Institute). While most activists had been raised as Orthodox, few local Bolsheviks had the type of preparation likely to assist them in the task of replacing the Orthodox worldview. As a result, local activists were highly dependent on centrally prepared lectures and materials, few of which could be tailored to local concerns. This material coming from Moscow had to be "dumbed down" to the level of its activists, who understood religion in the simplest terms—churches, priests, holidays—rather than as a worldview with many subjective elements.

The likelihood that local League activists would be ineffective was increased by the absence of women in the League's camp. With the exception of Mariia Chezhina in Iaroslavl' and Mariia Vronskaia in Pskov, no women were prominent in these League organizations; in Moscow, only a few occasionally appeared on Central Council protocols. At its congress in 1929, the League had resolved to increase its female membership to 40 percent, and although the League claimed to have approximately 1.5 million female members in 1932 (27.4 percent of its reported membership), lists of the Godless in Iaroslavl' and Pskov suggest far fewer women, to the extent that these lists mean anything.[70] Because Bolshevik propaganda regularly identified women as the source of the younger generation's religious beliefs, this dearth of women demonstrated that while the League

[70] These numbers are all highly suspect, expressed originally as "average percentages" from selected oblasts, without presentation of the original membership numbers. L. Tiurina, "Zhenshchiny-bezbozhnitsy i bor'ba za novyi byt," and V. Kalinin, "Dinamika rosta i sotsial'nogo sostava SVB," both in *Voinstvuiushchee bezbozhie v SSSR za 15 let*, ed. M. Enisherlov (Moscow, 1932), 269, 350.

may have been well organized among the converted, it was weakest where the need was considered greatest. In a similar mismatch, the Jewish background of the Pskov activists Arulin and Kopman may have increased the League's appeal to the local Jewish population, but it no doubt hindered propaganda work among the Orthodox peasantry.

In a reflection of *perebroska* and the general migration of labor during the First Five-Year Plan, the League's lower-level cadres were constantly shuffled about with apparent disregard for workplace stability or familiarity with local conditions. *Tekuchka*, or rapid job turnover, characterized not only much of the Soviet industrial working class[71] but also the regime's own administrative and propaganda cadres. Few names appeared on League protocols for more than a year or two, particularly at the lower levels. Many of these cadres were new to Pskov and Iaroslavl': Fedor Popov arrived in Iaroslavl' in 1927 and left in 1932. Shugaev resided in Iaroslavl' for a total of four years. Having come from Liubim, Veselov lived only three years in Iaroslavl', 1927 to 1930, before being sent to Tutaev. Dervoedov arrived from Siberia in 1930 and was soon executive secretary of the Iaroslavl' League; after two years, he disappeared. Among those activists with traceable records, Nikiforovskii spent the longest time in Iaroslavl', arriving in 1917 and staying at least through 1934. In an environment of chronic *perebroska*, investing significant effort in any given job, particularly a secondary concern such as the League, made little sense when the individual involved was soon transferred to entirely different work or to a different area. It is likely that many agitprop cadres sensed that the League itself was a transient phenomenon. Fedor Popov left his relatively high-ranking League position to study archival management. Under these conditions, few activists developed a primary identification with the League, or even with antireligious work in general. Passing through so many organizations and causes, these cadres may have seen themselves at most as general agents of modernization.

Cadres and Antireligion

Cadres were central to the rhetoric and reality of antireligion. To a great extent, the history of the League was the history of the appointment, training, and support of a nationwide network of cadres. Seeking to have a specialized propagandist in every rural district and many more in the cities,

---

[71] Hiroaki Kuromiya, *Stalin's Industrial Revolution: Politics and Workers, 1928–1932* (Cambridge: Cambridge University Press, 1988), 200–212, 220–226.

the League was overwhelmed by this process, and the search for cadres became a defining characteristic of the organization. What had started as a means to an end—the creation of a network to pursue the regime's ideological aims—had not only failed but had become an end in itself. Creation of the New Soviet Man in his guise as activist had become an all-consuming ethos rather than a goal to be met. While the League's growth offered a large number of administrative positions, and in theory the opportunity for promotion, these assignments were mostly empty, short-term sinecures until something better or the next job came along—hardly the road to advancement that has been associated with the expansion of Soviet bureaucracy.[72]

Although not necessarily the "scum of Communist society," as Nicholas Timasheff has called them,[73] the League's activists and rank-and-file members clearly added to rather than diminished the difficulties facing the regime in its effort to create an atheistic society. The creation of antireligious cadres was one of many unfinished revolutions that structured the political culture of the early Soviet period. The regime's long-term efforts to create a "Soviet working class," a high-quality Communist Party, and a "Soviet intelligentsia" also were depicted as necessary intermediate steps on the path to socialism. In each case, the results regularly fell short of expectations, and the focus of the endeavor remained on the means rather than on the end.

[72] Fitzpatrick, *Education and Social Mobility*.
[73] Nicholas Timasheff, *Religion in Soviet Society* (New York: Sheed & Ward, 1942), 101.

8

The Second Coming? The League of the Godless in the Late 1930s

In the Soviet Union, parasitic classes have been liquidated, oppression and exploitation have been destroyed. But capitalist survivals [*perezhitky*] remain
and have not been eliminated entirely from the consciousness of people.
Among them, religious prejudices play a not insignificant role.

—"Antireligioznaia propaganda," *Pravda*,
7 May 1937

Having reached its peak during the Cultural Revolution, the League of the
Godless receded to the point of invisibility in the mid-1930s. The Central
Council lost its newspaper, *Bezbozhnik*, in January 1935; most other
League journals ceased publication. Cells and councils evaporated, and the
claimed membership dropped from around five million to a few hundred
thousand. For some activists, the League's collapse could be hailed as a triumph: socialism and its junior partner, atheism, had been declared victorious at the Communist Party's Seventeenth Congress in 1934. The League's
decline also seemed natural to outside observers, who noted the onset of a
culturally conservative period in the mid-1930s—the so-called Soviet Thermidor, Great Retreat, or neo-NEP. Trotsky wrote of a "regime of ironical
neutrality" toward religion.[1] In this climate and given its unimpressive
record, the League seemed destined to disappear along with the most visible elements of the Cultural Revolution. The League's institutional format
also did not suggest longevity: most of the other single-issue advocacy
groups established in the 1920s were disbanded in the early 1930s.[2] It was
therefore all the more notable that the League experienced a renaissance in

---

[1] Nicholas Timasheff, *The Great Retreat* (New York: Dutton, 1946); Leon Trotsky, *The
Revolution Betrayed* (1937; New York: Pioneer Publishers, 1945), 154.
[2] A. P. Kupaigorodskaia and N. B. Lebina, "Dobrovol'nye obshchestva Petrograda-
Leningrada v 1917–1937 gg. (tendentsii razvitiia)," in *Dobrovol'nye obshchestva v
Petrograda-Leningrade v 1917–1937 gg.: Sbornik statei* (Leningrad: Nauka, 1989), 12–14.

the late 1930s, seemingly in response to evidence of continued, widespread religious belief that emerged during discussion of the Stalin Constitution in 1936 and on the suppressed census of January 1937.[3]

The persistence of religion was not necessarily surprising; the return of the League as an instrument of social change was. The League's second incarnation was almost indistinguishable from its first, with the same organizational patterns, institutional conflicts, rhetorical expression, and impotence. The League's weakness was worsened, moreover, by a lukewarm justification for its return. Unwilling to acknowledge explicitly the continuing strength of religion twenty years after the Revolution, the regime left the League in the late 1930s on the far periphery of Bolshevik ideology, countering "remnants" (*perezhitky*) of bourgeois consciousness among the population. According to contemporary commentators, the objective basis for religion had been eliminated with the construction of socialism, but these "remnants" persisted. Nevertheless, the League's significance in this later period was quite different from that of its first incarnation. No longer part of the NEP-era volunteer mobilization of society or a government-led intervention during the Cultural Revolution, the League was of almost entirely symbolic significance: the purported ideological vigilance of the late 1930s. A greater symbolism was perhaps unintended: that twenty years after the Revolution, the regime felt compelled to resuscitate this organization.

The Soviet polity in the late 1930s has attracted generations of scholars seeking to unravel the "mysteries" of Stalinism. Much of this literature has quite naturally focused on the purges,[4] the network of Soviet prison camps,[5] and high-level politics and personalities.[6] Broader interpretations

---

[3] For discussion of the constitution and subsequent elections, see J. Arch Getty, "State and Society under Stalin: Constitutions and Elections in the 1930s," *Slavic Review* 50, no. 1 (Spring 1991), esp. 26–27, 30–31. The results of the census of 1937 were not made public until the 1990s. See Iu. A. Poliakov, Ia. E. Vodarskii, V. B. Zhiromskaia, and I. N. Kiselev, eds., *Vsesoiuznaia perepis' naseleniia 1937: Kratkie itogi* (Moscow: Akademiia Nauk, 1991), 106–115.

[4] J. Arch Getty and Roberta T. Manning, eds., *Stalinist Terror: New Perspectives* (Cambridge: Cambridge University Press, 1993); J. Arch Getty, *Origins of the Great Purges: The Soviet Communist Party Reconsidered, 1933–1938* (Cambridge: Cambridge University Press, 1985); Robert Conquest, *The Great Terror: A Reassessment* (New York: Oxford University Press, 1990); Zbigniew Brzezinski, *The Permanent Purge: Politics in Soviet Totalitarianism* (Cambridge: Harvard University Press, 1956).

[5] Aleksandr I. Solzhenitsyn, *The Gulag Archipelago, 1918–1956: An Experiment in Literary Investigation*, 3 vols. (New York: Harper & Row, 1974).

[6] Robert Tucker, *Stalin as Revolutionary: A Study in History and Personality* (New York: Norton, 1973) and *Stalin in Power: The Revolution from Above, 1928–1941* (New York: Norton, 1990); Dmitri Volkogonov, *Stalin: Triumph and Tragedy* (New York: Prima, 1992); Oleg V. Khlevniuk, *In Stalin's Shadow: The Career of "Sergo" Ordzhonikidze* (Armonk, N.Y.: M. E. Sharpe, 1995) and *1937-i: Stalin, NKVD, i sovetskoe obshchestvo* (Moscow: Respublika, 1992).

of Stalinism have been ventured,[7] but despite the volume of literature, there is little consensus. The League's return speaks less to general assessments of this period than to one aspect of it—the purported ideological renewal associated with it. This view has been championed in the Western literature by Arch Getty's *Origins of the Great Purges*, and in a different framework by Stephen Kotkin's *Magnetic Mountain*. The history of the League in action in the late 1930s provides one arena to measure the ideological content of late 1930s Soviet political culture.

Revival

In early February 1937 the Central Committee's Orgbiuro discussed the refusal of sectarians in Belorussia to participate in the recent census, and the Orgbiuro ordered the Central Committee's Agitprop Department and the League Central Council to report on the condition of antireligious propaganda nationally.[8] On 29 April 1937, the Orgbiuro considered three separate submissions, one by the Central Committee's Cultural Enlightenment Department, another by the Agitprop Department (including an investigation of Iaroslavl' Oblast), and a third from the League's chairman, Emel'ian Iaroslavskii.[9] The three reports were almost identical in tone and conclusions. Following the accepted formula, they indicated that "clergy [*popovstvo*] of all religions are increasing their activism and still command quite significant resources." Iaroslavskii referred to the preliminary findings of the 1937 census and concluded that "the withdrawal of believing toilers from religion in many places had been clearly overestimated." He cited statistics indicating that half of all children born in Pskov District were baptized, 40 percent of burials included clerical participation, and 75 percent of students in one of the district's rural areas still attended church.[10] The report from the Agitprop Department cited "abnormally friendly" relations between clergy and government officials in Iaroslavl' Oblast. Local Communist officials knew of sectarian agitation at Krasnyi Perekop, but took no steps to oppose it. According to one account, "A major role in antireligious propaganda could be played by the Komsomol,

[7] Stephen Kotkin, *Magnetic Mountain: Stalinism as a Civilization* (Berkeley: University of California Press, 1995); Moshe Lewin, *The Making of the Soviet System: Essays in the Social History of Interwar Russia* (London: Methuen, 1985); Robert C. Tucker, *Stalinism: Essays in Historical Interpretation* (New York: Norton, 1977); Roy Medvedev, *Let History Judge: The Origins and Consequences of Stalinism* (New York: Knopf, 1971).

[8] RTsKhIDNI, f. 17, op. 114, d. 794, ll. 1–4.

[9] Ibid., d. 805, ll. 15–45.

[10] Ibid., ll. 24, 26, 32.

but until recently, Komsomol organizations limited themselves . . . to public demands for church closings." The Central Trade Union Council was criticized for not having discussed antireligious work even once from 1931 until November 1936, when specifically asked to do so by Iaroslavskii. The consequences of this indifference for the League were severe: "The USSR League of the Militant Godless has ceased to resist churchmen and sectarians as a serious force."[11] The tone of these accounts was similar to that of the reports written a decade earlier, employing the same rhetoric of a rising threat, self-criticism, and institutional blame. Having received these reports, the Orgbiuro appointed a commission to produce a letter to local Party committees directing them to improve their antireligious propaganda efforts.[12]

Between the Orgbiuro's first review of religion in early February and its second in late April, the Central Committee discussed the League at its famous plenum that met in late February and early March. In the main political report, Central Committee Secretary Andrei Zhdanov cited unsatisfactory Party and Komsomol antireligious work in the face of rising religious activism: "To this is added the situation that our League of the Militant Godless is, if not exactly at peace or in a state of appeasement with Mr. God [laughter] . . . , in any case paralyzed [laughter]." In response to Iaroslavskii's weak defense of the League, which not surprisingly amounted to blaming other institutions, Zhdanov pushed further, adding that it was difficult to understand how the League could consider itself in any way militant. Iaroslavskii shot back that not only the League but the entire antireligious apparatus was in a state of "anabiosis."[13] Despite this indictment, antireligious propaganda was not mentioned in the plenum's resolutions. Although Zhdanov's rise was linked to a purported new wave of ideological vigilance that ought to have benefited the League, it also was associated with the decline of other Stalin lieutenants, among them Iaroslavskii. According to Nikita Khrushchev, the message that Iaroslavskii was to be taken down a few pegs had been circulated among the Party's second-rank leaders after the plenum.[14] Whatever the personal slights, the plenum passed into history as the beginning of the mass arrests and the severe social, political, and institutional turmoil of the Great Terror—the same type of unstable environment in which the League had experienced its greatest nominal growth in 1929 and 1930.

---

[11] Ibid., ll. 11, 18, 22, 23, 29.
[12] Ibid., d. 626, l. 2.
[13] Ibid., op. 2, d. 612, vyp. 1, ll. 4–11. My thanks to Robert Thurston for this reference.
[14] N. S. Khrushchev, *Khrushchev Remembers* (Boston: Little, Brown, 1970), 82.

Iaroslavskii read into the plenum's general call for ideological renewal a specific mandate for the League's return, and although the Party's direct support for the League was lukewarm, it was forthcoming. Even before the Orgbiuro's directive of April, signs of antireligion's return were evident. In February, Iaroslavskii published an article in *Bol'shevik* that labeled efforts to dispense with antireligious propaganda "opportunistic."[15] Beginning in March, *Pravda* and *Izvestiia* covered the League again, mostly in highly critical articles, but their very publication was a sign of the League's recrudescence.[16] Even the Komsomol Central Committee adopted a resolution on antireligious propaganda in March.[17] In April, the League's Central Council secretariat resumed regular, frequent meetings.[18] On 7 May, for the first time in eight years, *Pravda*'s lead editorial was given over to antireligious propaganda.[19] The Central Trade Union Council fell in line in August with its first resolution on antireligious propaganda in six years and a lead editorial in *Trud* the next month.[20] During the course of 1937, the League's claimed membership rose from a few hundred thousand to nearly two million.[21] In February 1938, Iaroslavskii got his newspaper back and the League was sufficiently reestablished to hold the Fourth Central Council Plenum—its first since 1932.

Early 1938 represented the zenith of the League's return in Moscow. Again, however, its moment was brief and its achievements were fleeting.[22] In midyear, Iaroslavskii petitioned the Central Committee for additional support for the League, including permission to hold a national congress, but the Orgbiuro did not consider the request until seven months later, in

[15] E. Iaroslavskii, "Antireligioznaia propaganda v sovremennykh usloviiakh," *Bol'shevik*, 1937, no. 4 (15 February), 28–40.

[16] S. Petrov, "O voinstvuiushchikh i krotkikh Bezbozhnikakh," *Izvestiia*, 10 March 1937, 3; A. Snegov, "O voinstvuiushchikh durakakh," *Pravda*, 29 April 1937, 4; N. Kruzhkov, "Rezoliutsii vmesto propagandy," *Pravda*, 2 July 1937, 4; "Bogoboiaznennye redaktory," *Pravda*, 3 July 1937, 4; "Voinstvuiushchie golovotiapy," *Pravda*, 25 October 1937, 4. See also "Zametki ob antireligioznoi propagande," *Izvestiia TsIK*, 27 April 1937.

[17] V. A. Alekseev, *Shturm nebes otmeniaetsia?* (Moscow: Rossiia Molodaia, 1992), 157, 160.

[18] GARF, f. r-5407, op. 1, d. 106.

[19] "Antireligioznaia propaganda," *Pravda*, 7 May 1937.

[20] Em. Iaroslavskii, "Zadachi antireligioznoi propagandy," *Trud*, 15 April 1937, 2–3; L. Zimin, "Blagodushestvuiushchie Bezbozhniki," *Trud*, 27 August 1937, 3; "Ob antireligioznoi rabote proforganizatsii: Postanovleniia ot 26 avgusta 1937 VTsSPS," *Trud*, 10 September 1937; "Propaganda ateizma i profsoiuzy," *Trud*, 10 September 1937.

[21] "Bystree izzhit' nedostatki v rabote SVB," *Antireligioznik*, 1939, no. 11, 3. Reported membership climbed to 3.5 million by early 1941 (*Bezbozhnik*, 16 April 1941).

[22] For example, the print run of *Bezbozhnik* slipped by the end of the year to 155,000; by late 1939, the journal was being issued only every other month.

January 1939.[23] The reason for the delay, extraordinary even by Central Committee standards, remains unclear, as does the question whether Iaroslavskii's appeal ever had the Central Committee's backing. In any case, the Third Congress never convened. The League must have received some encouragement, however, because on 20 August another editorial on antireligious propaganda appeared in *Pravda*. The editorial was tepid toward the League, though, mentioning it only once and in passing. The responsibility for antireligious work was shifted back to traditional propaganda agencies: the Party, Komsomol, unions, and education authorities.[24] Nevertheless, official League membership across the nation continued to grow, climbing to more than three million reported members by November 1939.[25] However halfheartedly, the ruling echelon of the Bolshevik Party had mandated the League's return in two ill-defined waves, in 1937 and 1939. What was the local response to the League's reappearance? The few isolated instances of spontaneity and enthusiasm that had greeted the creation of the League in the mid-1920s were completely absent one decade later; this time, the League's local networks were produced entirely by Party agitprop departments. Initial attempts to resuscitate the League in Iaroslavl' were unsuccessful. In the summer of 1936, the Iaroslavl' Oblast Party created a League Orgbiuro and requested that its district committees assist in the "revival" of local League councils.[26] Whether these steps grew out of a specific incident, resulted from the renewed discussion of religion, or were simply measures taken as part of the establishment of Iaroslavl' Oblast remains uncertain.[27] In any case, they came to nothing. The autumn brought renewed efforts. After a planned conference of antireligious activists collapsed from lack of interest, the Iaroslavl' Oblast Party held a special meeting (*soveshchanie*) on 29 October to discuss antireligious propaganda.[28] When the Oblast Party ap-

---

[23] RTsKhIDNI, f. 17, op. 114, d. 899, ll. 125, 147ob. Iaroslavskii, Andreev, and Zhdanov were directed to review Iaroslavskii's proposal.

[24] "Za sistematicheskuiu antireligioznuiu propagandu," *Pravda*, 20 August 1939. Alekseev argues that the editorial was written by Iaroslavskii (*Shturm nebes otmeniaetsia?* 175–176). See also "Po bol'shevistski organizovat' antireligioznuiu propagandu," *Trud*, 14 September 1939, 1.

[25] "Bystree izzhit' nedostatki v rabote SVB," *Antireligioznik*, 1939, no. 11, 3.

[26] IaPA, f. 272, op. 223, d. 225, l. 18; d. 21, l. 6; d. 60, ll. 205–206.

[27] On 11 March 1936, the VTsIK Presidium created Iaroslavl' Oblast out of the former Ivanovo Industrial Oblast. The oblast's boundaries corresponded to those of the former province, plus much of former Kostroma Province (*Iaroslavskaia oblast': Spravochnik po administrativno-territorial'nomu deleniiu, 1917–1927* [Iaroslavl', 1972], 66). The establishment of an entirely new administrative, political, social, and economic apparatus extended over a period of several months.

[28] *Antireligioznik*, 1936, no. 6, 44.

proved the conference's resolutions on 3 November, the organizational process began again with a newly appointed *oblast orgbiuro* and twenty-eight district and city councils.[29]

The new year (1937) brought additional Party resolutions on antireligious propaganda. The First Iaroslavl' Oblast Party Conference called for "the wide deployment of antireligious propaganda among the laborers of the towns and especially on the collective farms, and the strengthening of League district councils through appointment of politically reliable comrades."[30] In February and March, the Oblast Party assessed the fulfillment of its November 1936 decision in several districts and declared it to be, not surprisingly, "highly unsatisfactory." Another investigation in July and several critical articles in *Severnyi rabochii*, including a lead editorial on 10 September, pointed to the League's continued marginal existence.[31] In October 1937, one year after the first attempt failed, the Iaroslavl' Oblast League of the Militant Godless was finally able to mount a conference.[32]

The League's organizational status and activity in Iaroslavl' Oblast after 1937 varied widely, and the following years brought many conflicting accounts. In March 1938, a rural Party committee that had been severely reprimanded for laxity a year earlier claimed that antireligious work was flourishing, with 1,341 League members in 45 cells, an elected (rather than appointed) district council, and a high level of activism. In June, the Iaroslavl' Oblast Party also noted an improvement in antireligious propaganda, including the establishment of a League council in each district. Despite this reported progress, later in the year the Iaroslavl' District Party leveled a blunt attack on the local League organization for having only 23 cells and 268 members; of those cells, only 11 were in any way active.[33] The situation in 1939 was no less confused. In July, a planned conference appears to have been replaced by an "expanded plenum" of the oblast council.[34] On 28 August, eight days after *Pravda*'s lead editorial on antireligious propaganda, *Severnyi rabochii* published a highly critical assessment of the League in Iaroslavl' District: "In the District Party, they have

[29] *Materialy k otchetu orgbiuro TsK VKP(b) po Iaroslavskoi oblasti'* (Iaroslavl', January 1937), 56. At the time, Iaroslavl' Oblast consisted of twenty-eight districts and three major cities. See IaPA, f. 272, op. 223, d. 42, ll. 6, 133–136, 138; f. 273, op. 68, d. 265, l. 321.

[30] *Resheniia pervoi Iaroslavskoi oblastnoi partiinoi konferentsii* (Iaroslavl', 1937), 22.

[31] IaPA, f. 272, op. 223, d. 356, l. 4; f. 272, op. 223, d. 686, ll. 1–14; *Severnyi Rabochii*, 28 May, 3 August, 10 September, and 16 September 1937.

[32] *Severnyi rabochii*, 28 October 1937; IaPA f. 272, op. 223, d. 421, l. 4.

[33] IaPA, f. 272, op. 223, d. 1073, ll. 41–42; d. 811, ll. 16–18; f. 274, op. 2, d. 28, ll. 306, 310.

[34] Ibid., op. 223, d. 1214, l. 16; *Severnyi rabochii*, 22 August 1939.

already become accustomed to poor League work and make no effort to revitalize this most important organization."[35] Additional resolutions on antireligious propaganda were apparently issued by the Oblast Party on 11 November 1939 and on 26 January 1940.[36] The same pattern of newspaper articles, Party resolutions, and little actual propaganda activity under the League's auspices characterized 1940 and 1941.[37] Around Easter 1941, the *obkom* removed the League's chairman and executive secretary, charging that the "quality and ideopolitical purposefulness of antireligious propaganda remain at a very low level."[38] In early June, the Party ordered the Iaroslavl' League to review its existing cells and identify persons willing to serve as cell secretaries and in district councils.[39] The German invasion on June 22 rendered this decree moot.

What did the late Iaroslavl' League achieve in organizational terms, the all-important benchmark of Bolshevik political culture? Whereas in the late 1920s and early 1930s the number of League members was used to indicate both the League's health and, so it was presumed, the spread of atheism, in the late 1930s the number of League members was a less prominent marker, probably because there were far fewer of them. However artificial the earlier figures may have been, they reflected at least some penetration into society. In this later period, however, when the League existed in most cases only in the "webs of insignificance" spun by party agitprop departments,[40] the benchmark was not cells and members but whether a League council existed in each district. These councils represented a purely administrative achievement and one that required no popular participation. When membership numbers were actually tallied, they highlighted the League's failure to reach its previous organizational heights. As of January 1937, the Iaroslavl' Oblast Party claimed 91 League cells and 1,703 members. In mid-1938, reported membership stood at 19,631, and on the eve of World War II, the Iaroslavl' Oblast League supposedly consisted of 21,142 individuals.[41] In 1933, by contrast,

[35] *Severnyi rabochii*, 28 August 1939.

[36] Ibid., 21 March 1940.

[37] Ibid., 21 March, 12 April, and 20 December 1940; 4 and 6 April 1941; IaPA, f. 273, op. 68, d. 535, ll. 145–146.

[38] IaPA, f. 272, op. 224, d. 124, ll. 31, 36.

[39] IaPA, f. 272, op. 224, d. 65, l. 12.

[40] My apologies to Clifford Geertz and Max Weber. See Geertz, *The Interpretation of Cultures* (New York: Viking, 1973), 5.

[41] *Materialy k otchetu orgbiuro TsK VKP(b) po Iaroslavskoi oblast'*, 56; IaPA, f. 272, op. 223, d. 919, l. 68; f. 272, op. 224, d. 124, l. 36. According to Oleshchuk's report to the League's Fourth Plenum in February 1938, there were 14,000 members in the entire oblast, all but 2,000 of whom were in the cities (*IV raschirrenyi plenum tsentral'nogo soveta soiuza voinstvuiushchikh Bezbozhnikov* [Moscow: OGIZ/GAIZ, 1938], 26). Reconciliation of these

there were purported to have been 27,000 members in the city and suburbs of Iaroslavl' alone. Keeping in mind that the membership numbers
for both the early and late League were highly doubtful, we still must
see the Iaroslavl' League in the late 1930s as a Potemkin village of antireligion.

The League's return to Pskov Okrug (reestablished in 1935) was
marked by even greater difficulties. Even the League's national resurgence
in 1937 by-passed Pskov, despite numerous resolutions on antireligious
propaganda from the oblast capital, Leningrad. In February and June
1937, in rare instances when the system of soviets was the initiator of antireligious propaganda, the Leningrad Oblast Executive Committee issued
letters on the need to improve antireligious propaganda, including assistance to the League of the Godless.[42] Nevertheless, in a biting article in
Pskovskii kolkhoznik on 17 April, O. Rubanov recounted how he had
spent hours just trying to find the office of the League City Council. The
League's secretary had regularly sent glowing reports to Leningrad which
turned out to be the "fruit of the author's idle fantasy."[43] In April, the
Oblast League reported that the Pskov Okrug organization (still characterized as an *orgbiuro*) "had stirred," but that district councils were formally organized in only three of the *okrug*'s twelve districts. Although
generally critical, articles and editorials in *Pskovskii kolkhoznik* around
Easter also heralded the League's return.[44] In October, the Pskov Okrug
League was sufficiently functional to convene a conference, the first in
Pskov since the return of the League to the national stage over eighteen
months earlier and one year after Iaroslavl''s conference. The gathering
was said to represent 139 cells and 4,488 members.[45]

The organizational activity of 1938 was not sustained. An investigation
in January 1939 found little activity, and the Pskov League proved unable
to meet even the most minimal, bureaucratic expectations of existence in
Bolshevik political culture: the Okrug Council had met only once since its
creation, it had no plans, it had passed no resolutions, and it had conducted no investigations. Reported League membership declined. After

---

numbers is less important than their indication of the League's uncertainty, nationally and locally, of the number of dues-paying or even paper members.

[42] PPA, f. 3, op. 2, d. 1113, ll. 9–10; TsGAIPD Spb., f. 24, op. 8, d. 437, ll. 13–15, 28, 84.
By this time, such a flagrant violation of the separation of Church and State came as no surprise. Still, such statements in regard to antireligious propaganda were rarely issued by government executive bodies.

[43] *Pskovskii kolkhoznik*, 17 April 1937.

[44] TsGAIPD Spb., f. 24, op. 10, d. 420, l. 54ob; *Pskovskii kolkhoznik*, 6 and 23 April 1938.

[45] *Pskovskii kolkhoznik*, 11 June 1939.

climbing to 5,623 members in 204 cells in late 1938, the claimed number of Godless fell to 3,596 in 161 cells in early 1939. Three months later, membership had recovered to 4,050, but these members were organized in just 89 cells. According to one account, members existed on paper only, neither having membership cards nor paying dues. An editorial in *Pskovskii kolkhoznik* in June added that only two or three of the forty cells in Pskov were in any way active, and that the Pskov City League had not met once since August 1938.[46] The one achievement on the propaganda front in 1939 was the opening of an antireligious museum in the city's Troitskii Sobor, complete with a Foucault pendulum suspended from the ceiling.[47] The League's role in this project, if any, remains unclear, and on Orthodox Christmas 1940, *Pskovskii kolkhoznik* characterized the League in a lead editorial as in a "sorry state."[48] This malaise was not for lack of Party directives. Decisions to strengthen antireligious propaganda were passed by Party committees at the *okrug* and oblast levels on 31 August and 31 December 1939.[49]

The middle of 1940 brought another attempt to organize the Pskov League. The precise impetus for this effort remains unclear, though it may have been connected with the annexation of the nearby Baltic lands in the summer of 1940, including the famed Pechora Monastery, which had survived the depredations of the 1920s and 1930s as Estonian territory.[50] After publication of several newspaper articles on antireligious work, the Pskov Okrug Party passed a resolution on antireligious propaganda in August directing local Party committees to hold League conferences (on a nonwork day) to reelect district councils.[51] The Pskov City-District Council held its conference only in late January 1941, and according to a newspaper account, the participants "noted the total inactivity and placidity of the League City Council."[52] During the Easter season, two more editorials on the need for antireligious propaganda appeared in *Pskovskii kolkhoznik*.[53]

While the League's record in Pskov was utterly monotonous, it differed in some ways from that of Iaroslavl'. The Pskov League offers a view of

---

[46] PPA, f. 3, op. 2, d. 1139, ll. 1–3, 25–28; TsGAIPD Spb., f. 24, op. 10, d. 421, l. 71; *Pskovskii kolkhoznik*, 11 June 1939.

[47] PPA, f. 3, op. 2, d. 1139, l. 28; *Pskovskii kolkhoznik*, 17 September 1939.

[48] *Pskovskii kolkhoznik*, 6 January 1940.

[49] PPA, f. 3, op. 2, d. 1152, l. 5; *Pskovskii kolkhoznik*, 22 May 1940.

[50] See the editorial "Bol'she vnimaniia antireligioznoi propagande," *Krasnaia zvezda*, 8 August 1940.

[51] PPA, f. 3, op. 2, d. 1152, ll. 12–13, 18; *Pskovskii kolkhoznik*, 28 April and 14, 18, and 22 May 1940.

[52] *Pskovskii kolkhoznik*, 2 February 1941.

[53] Ibid., 19 March and 19 April 1941.

relations between the Leningrad Oblast authorities and those of Pskov Okrug. While the Pskov Party was directly subordinate to the Leningrad Obkom, *okrug* status provided it with its own substantial Party apparatus and an intermediate level of social organizations, including the League. While Oblast Party committees had real power and district-level authorities were strictly executive, *okrug* organizations were suspended somewhere between the two. The consequences of this structure for the League appear to have been entirely negative. Although the signals to recreate the Pskov League came from Leningrad, oblast authorities generally took less interest in districts incorporated within *okrugy* than those directly subordinate to the Oblast Party. At the same time, *okrug* authorities often ignored directives from Leningrad. According to a report in July 1939, directives from the Leningrad Oblast Council received in Pskov were "filed, but not fulfilled."[54] The additional level of bureaucracy may also explain why Pskov was a year behind Iaroslavl' in its League revivals. Clearly the "transmission belt" of social organizations from the Communist Party to society was very frayed and performed unevenly throughout the country.[55] Despite the uniform pallor that settled over the Soviet polity, in practice much variety remained.

Antireligion in the Late 1930s

With minor variations, the League's experience in Iaroslavl' and Pskov was a model of the largely unaltered organizational formalism of the League's earlier existence. Other elements of the political culture also remained constant, or sported a gloss that reflected contemporary forms. In particular, the institutional relationships and their rhetorical expression were received nearly intact from the earlier period. Indeed, the League's weaker overall condition provided even greater opportunities for blaming local Party, Komsomol, trade union, and education bodies. A typical report from Iaroslavl' in 1938 criticized Party and Soviet leaders for not understanding the full political import of antireligious work: "individual district party committees . . . adopted a lowest-common-denominator" approach.[56] Not surprisingly, the League found the Komsomol's support

---

[54] TsGAIPD Spb., f. 24, op. 10, d. 421, l. 71.

[55] Alfred G. Meyer, *Communism* (New York: Random House, 1960), 43.

[56] IaPA, f. 272, op. 223, d. 811, ll. 16–17. In Russian, *khvostistskaia liniia.* According to the *Oxford Russian Dictionary, khvostizm* (tailism) is "the limitation of revolutionary aims to those intelligible to backward masses"; in this case it also suggests the tail wagging the dog, that is, the shortcomings of a system in which the masses dictate policy to the vanguard.

wanting, and throughout the mid- and late 1930s, the League Central Council and the Komsomol Central Committee engaged in continuous conflict.[57] The Komsomol's attitude toward the League locally was much simpler: utter indifference. In 1938, *Pskovskii kolkhoznik* quoted a Komsomol official at the Krasnyi Shveinik plant in Pskov as saying that he saw no purpose for the League.[58] Local trade unions seemed no more interested in the League than the Komsomol, and *Pskovskii kolkhoznik*'s lead editorial in early 1941 sounded a sarcastic note when it pointed out that "as strange as it may seem," trade unions had distanced themselves from the League.[59]

Conflicting signals continued to emanate from the center. Even the Komsomol Central Committee's position underwent several transformations as it did battle with the League Central Council.[60] While these clashes remained largely "inside the Moscow Ring Road," to attentive local activists they offered more of the on-again, off-again style of political communication that had characterized the League from its inception. The League's demise in the mid-1930s and the apparently benign indifference toward religion in the Stalin Constitution of 1936 seemed to signal an end to the antireligious campaigns.[61] In August 1936 the Leningrad Oblast League Council even discussed changing the League's name to a milder "Society for Scientific Enlightenment and Antireligious Propaganda."[62] Believers, too, sensed a change. According to a Party report, church attendance in a rural area near Pskov in early 1937 had risen as a result of the new constitution, and believers who earlier feared for their jobs now openly attended church.[63] The would-be liberalism of 1936 was as short-lived as it was deceptive. The burst of political activism and institutional self-justification the following year brought a decisive return to aggressive antireligious propaganda, a resurrected League, arbitrary church closings, and arrests of clergy. By 1938, Iaroslavskii was once again seeking to have the Central Committee issue directives mandating caution in antireligious

---

[57] Alekseev, *Shturm nebes otmeniaetsia?* 138–163.

[58] *Pskovskii kolkhoznik,* 6 April 1938.

[59] Ibid., 19 March 1941.

[60] See Alekseev, *Shturm nebes otmeniaetsia?* 145–152.

[61] Ibid., 148–150; John Shelton Curtiss, *The Russian Church and the Soviet State* (Boston: Little, Brown, 1953), 273–275. See Nicholas Timasheff, *Religion in Soviet Russia* (New York: Sheed & Ward, 1942), 112–132, for more details on what Timasheff labels the regime's "New Religious Policy," a play on words recalling the NEP's softening of previous economic policy. The wartime alliance of the Soviet Union and the United States provides the important context for Timasheff's assertions, made in 1942.

[62] TsGAIPD Spb., f. 24, op. 8, d. 326, l. 219.

[63] PPA, f. 3, op. 2, d. 1102, l. 110.

matters. As in the 1920s, the League wended its way between what it saw as two extremes: total neglect of antireligious propaganda and "excesses" by local activists and Komsomol members.[64] To a greater extent than in the 1920s, of course, the main threat to antireligious propaganda was seen in "opportunistic" neglect.

Neither the League's penury nor its penchant for blaming others for its woes abated in the late 1930s. In the summer of 1938, Iaroslavskii called the League's financial condition "catastrophic," and he protested that, despite Central Committee directives, local Party committees still failed to fund League councils.[65] The pretense of relying on dues long since abandoned, local League councils existed on subsidies from governmental, Party, and trade union authorities, but these subsidies were received far less frequently than they were promised. The situation in Pskov was particularly severe; in 1939, the Pskov Okrug Council repeatedly turned to the Party for assistance after being denied, it charged, its budgeted subsidy from the Okrug Executive Committee of Soviets. (By this time, this shameless violation of the separation of Church and State surprised no one.) In a personal appeal to the first Party secretary, the head of the Pskov League spoke of the League's "hopeless" financial situation.[66]

With the passing of a decade, the League had of course changed, but certain aspects of its political culture remained and were even accentuated in the climate of high Stalinism. First, the League was even more introspective and oriented away from the outside community that it theoretically served. It was even less involved than earlier in the actual suppression of religion, which in this period was almost exclusively an administrative affair, with little effort expended to rally public support. Beginning in 1937, the mostly rural churches that remained open found their clergy arrested or taxed out of their parishes. Their unused churches were then formally closed during the next few years by local authorities citing inactivity or the nonpayment of taxes. The League was nowhere visible in this process. In rural Danilov Region (Iaroslavl' Oblast), twenty-one churches were formally closed between 1937 and 1939 compared to only two from 1929 to 1931. By 1939, of twenty-three churches in Pskov Region, nineteen had been closed and most of their clergy arrested as enemies of the

---

[64] See, for example, Oleshchuk's presentations of incorrect work of both stripes in "Boevye voprosy antireligioznoi propagandy," *Bol'shevik*, 1938, no. 16 (15 August), 28–43, and "Kommunisticheskoe vospitanie mass i preodolenie religioznykh perezhitkov," ibid., 1939, no. 9, 38–49.

[65] RTsKhIDNI, f. 17, op. 114, d. 899, l. 147.

[66] PPA, f. 3, op. 2, d. 1139, ll. 10–12, 18, 20. There is no indication of the final disposition of these requests.

people. Only 950 religious communities remained registered in the entire RSFSR by 1940; the Russian Orthodox Church was at its nadir.[67]

The second distinctive element of the League's political culture in the late 1930s—the rhetorical role of "wreckers" and "enemies of the people"—drew its theme directly from the Great Terror, but again it focused attention within the League and augmented an already strongly rooted tendency toward introspection. This theme was taken up with particular enthusiasm because it could explain the League's (and other institutions') earlier failings. In published propaganda, speeches, and internal reports, the League's checkered past was attributed to enemies of the people who had penetrated League councils. In 1938, Anatolii Lukachevskii, the League's deputy chairman and its de facto administrative head for nearly ten years, was arrested. Oleshchuk, who just barely escaped arrest himself, explained that "owing to the dulling of our revolutionary vigilance, to the absence of self-criticism over a long period of time, the Trotskyist spy Lukachevskii remained in the leadership."[68] Lukachevskii's achievement as a Trotskyist spy was all the more impressive in view of the fact that his direct superior, Iaroslavskii, headed the Party Control Commission, the Party's internal watchdog.

The Leningrad League in late 1937 blamed its failures on the arrested former leadership, including the chairman, Nikolai Matorin, who was charged with being a Zinovievite. As an example of the wreckers' brazenness, one investigation reported that a Godless collective farm in Pskov Okrug had even been named for "the people's enemy Matorin."[69] An investigation in Pskov in February 1939 found a "non-Bolshevik line" that was "explained largely by wrecking, which led to the collapse of the Okrug League organization."[70] The discovery of "wreckers" and "enemies of the people" throughout the League's network provided the rationale to continue demands for assistance. However fantastic, the "enemies" scenario presented a "reasonable" (at the time) explanation for the failure

---

[67] GARF, f. r-6991, op. 1, d. 9, l. 141; PPA, f. 3, op. 2, d. 1139, l. 2. The total number of churches in Pskov Region in this account is less than in earlier reports. M. I. Odintsov, *Religioznye organizatsii v SSSR nakanune i v gody velikoi otechestvennoi voiny, 1941–1945 gg.* (Moscow: Rossiiskaia Akademiia Gosudarstvennoi Sluzhby, 1995). In English, see Nathaniel Davis, *A Long Walk to Church* (Boulder: Westview, 1994), 10–13.

[68] *IV rasshirennyi plenum*, 18. According to Oleshchuk's son, Iaroslavskii intervened at the last minute to prevent Oleshchuk's arrest. Interview with Iurii F. Oleshchuk, Moscow, 25 May 1992.

[69] TsGAIPD Spb., f. 24, op. 10, d. 317, l. 2. There is circumstantial evidence that the former head of the Pskov Okrug League in the 1920s, Ivan Nikitich Sigov, was promoted to the Leningrad Oblast League and was also arrested in 1936.

[70] PPA, f. 3, op. 2, d. 1139, l. 6.

of Bolshevik plans and one that did not challenge the basic structure of the system; it maintained the focus on cadres, now on their political loyalty rather than on their numbers, *peregruzka*, and *perebroska*.[71]

Mediocre Cadres—Irrelevant Labor

Stalin's notorious 1935 statement about cadres ironically was most relevant to the League in the 1920s, when capable agitprop cadres were scarce and the challenge at hand was more evident. By the late 1930s several factors had ameliorated this shortage, at least in quantitative terms. First, after twenty years the Soviet regime had had ample opportunity to produce its own personnel. Second, the limited scope of League propaganda in the late 1930s obviated the need for specialists. This propaganda, as we shall see, was delineated by a few set and simple topics that had little to do with religion, and therefore specialists trained in the history of religion and well versed in the Bible were no longer needed. Finally, in a measure to combat just the sort of bureaucratic growth represented by the League, the Council of People's Commissars in August 1935 prohibited voluntary societies from having paid employees at the district level.[72] A prominent theme in Bolshevik discourse in the 1930s was the battling of bureaucracy, but this move made it all the more improbable that the League could be recreated as an organization that had defined itself in terms of such cadres. Trying to cast this restriction of bureaucracy in a positive light, the Leningrad Oblast League commented that the previous system of paid workers had undermined the "principle of public involvement [*obshchestvennost'*] in the work of our voluntary society."[73] Although cadres were no longer the central issue for the League, the individuals working for the later League still posed an obstacle to the realization of Bolshevik plans.

Not surprisingly, there were even fewer professional propagandists in the mid- to late 1930s than there had been a decade earlier. Now the Party directed secondary agitprop cadres (museum workers, teachers, trade union officials) to run League councils. Moreover, the League's normally

---

[71] For more on the use of conspiracies to explain why things did not work as planned, see Gabor Tamas Rittersporn, "The Omnipresent Conspiracy: On Soviet Imagery of Politics and Social Relations in the 1930s," in *Stalinism: Its Nature and Aftermath: Essays in Honor of Moshe Lewin*, ed. Gabor Rittersporn and Nick Lampert (Armonk, N.Y.: M. E. Sharpe, 1992), 101–120.

[72] TsGAIPD Spb., f. 24, op. 8, d. 326, l. 204; N. Z., "Perestroika raboty SVB v sviazi s uprazdneniem platnykh rabotnikov v raionakh," *Antireligioznik*, 1935, no. 5, 42–43.

[73] TsGAIPD Spb., f. 24, op. 8, d. 326, l. 204.

high turnover was aggravated by the turbulent times. The League in Iaroslavl' had no fewer than four (possibly five) chairmen and three executive secretaries; Pskov had at least four leaders between 1937 and 1940. The first Iaroslavl' chairman was Mikhail Popov, a professional Godless from Ivanovo who had been deputy head of the Ivanovo League in the late 1920s and early 1930s. At the time of his appointment, he worked as the Iaroslavl' correspondent for the newspaper *Za industrializatsiiu* (For Industrialization). He was appointed chairman of the Oblast Orgbiuro in July 1936, but in early 1937 he was transferred to Kostroma to serve as editor of the local newspaper. He was arrested by the NKVD in July 1937.[74]

The first executive secretary of the revived Iaroslavl' League was Viktor Mikhailovich Kovalev, who had been active in the Iaroslavl' Uezd League in the late 1920s. In July 1936 he was transferred from a trade union position on the Volga docks to the post of oblast League executive secretary. In November he moved to the local history museum, though he remained an instructor for the League through 1938. At the League's October 1937 conference, Kovalev was denounced for wrecking, but his association with the League continued. From 1938 until the outbreak of the war, he was director of the Iaroslavl' Antireligious Museum in the Il'ia Prorok Church.[75]

The conference in October 1937 brought the "election" of a new chairman, Aleksandr Dmitrievich Antamonov. Before coming to the League, Antamonov had worked in various Party propaganda positions in Iaroslavl', including that of deputy editor of *Severnyi rabochii*. In June 1938, the oblast Party appointed him to work full-time in the League, but the following year, Antamonov resumed work for the oblast Party as a lecturer.[76] At the same October (1937) conference, a former trade union official, Konstantin Evlamplievich Anan'ev, was elected executive secretary of the oblast League; he had earlier headed the League's council in the Kirov District of Iaroslavl'. As executive secretary, Anan'ev traveled to Moscow in January 1938 to give an account of the Iaroslavl' League and to attend the League's Fourth Plenum the following month. Anan'ev's association with the League ended in August 1939.[77] For at least part of 1939, Pavel

---

[74] Biographical abstract, IaPA; IaPA, f. 272, op. 223, d. 21, l. 6; f. 273, op. 68, d. 267, l. 286; *Severnyi rabochii*, 23 September 1936.

[75] Biographical abstract, IaPA; IaPA, f. 272, op. 223, d. 19, l. 14, and d. 21, l. 6; f. 273, op. 68, d. 267, l. 286.

[76] Biographical abstract, IaPA; IaPA, f. 272, op. 223, d. 811, l. 18; *Severnyi rabochii*, 28 October 1937.

[77] Biographical abstract, IaPA; IaPA, f. 276, op. 1, d. 244, ll. 131, 139; GARF, f. r-5407, op. 1, d. 107, l. 151.

Ivanovich Korkin, a teacher at Krasnyi Perekop, served as League chairman. Korkin had been active in the League over a decade earlier, having served briefly on the provincial council and as secretary of the Second District Council.[78] Korkin's immediate replacement, if there was one, remains unknown, but in May 1940, Gennadii Vasilievich Glazunov became League chairman, a position he held until April 1941. Glazunov ran a workers' club in Iaroslavl' from August 1939 to May 1940, when he assumed two concurrent positions, in the MOPR Obkom and as chairman of the League council.[79]

We know little about the Pskov League's leaders beyond their names. Aleksandr Ivanovich Gorshkov, a teacher and Party propagandist, was appointed chairman of the *okrug* organizational bureau on 20 January 1938. Several years earlier, he had served briefly as director of the Antireligious Correspondence Institute in Leningrad. He remained chairman until October (the first Pskov League conference), when he returned to full-time Party work.[80] Gorshkov was succeeded by Aleksandr Mikhailovich Shkaradnykh, who was "elected" chairman in October 1938.[81] Another activist, A. I. Nikitin, was visible as a contributor of newspaper articles throughout much of the late 1930s, and he was identified as chairman in 1940. At the time, Nikitin worked in the Pskov Okrug education authority.[82]

Clearly there were little continuity of leadership. Not only were the former League leaders gone, the local full-time staff also were absent. Only Kovalev, Korkin, and Konstantin Karasev provided any connection to the past. Popov was the only "professional" Godless, but he came from another city. With the exception of Antamonov and Popov, the later Godless were all teachers and trade union officials—that is, secondary or tertiary cadres in the Bolshevik hierarchy. This generation of League leaders, nevertheless, was better educated than its predecessors, at least formally. Several—Korkin (1932–1936), Shkaradnykh (1927–1930), and Gorshkov (1931–1935)—had received training at the Krupskaia Institute in Leningrad. Antamonov had attended the Soviet Party school in Vladimir from 1927 to 1929 and the Iaroslavl' Pedagogical Institute from 1930 to 1934. Glazunov studied at the Higher Trade Union School in Leningrad.

Although the Soviet system of preparing political cadres had overcome some of its previous haphazardness, it was far from perfected. Kovalev's

[78] Biographical abstract, IaPA; IaPA, f. 261, op. 1, d. 247, l. 100.
[79] Biographical abstract, IaPA. MOPR was one of the few other voluntary societies to survive into the late 1930s.
[80] PPA, f. 3, op. 2, d, 1139, ll. 25–28; op. 3, d. 325.
[81] Ibid., op. 3, d. 1328.
[82] Ibid., op. 2, d. 1139, l. 6; d. 1152, l. 17.

formal education consisted only of primary school and political literacy training,[83] and the leader of the Iaroslavl' District League in late 1938, M. I. Kotovskii, spent three years at a rural grammar school and six months at the Briansk Forestry Institute. Moreover, extensive education was certainly no guarantee of quality. Anan'ev had studied for several years in Moscow at the Central Textile School and the Higher Trade Union School (in a course for propagandists), yet a report in 1941 ridiculed his performance as a lecturer: "Lacking not only specialized but also sufficient general preparation, [having been] assigned to lecture on 'sleep and dreams,' he caused such a scandal that he was no longer permitted to lecture on this topic."[84] Incidental information on another low-level activist, Grigorii Domashnyi, who headed the Iaroslavl' League's lecture bureau from September 1939 to May 1941, suggests continuing basic quality problems with the newly minted Soviet intelligentsia. Domashnyi's education amounted to a rural grammar school and occasional short-term training courses, and an investigation in 1941 criticized the "extremely low ideological-theoretical level" of his bureau's lecturers. It cited a specific incident in which Domashnyi appeared before a conference of teachers and spoke such "nonsense" that he was forced to apologize.[85]

These colorless individuals represented the norm for antireligious propagandists in the late 1930s. They were characterized by high turnover, limited education, and a narrow operating scope. *Severnyi rabochii* put it succinctly in 1941: "Those recommended to work in the district League council are, as a rule, incompetent in antireligious work, and uninterested in it."[86] To some degree, the constraints on antireligious activists and their own abilities roughly corresponded: they were mediocre cadres engaged in irrelevant labor. Into the late 1930s, the lack of high-quality cadres underscored the tremendous gap that still existed between the expectations within Bolshevik political culture—that the League's network would be staffed by able propagandists—and a Soviet political landscape that remained poor in competent activists. This poverty was only worsened by the Terror, which struck disproportionately among well-educated cadres and therefore guaranteed the limits on the regime's abilities.

[83] Biographical abstract, IaPA.

[84] IaPA, f. 272, op. 224, d. 142, l. 45.

[85] Biographical abstract, IaPA; IaPA, f. 272, op. 224, d. 142, ll. 44–45. In an interview in the village of Kurba, Iaroslavl' Oblast, 19 May 1992, Domashnyi claimed to have headed his village's postwar committee to protect historical and cultural monuments, and in that capacity to have helped preserve the local church.

[86] *Severnyi rabochii*, 18 January 1941.

The one exception to the late League's bland fare was Konstantin Evlamplievich Karasev. In the late 1930s, Karasev was well into his sixties and among the oldest League officials in the country. Karasev had worked as a zemstvo bureaucrat in Iaroslavl' before serving in the tsarist army in World War I. After the Revolution, Karasev occupied a series of increasingly high-level local Party and Soviet administrative positions, including three years as head of an NKVD youth labor colony in the mid-1930s. Karasev's League experience was extensive but intermittent. From 1925 to 1929, he served as the head of agitprop for the Party in Poshekhon'e-Volodar'e Uezd (Iaroslavl' Province), and in that capacity, he attended League conferences in Iaroslavl' in 1926 and 1928. His association with the League was resumed in November 1936, when the Iaroslavl' Party appointed him executive secretary of the Oblast Council. He was either replaced in October 1937 or moved to another job within the League, but in August 1939 he returned to his former position, and he remained there until April 1941.

What distinguished Karasev was not only his age but also his religious background. He wrote in 1936 in his Party autobiography that around the turn of the century,

> in search of truth, I was attracted to religious-philosophical teachings. Under the influence of Warsaw gold-tongues [*zlatoustov*]—Orthodox missionaries on one side and life's contradictions, evil's foulness, deceptions, vulgarities, and the other charms of capitalist society on the other side, . . . I became a strong believer in God. . . . Arming myself with God's word, I devoted myself to serving society and hapless people. . . . I went to the oppressed . . . to the hurt. . . . I did not have to go far. All of Russia was one hungry house.

Karasev lived in the countryside "as an independent artist, teaching not in school but in the peasant hut, teaching the word of God, not in church but on the street." As Karasev wandered through Tver Province, people began to call him holy. Hiding to avoid the draft, Karasev began his transformation: "On pilgrimage, I wandered on foot from churches to monasteries, and carrying out my mother's wish, I visited the 'holy' cloister of Serafim of Sarov. Having seen enough priestly vileness [*popovskie merzosti*], base religious-monastic machinations, and not finding anywhere the presence of God's works, I became an atheist—an active Godless."[87] With this background, Karasev was certainly qualified for his work in the League,

[87] IaSA, f. 3362, op. 1, d. 4, ll. 89–96, 169–174; f. 272, op. 35, d. 5283.

but his past cannot fully explain his shift to a position that everyone knew was thankless and without prospects. Karasev's transfer may have served as a minor demotion during turbulent times; more likely, however, is the simple explanation that the sixty-four-year-old Karasev was given an undemanding sinecure before retirement.

High Stalinist Propaganda

The League's propaganda in the late 1930s was as uninteresting as its activist core, but it revealed how the League sought to retain its sense of purpose. Unlike the number of open churches or active clergy (greatly reduced by this time), the threat posed by "remnants" was not so easily incorporated into the League's activities. Instead, the League-printed materials provided a steady diet of basic science, archaeology, reports on faraway places (the cultural developments of Buriat-Mongolia), and lots of ancient history ("antireligious themes in popular culture" based on medieval limericks).[88] Reflecting the League's generally low standing, its propaganda efforts in this period were limited strictly to the Christmas and Easter seasons, and the forms were reduced from the bewildering complexity of the late 1920s to the simplest: lectures and discussions. The number of lectures delivered and the claimed size of the audiences served as the framework for League accounts of antireligious propaganda activity.

The general political climate also placed limitations on the League's activities. Whereas the late 1920s had offered a new campaign a week, a decade later a handful of overall themes set the tone for all propaganda ventures. Beyond the regular panegyrics to Stalin's insightful analysis of religion or homage to the beloved Kirov,[89] there were discussions of the Stalin Constitution (1936), the elections to the soviets (1937–1939), the purges (1936–1938), Stalin's *Short Course* (1938–1939), and the defense of the Soviet Union (1936–1941). The League necessarily kept close to these subjects and presented them with a gloss of relevance and self-justification. During the election campaigns, for instance, League propaganda focused

---

[88] B. Kandidov, "Rost kul'tury i bezbozhiia v Buriat-Mongolii," *Bezbozhnik*, 1936, no. 3, 10; D. Tret'iakov, "Antireligioznye motivy v narodnom tvorchestve," ibid., 1939, no. 7, 13.

[89] For example, P. Fedoseev, "Tovarishch Stalin o bor'be s religiei," *Bezbozhnik,* 1939, no. 6, 4–6, and his "Stalin o religii," ibid., no. 7, 4–6; M. Shakhnovich, "S. M. Kirov protiv tsaria i religii," ibid., 1940, nos. 7–8, 2–4. Other atheistic heroes profiled included Stakhanov, Gorky, and Pushkin: "A. G. Stakhanov o religii," ibid., 1936, no. 3; E. Iaroslavskii, "Gorkii byl velikim ateistom," ibid., no. 7, 3, and "Ateizm A. S. Pushkina," ibid., no. 12, 11–15.

on keeping clergy and active laity from being elected to the soviets. A League propagandist reported that a priest arrested in 1937 for counter-revolutionary activity in Siberia had admitted that he had dreamed that Bukharin and Aleksei Rykov would come to power, but after their arrest, he had decided to pursue his goals "from below."[90] On its front and rear covers, the journal *Bezbozhnik* depicted Orthodox clergy, Old Believers, and sectarians trying to enter the local soviet and being denied.[91] In a radio address, Iaroslavskii cited a supposed episode in a rural council of Iaroslavl' Oblast where local religious leaders held a mock election for their candidates.[92]

Clergy and sectarians were regularly depicted as counterrevolutionaries, and often as the agents of fascist powers.[93] According to a writer in *Izvestiia* in late 1937, "numerous incidents testify to the fact that church and sectarian leaders more and more are linked to the foreign intelligence services of fascist countries and enter their service, acting hand in hand with Trotskyists, Bukharinists, and other swine."[94] Attacks on Nazi Germany, including a contrast between the Christmas tree (*elka*) recently reintroduced to Soviet Russia and the German *Tannenbaum*,[95] were a central theme of this discourse until the autumn of 1939, when the attacks abruptly disappeared. The threat of unidentified foreign conspirators remained, however, and *Bezbozhnik* suggested that crosses beside the roads in western Ukraine had been put there as guideposts for unnamed foreign enemies.[96]

The League's propaganda in the late 1930s was perhaps more revealing than its creators intended. Repeated commentary on the threat to kolkhozes from religion suggested that the Church remained a cultural force in the countryside nearly a decade after collectivization. In many cases, accounts were little changed from twenty years earlier. The journal *Bezbozhnik* reported that the kolkhoz farmers in one rural district had spent four days celebrating the holidays of Ascension and Nikola.[97] Another account "explained" yet again Joshua's miracle of halting the sun.[98] The number of antireligious lectures also indicated that the regime continued to regard religion as a major issue. District Party committees in the late

[90] F. M. Putintsev, *Vybory v sovety i razoblachenie popovshchiny* (Moscow: OGIZ/GAIZ, 1938), 36.
[91] *Bezbozhnik*, 1937, no. 6, 13, front cover of no. 7, rear cover of no. 11.
[92] Ibid., no. 8, 2–8. See also "Dadim otpor proiskam popv i sektantov," ibid., 13–15.
[93] *Pskovskii kolkhoznik*, 15 November 1937.
[94] A. Iurin, "Tserkovniki i sektanty na sluzhbe fashizma," *Izvestiia*, 22 November 1937, 4.
[95] "Elka v fashistskoi germanii," *Bezbozhnik*, 1936, no.12, 17.
[96] I. Kryvelev in *Bezbozhnik*, 1940, nos. 11–12, 6–7.
[97] P. Kashirin, "K novym pobedam kolkhoznogo stroia," *Bezbozhnik*, 1939, no. 7, 2–3.
[98] G. Gurev, "Chudo iisusa navina," *Bezbozhnik*, 1938, nos. 8–9, 16.

"You are waiting in vain at the church door, priest. We live wonderfully without icons and God!": Moscow, 1939. (The Hoover Institution Archives, Poster Collection, RU/SU 1829.)

1930s regularly forwarded up the chain of command the number of lectures delivered, their topics, and the sizes of their audiences. These reports placed religion among the regime's most prominent propaganda themes, particularly in the countryside. The Ermakov District Party (Iaroslavl' Oblast) claimed that during 1940 its staff had delivered fourteen antireligious lectures (for a combined audience of 593), fourteen on Stalin's *Short Course* (for 958) and twenty-eight on the Soviet Union's international situation (for 2,256). For roughly the same period in rural Poshekhone-Volodar'e, sixty-three lectures were read on the international situation, sixty-four on the history of the Party, forty-nine on antireligious themes (mostly in April), and a total of forty on other topics. These numbers meant little—it was common practice to exaggerate the size of the audience and even the number of lectures delivered—but antireligious work was still the only such social concern to be included in the agitprop lecture repertoire.[99] In other ways as well, the bland fare of the late 1930s revealed how far the regime still had to go to create its ideal countryside. An

[99] IaPA, f. 272, op. 223, d. 177, l. 30; f. 261, op. 1, d. 360, ll. 9, 14.

antireligious training guide for Party and Red Army propagandists issued in 1940 still covered the basics: evolution, the solar system, the weather, rudimentary science, primitive Marxism, the threat of sectarianism. It was as if twenty-five years of socialization had not advanced the population's ideological benchmark, so the regime was starting over again.[100]

The League of the Godless and Stalinism

Why did the League return in the late 1930s? The existing literature largely sidesteps the issue. John Shelton Curtiss does little more than note the League's rise in membership, while V. A. Alekseev keeps close to the Komsomol/League conflict. G. V. Vorontsov neatly ends his study in 1937, as if to declare victory and retreat. Dimitry Pospielovsky treats the 1930s as one period, and even writes that 1937 represented a downturn in the League's fortunes.[101] One thing is certain: Despite the regime's rediscovery of religion, the League was not really expected to overcome it. As an agency of social transformation, the League was poorly suited for this task and had proved so over many years. Given its record, no one, not even Iaroslavskii, could seriously have thought that the League's revitalization would have a significant impact on the dissemination of atheism. As for religion, the regime resorted without hesitation to direct methods of suppression.

Just as the League's initial growth reflected the foment of the Cultural Revolution, so the League's return was a manifestation of renewed instability in the late 1930s. Yet this period of turmoil was not linked to comprehensive social transformation, and therefore the League's role is less clear than it was during the Cultural Revolution of 1928–1931. The traditional explanation of the Great Terror as Stalin's attempt to remove all possible competitors provides a role for the League as an instrument of vigilance. However useful, if only on a symbolic level, the League may have been for finding "enemies," in practical terms it *was* the enemy: the League lived off the bloated bureaucracy that was the object of persecution from above and below. The revisionist characterization of the purges

---

[100] *Programma po antireligioznomu samoobrazovaniiu partiino-politicheskikh rabotnikov i propagandistov Krasnoi Armii* (Moscow: Voenizdat, 1940).
[101] Curtiss, *Russian Church and the Soviet State*, 279; Alekseev, *Shturm nebes otmeniaetsia?*; G. V. Vorontsov, *Leninskaia programma ateisticheskogo vospitaniia v deistvii* (Leningrad: Leningradskii Gosudarstvennyi Universitet, 1973); Dimitry V. Pospielovsky, *A History of Marxist-Leninist Atheism and Soviet Anti-religious Policies*, vol. 1 (New York: St. Martin's Press, 1987), 65.

as a "wave of popular radicalism" that included elements of ideological renewal reflecting the influence of Andrei Zhdanov also offered a niche for the League.[102] In this period of cultural conservatism, however, the League's social militancy existed in name only. Yes, churches were again closed and clergy arrested, but this was an exercise in power, not cultural transformation. While the League's revival suggested an effort by the regime to create an ideological framework for the purges, the effort seemed halfhearted, and the result was, characteristically, bureaucratic and lacking in substance. Atheism and other high-visibility topics in the 1930s, such as Stakhanovism, Soviet polar exploration, and Soviet achievements in aviation, served to justify the operation of power politics below, or at a minimum to distract public attention from it.

Whatever its origins, the League's return illuminated fundamental aspects of the Bolshevik political process in the late 1930s. Institutional conflict remained at the fore. The League still defined and justified itself in terms of what other institutions (the Party, Komsomol, trade unions, education authorities) were not doing in regard to antireligious propaganda. In particular, antireligious propaganda and its failings were employed as a stick, or rather more a twig, in the battle of the League and Komsomol to manifest their zeal. Here a good offense of criticism was the best defense.[103] The rhetoric of indictment remained structured so that the actual institutions themselves were rarely faulted. It was the traitorous wreckers within who were blamed—once again the focus was on cadres. The way to deal with an ineffective League council was to label its members "wreckers" and appoint new ones. In the late 1930s this chronic form of interaction fed off of and contributed to the frenzy of incrimination that was the Great Terror. In the absence of a substantial, organized religious opposition, the later League revealed its essence: a series of bureaucratic interactions internal to the Bolshevik polity, an ephemeral entity operating narrowly within existing bureaucratic boundaries.

---

[102] Getty, *Origins of the Great Purges*. See also Sheila Fitzpatrick, "How the Mice Buried the Cat: Scenes from the Great Purges of 1937 in the Russian Provinces," *Russian Review* 52, no. 3 (July 1993): 299–320.

[103] Oleg Khlevniuk narrates a similar conflict between the NKVD and the party in *1937-i: Stalin, NKVD, Sovetskoe obshchestvo* (Moscow: Respublika, 1992), 229.

Epilogue and Conclusion

The German attack on the Soviet Union in June 1941 brought an immediate end to the public activities of the Militant Godless. The Central Council ceased publication of its various journals, and most local League councils disappeared for the final time.[1] Iaroslavskii continued to serve the Party as a high-level official and propagandist until his death of natural causes in 1943, at the age of sixty-five. While the League receded, the Orthodox Church quickly gained a higher profile.[2] Numerous churches in Soviet-controlled regions reopened (as did many in German-occupied areas), some clergy returned to their former positions, and public displays of religious patriotism were permitted, though not exactly encouraged. Stalin even met with the leading hierarchs of the Russian Orthodox Church in September 1943 and permitted the convening of a Church

---

[1] Throughout the war, a skeleton staff of the Central Council delivered patriotic lectures and chronicled the religious revival. Minimal League operations with similar functions existed in a number of Russian cities.

[2] The literature in English on the Russian Orthodox Church during the war is very limited, but Russian scholars are beginning to discuss the period in greater detail. See M. I. Odintsov, ed., *Religioznye organizatsii v SSSR nakanune i v gody Velikoi otechestvennoi voiny, 1941–1945* (Moscow: Rossiiskaia Akademiia Gosudarstvennoi Sluzhby, 1995); M. A. Vyltsan, "Prikaz i propoved': Sposoby mobilizatsii resursov derevni v gody voiny," *Otechestvennaia istoriia*, 1995, no. 3, 69–80; Protoierei Vladislav Tsypin, "Patrioticheskoe sluzhenie russkoi pravoslavnoi tserkvi v Velikuiu Otechestvennuiu Voinu," *Novaia i noveishaia istoriia*, 1995, no. 2, 41–47; M. V. Shkarovskii, "V ogne voiny: Russkaia pravoslavnaia tserkov' v 1941–1945 gg. (po materialam Leningradskoi eparkhii)," *Russkoe proshloe*, 1994, no. 5, 259–316. In English, see Wassilij Alexeev and Theofanis G. Stavrou, *The Great Revival: The Russian Church under German Occupation* (Minneapolis: Burgess, 1976); Harvey Fireside, *Icon and Swastika: The Russian Orthodox Church under Nazi and Soviet Control* (Cambridge: Harvard University Press, 1971).

council that elected Metropolitan Sergei as patriarch. In foreign policy matters, the Orthodox Church soon became an active junior ally of the regime. Toleration of the Orthodox Church continued in the immediate postwar period and Church officials, including the newly elected Patriarch Aleksei, were visible in Soviet propaganda efforts abroad.

The regime's own propaganda apparatus remained muted in regard to antireligious matters. A Central Committee resolution of 1944 on propaganda spoke only of the need to overcome "remnants of ignorance, superstition, and prejudice."[3] While the central Komsomol apparatus took an increasingly aggressive stance toward religion in the late 1940s,[4] the tenor and scope of official antireligious propaganda efforts remained muted as long as Stalin lived.[5] The League's juridical successor, the All-Union Society for the Dissemination of Political and Scientific Knowledge—known as the Knowledge Society (Obshchestvo Znaniia)—was created in 1947, but its mandate was broad and it did not at first pursue antireligious propaganda vigorously.[6]

This attitude of diffused hostility toward religion lasted until Khrushchev launched a fierce new attack in 1959.[7] Churches and monasteries were again closed, religious instruction was sharply curtailed, and new restrictions were placed on parishes and clergy. In 1960, the Knowledge Society began publication of *Nauka i religiia* (Science and Religion), a journal near in spirit to *Bezbozhnik* and *Antireligioznik*. Khrushchev's replacement by Brezhnev in 1964 ended this cycle of religious persecution, and during the Brezhnev era, the Orthodox Church was again minimally tolerated.[8] The major exceptions were religious activists among the dissidents, who were persecuted in the 1970s and early 1980s.

The postwar antireligious propaganda efforts differed sharply from those of the 1920s and 1930s. Except during the years from 1959 to 1964, the regime's antireligious propaganda was less virulent and focused on

---

[3] John Shelton Curtiss, *The Russian Church and the Soviet State* (Boston: Little, Brown, 1953), 302–303.

[4] Alekseev, *Shturm nebes otmeniaetsia?* 200–208.

[5] Curtiss, *Russian Church and the Soviet State,* 304–326. The campaign against Jews in the late 1940s is a notable exception, but it may be seen as more ethnic than antireligious in motivation.

[6] The League was officially disbanded by the same Sovnarkom decree of 1947 that created the Knowledge Society. MIR, f. 29, op. 1, d. 5, ll. 1–2.

[7] Khrushchev mounted a short-lived attack on religion soon after coming to power in 1954. After one hundred days, this campaign was called off, apparently because of widespread popular discontent. See John Anderson, *Religion, State and Politics in the Soviet Union and Successor States* (Cambridge: Cambridge University Press, 1994), 6–67.

[8] Ibid., 68–136.

long-term development rather than immediate social transformation. Perhaps the most important distinction from our perspective is that the Bolshevik leadership no longer felt the need for an entirely separate organization to promote atheism. Perhaps having learned from the experience of the League, the Communist Party (and the Komsomol) directly took charge of promoting atheism. The regime was sufficiently established to do without the services of nonparty activists or to need organizational manifestations of socialism's success that introduced only confusion and conflict into the process of social engineering.

What, then, was the League's ultimate significance in the Bolshevik battle against religion? As noted in the Introduction, several methodological difficulties stand in the way of isolating the League's contribution from the other pressures brought to bear on religion. First, the regime's determination to counter religion by all means possible blurred the distinction between administrative policy and explicit propaganda measures. The initial legislation against the Church, the nominally disinterested investigations of reliquaries, the prosecution of Church leaders on trumped-up charges, and the encouragement of the Renovationist Church—these early measures served propaganda purposes in addition to their primary goal of undermining the Orthodox Church as an institution. The same problem arose at the end of the 1920s when the Party adopted a policy of forcibly closing churches and arresting clergy. The demographic upheaval resulting from the regime's concomitant policy of forced collectivization and rapid industrialization also created tremendous obstacles to the maintenance of stable religious communities. The overlap of the efforts to weaken religion and to promote atheism might make examining the League's role seem artificial, especially given its organizational impotence. This view, however, discounts the Communist Party's repeated efforts to support the League. It also ignores the manifest importance of propaganda and its organizational forms in Bolshevik political culture. Moreover, the League was distinguished from those other forces by virtue of nominally fulfilling a constructive role—the promotion of atheism, not just the demolition of Orthodoxy. The League's mere existence contributed, if only symbolically, to the atmosphere of radical cultural creation characteristic of the Soviet Union in the 1920s and 1930s.

Second, any quantitative assessment of the level of religious belief is problematic. While local authorities kept close account of the membership of individual sectarian groups, the State had no way of accurately measuring loyalty toward Orthodoxy in the population at large. The census of January 1937 included a question on religion—whether the respondent was a believer or a nonbeliever—but even now that those numbers have become available,[9] they do not do justice to the complexity of the issue, for there were many intermediate positions, even among Communists, between the would-be opposites of religious belief and militant atheism. These were categories—words—imposed on people from without (even if later internalized) that rarely corresponded to the way people lived their lives. Moreover, despite the rather open discussion of religion during 1936, respondents did not necessarily answer the question on the 1937 census honestly. An answer could have been interpreted as a statement of political support or opposition to the regime, quite distinct from an individual's genuine feelings about religion.

Despite these caveats, the census numbers still testify to the distance remaining before a completely atheistic society was attained. Of the reported adult population (over age fifteen) of 98,410,000 in 1937, only some 42,243,000, or 42.9 percent, stated that they were nonbelievers.[10] Although these numbers remained secret at the time, Iaroslavskii did publicly acknowledge that a large percentage of the population retained religious beliefs. In November 1937, he claimed that one-third of the rural population and two-thirds of the urban population—far less than half the total population—had become atheists.[11] Paradoxically, Soviet expansion in 1939 and 1940 brought millions of new believers, many of them Orthodox, into the Soviet orbit. The religious renaissance that accompanied the regime's final demise beginning in the late 1980s offers further evidence—even if this recrudescence has proved uneven—that the effort to engineer an atheistic society was a failure.

Although the extent of secularization in the 1920s and 1930s remains uncertain, it clearly had little to do with the organization specifically created to promote atheism. While one might reasonably argue that the message of atheism as an essentially hollow negation of religion could not be dictated to an entire population or be sustained as a mass outlook, the League's failure casts doubt on the capability of government-sponsored propaganda to transform the beliefs of the majority of society in a thorough, persuasive, and enduring manner. The parallel efforts of the Mexican revolutionaries to counter Catholicism in the 1930s also yielded unim-

---

[9] Iu. A. Poliakov, Ia. E. Vodarskii, V. B. Zhiromskaia, and I. N. Kiselev, eds., *Vsesoiuznaia perepis' naseleniia 1937: Kratkie itogi* (Moscow: Akademiia Nauk, 1991). On Stalin's insistence that this question be on the census in direct violation of Soviet law, see A. Berezin, "Iz vsekh ofitsial'nykh aktov," *Nauka i religiia*, 1990, no. 2, 17.

[10] *Vsesoiuznaia perepis' naseleniia*, 106–107.

[11] E. Iaroslavskii, "Antireligioznuiu propagandu nado vesti sistematicheski," *Antireligioznik*, 1937, no. 11, 2.

pressive results.[12] Even the vaunted Nazi propaganda machine may have been less effective than previously imagined.[13] The failure of one aspect of the Bolshevik ideological program did not, of course, preclude success in other important areas, such as the eradication of illiteracy, the establishment of primary education, and basic political indoctrination, but it does qualify the depth of Soviet achievements. The regime's propaganda organs were far from successful in convincing the population of the guilt of many "enemies of the people," for instance.[14]

Early in the Soviet period, the Bolshevik propaganda state may have been effective for a society still enthusiastic about the possibilities of creating a just society, but that honeymoon period was short, leaving a bureaucratic legacy of competing institutions and official discourses.[15] Indeed, atheism as a worldview probably suffered from its association with the impotent, bureaucratized League and the "hooliganish" Komsomol, to the extent that those individuals sympathetic to the issue may not have been willing to express their agreement through these regime-sanctioned vehicles. Make no mistake: many millions who might have believed in God under a continuation of the Old Regime lost their faith in this period; others found faith in Stalin or socialism, or in nothing at all. The League, however, played no substantial role in these developments.

Although the extent of secularization in the 1920s and 1930s can only be conjectured, the possible sources for it lie beyond the League. The damage to the Orthodox Church as an institution and as a network of visible clergy and churches certainly was important. Perhaps more decisive was the general transformation of Soviet society in those decades. The reconstruction of quotidian existence for millions of Soviet citizens challenged the traditional order and provided little space for religion, even for the "modernized" sectarians and Renovationists. The movement to the cities; the creation of new communities in which churches were never built and in which clergy were rarely, if ever, seen; the absence of structured religious education and its replacement by a secular, if not always militantly atheistic, education; the new culture of the radio and the airplane—all

---

[12] Adrian A. Bantjes, "Burning Saint, Molding Minds: Iconoclasm, Civic Ritual, and the Failed Cultural Revolution," in *Rituals of Rule, Rituals of Resistance: Public Celebrations and Popular Culture in Mexico*, ed. William H. Beezley, Cheryl Martin, and William French (Wilmington, Del.: SR Books, 1994), 261–284.

[13] David Welch, *The Third Reich: Politics and Propaganda* (London: Routledge, 1993).

[14] See Oleg Khlevniuk, *1937-i: Stalin, NKVD, i sovetskoe obshchestvo* (Moscow: Respublika, 1992).

[15] Peter Kenez, *The Birth of the Propaganda State* (Cambridge: Cambridge University Press, 1985). The early focus of Kenez's study obscures the later outcome.

these things competed for the private and public spaces once occupied in large part by Orthodox and popular religious culture. The presence of icons in many Soviet apartments and homes through the 1930s testified to continued religious belief, but not at its former level of visibility.[16] Ironically, the effort to engineer secularization in Russia coincided with a period of flourishing religious expression in Western Europe after a century of apparent religious decline.[17]

The League's very failure to achieve its direct aims nevertheless illuminates salient features of Bolshevik political culture. The League reflected the Bolsheviks' bureaucratic manner of envisioning, executing, and measuring social change—whether secularization or the numerous other forms of modernization launched by the regime. But how else, a reasonable person might ask, would one track the implementation of a social policy if not by some form of empirical accounting? In the League's case, the real question is one of degree and meaning. At a certain point the numbers became more than just a neutral means of expressing social change and became an end in themselves: antireligion. The League and the interpretation of social transformation it represented crossed the point beyond which quantitative representations of social transformation lost their direct significance.

The League of the Militant Godless also provides clear evidence of the stress that Bolshevik political culture placed on a uniform standard of organizational development, even at the expense of the organization's activities. The League was expected to mimic the Party's nationwide network by engaging in a wide array of centrally sanctioned activities. Down to the district level, League councils were to have research departments, international sectors, sections working with other voluntary societies, divisions tracking sects, and so on. The atmosphere of antireligion was one of an administrative all-or-nothing, in which the League often existed in elaborate forms only on paper, if at all. (Ironically, the homogenization of political and social practices—at least officially—militated against secularization, which is usually associated with the diversification of everyday experiences.)

A direct consequence of this orientation was a tendency to view the League not from the perspective of what it had achieved but according to how short it fell from Bolshevik high standards. The gap between the League's organizational expectations and its reality compelled it not to articulate more realistic organizational goals, but instead to demand addi-

---

[16] Hoover Institution Archives, Harvard Interview Project of Soviet Refugees, Boxes 1–15, Schedule A Interviews, Question F–4.

[17] In France, for example, see Eugen Weber, *The Hollow Years* (New York: Norton, 1994), 186–206.

tional support from the Communist Party and other institutions. These supplications were part of the larger context of institutional conflict that was a central aspect of Bolshevik political culture (glossed over by ideological interpretations of the Soviet polity). Studies of Bolshevik administration, now made easier by greater access to source materials, need to redress this imbalance.[18]

The League's constant exasperation over its inability to find and retain high-quality activists highlights the role played by cadres in the Bolsheviks' plans for social modernization. As commodities in high demand, cadres were the linchpin of the League's existence, and the unending search for cadres and efforts to retain them displaced propaganda activities as the League's first priority in the 1920s. The absence of such cadres also provided a ready explanation for the League's failings. The League was not alone in this regard. Given the labor-intensive nature of many early Bolshevik propaganda campaigns, finding enough high-quality cadres was a pressing concern throughout the Bolshevik world. In the process of serving this need, the line between means and end in the creation of the New Soviet Man became blurred.

Language played a critical role in Bolshevik political culture, and not just as a medium to describe institutions such as the League. A highly stylized rhetoric served as a high ground in the competition for legitimacy and resources. This rhetoric became a nearly autonomous sphere of activity that only partly reflected the material conditions of "objective reality." The world of official rhetoric was expressed in an endless series of resolutions, investigations, charges of deviation, criticisms of other institutions, and other everyday political communications—all of which formed a comprehensive internal discourse. In this world, challenges were defined and redefined, policy was developed and reversed, battles were won and lost, goals were achieved and final judgments made, all within a closed bureaucratic circle and with few tangible effects on the outside world. Antireligion offered not only the Potemkin organization of the League but also a Potemkin political process masking division, competition, and the pursuit of ulterior interests.

The League's actual work supported the Bolshevik approach to propaganda, which was concerned as much with form as with content. The tendayers, the campaigns, the shock work, and their swift interchange often amounted to little more than a compilation of the familiar organizational

---

[18] See, for instance, James W. Heinzen, "Politics, Administration, and Specialization in the Russian People's Commissariat of Agriculture, 1917–1927," Ph.D. diss., University of Pennsylvania, 1993.

and rhetorical forms. The League's message was equally compromised by rapidly shifting campaigns that reflected the regime's many challenges and limited resources. Despite the hyperbole about evil clergy, ever-ascendant religion, and heroic bearers of a new, atheistic Soviet culture, the League's propaganda in the 1920s still might plausibly be seen as a weapon in the battle against religion. When organized religion had all but disappeared in the 1930s, according to the regime's own logic the League was left without a purpose and became a superfluous organ of general propaganda.

The regime was well aware that many of its most visible efforts were being seriously undermined by their bureaucratic character, and the Soviet and Party press in the 1920s and 1930s characteristically bristled with campaigns against bureaucracy.[19] In one way, the constant harping on bureaucracy only added to the problem, displacing reconsideration of how the regime defined and achieved its goals. If only bureaucracy could be overcome, the logic held, the system would run smoothly and achieve its stated ends. The history of the League suggests that the problem of bureaucracy ran far deeper and could not be isolated or removed; it stood at the very center of Bolshevik political culture.

The challenges posed by bureaucracy were not entirely created by the Bolsheviks. An obvious but often overlooked source of Bolshevik political culture was the notoriously bureaucratic imperial Russian polity. Robert Tucker, among others, has pointed to the continuities in tsarist and Stalinist political practice.[20] The bureaucracy's ability to impede reform during the late tsarist period has been amply documented,[21] and the Soviet state and Bolshevik Party inherited the administrative culture of the Romanov autocracy.[22] Lenin himself acknowledged the persistence of a Russian bu-

[19] Daniel T. Orlovsky, "The Anti-bureaucratic Campaign of the 1920s," in *Reform in Modern Russian History*, ed. Theodore Taranovski (Washington, D.C.: Woodrow Wilson Center, 1995), 290–310.

[20] Robert C. Tucker, "Stalinism as Revolution from Above," in his *Stalinism: Essays in Historical Interpretation* (New York: Viking, 1977), esp. 96–101; Steven White, *Political Culture and Soviet Politics* (London: Macmillan, 1979).

[21] Daniel Orlovsky, *The Limits of Reform: The Ministry of Internal Affairs in Imperial Russia, 1802–1881* (Cambridge: Harvard University Press, 1981); Francis Wsiclo, *Reforming Rural Russia: State, Local Society, and National Politics, 1855–1914* (Princeton: Princeton University Press, 1990); W. Bruce Lincoln, *The Great Reforms: Autocracy, Bureaucracy, and the Politics of Change in Imperial Russia* (DeKalb, Ill.: Northern Illinois University Press, 1990); Neil B. Weissman, *Reform in Tsarist Russia: The State Bureaucracy and Local Government, 1900–1914* (New Brunswick: Rutgers University Press, 1981).

[22] For a lucid discussion of the Soviet Union's bureaucratic inheritance, see Roger Pethybridge, *The Social Prelude to Stalinism* (New York: St. Martin's Press, 1974), 15, 268–269. See also Daniel Orlovsky, "The Lower Middle Strata in Revolutionary Russia," in *Between Tsar and People*, ed. Edith Clowes, Samuel Kassow, and James West (Princeton: Princeton University Press, 1991), and "State Building in the Civil War Era: The Role of Lower-Middle

reaucracy "hardly affected by the Soviet spirit."[23] The Bolsheviks' determination to modernize society rapidly also contributed to this bureaucratic outcome. Moshe Lewin has described how the Soviet path of "telescoped" development led to the emergence of a bureaucratic power elite that supplanted the immature working class and peasantry.[24] The same interpretation can be extended to the social realm, where artificial constructs of modernization such as the League operated.

Finally, the Enlightenment tradition that inspired most European radical movements from Saint-Simon to Lenin promoted a belief in progress through the superior organization of society. According to Nikolai Berdiaev, Lenin "had a boundless faith in the social regimentation of man. He believed that compulsory social organization could create any sort of new man."[25] The Bolsheviks were steeped in this organizationalism, and its application did not necessarily correspond well to the challenges at hand. The Komsomol may have been good at mobilizing youthful enthusiasm for short periods of time, and the Party may have been adept at exercising political control, but this approach did not extend as well to the propaganda realm, where the goals were more intangible and difficult to conceptualize and achieve. Thus the regime defined and offered its utopian aims as structures and forms that were ultimately hollow. As a prominent Bolshevik propagandist wrote on the occasion of the tenth anniversary of the Revolution, the proletariat had seized power with the goal of "transforming life, so to speak, into organized happiness."[26] Happy or not, it would be organized.

Strata," in *Party, State, and Society in the Russian Civil War*, ed. Diane P. Koenker, William G. Rosenberg, and Ronald Grigor Suny (Bloomington: Indiana University Press, 1989), 180–209; Don Karl Rowney, *Transition to Technocracy: The Structural Origins of the Soviet Administrative State* (Ithaca: Cornell University Press, 1989); Walter M. Pintner and Don K. Rowney, eds., *Russian Officialdom: The Bureaucratization of Russian Society from the Seventeenth to the Twentieth Century* (Chapel Hill: University of North Carolina Press, 1980).

[23] Moshe Lewin, *Lenin's Last Struggle* (New York: Monthly Review Press, 1968), 86.

[24] Moshe Lewin, "The Social Background of Stalinism," in Lewin, *The Making of the Soviet System: Essays in the Social History of Interwar Russia* (London: Methuen, 1985), 114. See also Merle Fainsod, "Bureaucracy and Modernization in the Russian and Soviet Case," in *Bureaucracy and Political Development*, ed. Joseph La Palombara (Princeton: Princeton University Press, 1963), 233–267; and on the legitimacy of understanding characteristics of modernization within a national context, Michel Crozier, *The Bureaucratic Phenomenon* (Chicago: University of Chicago Press, 1964).

[25] Pethybridge, *Social Prelude to Stalinism*, 39, 272, citing Nicholas Berdiaev, *The Origin of Russian Communism* (Ann Arbor, 1960), 127.

[26] S. Smidovich, "Reorganizatsiia byta za 10 let proletarskoi revoliutsii," *Kommunistka* 8, no. 10 (October 1927): 72. My thanks to Heather Coleman for this reference.

Selected Primary Sources

Archival Sources

Moscow

RTsKhIDNI: Rossiiskii Tsentr Khraneniia i Izucheniia Dokumentov Noveishei Istorii (Russian Center for the Preservation and Study of Contemporary Historical Documents; formerly Central Party Archive of the Marx-Engels Institute,
TsPAIML)

f. 17, op. 3	Central Committee, Political Bureau and others
f. 17, op. 60	Central Committee, Agitprop Department
f. 17, op. 112, 113, 114	Central Committee, Secretariat and Organizational Bureau
f. 89, op. 4	Iaroslavskii's personal file concerning religious matters and antireligious propaganda

GARF: Gosudarstvennyi Arkhiv Rossiiskoi Federatsii (Government Archive of
the Russian Federation; formerly Central State Archive of the October Revolution and Socialist Construction, TsGAOR)

f. 5407	All-Union League of the Militant Godless

TsKhDMO: Tsentr Khraneniia Dokumentov Molodezhnykh Organizatsii (Center
for the Preservation of Documents of Youth Organizations; formerly Central
Archive, All-Union Leninist Communist Union of Youth, TsAVLKSM)

f. 1, op. 1, 3, 23	Central Committee of the Komsomol

Leningrad

TsGAIPD SPb: Tsentral'nyi Gosudarstvennyi Arkhiv Istoriko-politicheskikh
Dokumentov Sankta-Peterburga (Central State Archive of Historical-Political
Documents of St. Petersburg; formerly Leningrad Party Archive, LPA)

f. 24, op. 8, 10   Leningrad Oblast Party Committee

Pskov

PPA: Pskov Party Archive; officially Oblastnoi Tsentral'nyi Arkhiv Dokumentov
Partii i Obshchestvennykh Dvizhenii (Central Oblast Archive of Documents of
Parties and Social Movements; formerly Archive of the Pskov Oblast Party
Committee, PAPO)

ff. 1, 3, 5, 6   Pskov provincial, okrug, district, and city Party
                      committees

PSA: Pskov State Archive; officially Gosudarstvennyi Arkhiv Pskovskoi Oblasti
(Government Archive of Pskov Oblast)

f. 247   Pskov provincial, okrug, district, and city councils
                      of the League of the Godless

Iaroslavl'

IaPA: Iaroslavl' Party Archive; officially Tsentr Dokumentatsii Noveishei Istorii
Iaroslavskoi Oblasti (Center for the Documentation of Contemporary History
of Iaroslavl' Oblast; formerly Archive of the Iaroslavl' Oblast Party Committee, PAIaO)

ff. 1, 22, 272   Iaroslavl' provincial, oblast, okrug, district, and
                      city Party committees

IaSA: Iaroslavl' State Archive; officially Gosudarstvennyi Arkhiv Iaroslavskoi
Oblasti (Government Archive of Iaroslavl' Oblast)

ff. 2410, 3362, 3378, 3516 Iaroslavl' provincial, okrug, district, and city
                      councils of the League of the Godless

Newspapers and Journals

(All based in Moscow unless otherwise indicated)

Antireligioznik
Bezbozhnik (newspaper)

Bezbozhnik (journal)
Bezbozhnik u stanka
Bol'shevik
Izvestiia TsK KPSS
Izvestiia TsK VLKSM
Kommunisticheskaia revoliutsiia
Kommunistka
Pod znamenem marksizma
Pravda
Pskovskii kolkhoznik (Pskov)
Pskovskii nabat (Pskov)
Revoliutsiia i tserkov'
Severnyi rabochii (Iaroslavl')
Sputnik kommunista
Trud
Vestnik agitatsii i propagandy

Selected Primary Sources

Belkin, B. *Bor'ba s biurokratizmom: Vazhneishaia zadacha sovetskikh iacheek.* Moscow: Mosoblpartizdat, 1933.

Burkin, N. *Monastyri v Rossii, ikh eksploatatorskaia i kontrrevoliutsionnaia rol'.* Moscow: Bezbozhnik, 1931. (10,000 copies.)

IV raschirrenyi plenum tsentral'nogo soveta soiuza voinstvuiushchikh bezbozhnikov. Moscow: OGIZ/GAIZ, 1938.

Chetyre gody raboty: Otchet vtoromu vsesiouznomu s"ezdu bezbozhnikov. Moscow, 1929.

Dvenadtsatyi s"ezd RKP(b): Stenograficheskii otchet. Moscow: Politicheskoi Literatury, 1968.

Enisherlov, M., ed. *Voinstvuiushchee bezbozhie v SSSR za 15 let.* Moscow, 1932.

Galaktionov, M. *Lenin o religii i bor'be s nei.* Moscow: OGIZ/GAIZ, 1933. (25,000 copies.)

Garkavenko, F., ed. *O religii i tserkvi: sb. dokumentov.* Moscow: Politicheskoi Literatury, 1965.

Gorev, Mikh. *Troitskaia lavra i Sergei Radonezhskii.* Moscow: Narodnyi Kommissariat Iustitsii, 1920.

Iaroslavskaia guberniia v tsifrakh statisticheskii spravochnik. Iaroslavl', 1927.

Iaroslavskii, E. *Bibliia dlia veruiushchikh i neveruiushchik.* 10th ed. Moscow: OGIZ/GAIZ, 1938. (20,000 copies.)

———. "Zadachi i metody antireligioznoi propagandy." In *Voprosy propagandy v derevne.* Moscow/Leningrad: Gosizdat, 1926. (10,000 copies.)

Kandidov, Boris. *Iaponskaia interventsiia v Sibiri i tserkov'.* Moscow: OGIZ/GAIZ, 1932. (20,000 copies.)

———. *Vreditel'stvo, interventsiia i tserkov'.* Moscow: Bezbozhnik, 1931. (30,000 copies.)

Kommunisticheskaia partiia Sovetskogo Soiuza v rezoliutsiiakh i resheniiakh s"ezdov, konferentsii i plenumov TsK. 2 vols. 7th ed. Moscow, 1953.

Kommunisticheskaia partiia Sovetskogo Soiuza v rezoliutsiiakh i resheniiakh s"ezdov, konferentsii i plenumov TsK, vol. 5 (1929–1932). 9th ed. Moscow, 1984.

Lunacharskii, A. V. *Khristianstvo ili kommunizm: Disput s mitropolitom A. Vvedenskim.* Leningrad: Gosizdat, 1926. (10,000 copies.)

Materialy k XXII Iaroslavskoi gubernskoi partiinoi konferentsii: Otchet gubernskogo komiteta VKP(b). Iaroslavl', 1929.

Materialy k otchetu orgbiuro TsK VKP(b) po Iaroslavskoi oblasti. Iaroslavl', January 1937.

Meshcheriakov, N. *Popovskie obmany: Fakty i dokumenty.* Moscow: Gosizdat, 1919.

Otchet Iaroslavskogo gubernskogo komiteta VKP(b) za period dekabria 1925 - dekabria 1926. Iaroslavl', 1926.

Otchet Iaroslavskogo gubernskogo komiteta VKP(b) za period ianvaria-noiabria 1927. Iaroslavl', 1927.

Otchet Iaroslavskogo gubkoma VKP(b): Za period V/24IV/25. Iaroslavl', 1925.

Otchet o rabote Iaroslavskogo gubernskogo komiteta partii za fevral'-mai mes. Iaroslavl', 1929.

Otchet o rabote Iaroslavskogo okruzhnogo komiteta partii za iiun'-mai mes, 1929-1930. Iaroslavl', 1930.

Otchet o rabote Iaroslavskoi okruzhnoi KK VKP-RKI k 2-i Iaroslavskoi okruzhnoi partkonferentsii za iiun' 1929-mai 1930 g. Iaroslavl', 1930.

Otchet Pskovskogo gubkoma RKP(b) k XV gubpartkonferentsii. Pskov, 1924.

Otchet raboty: Mart 1923-fevral' 1924. Iaroslavl', 1924.

Otchet Rybinskogo gubkoma RKP(b) za 1922. Rybinsk, 1923.

Pervaia vseobshchaia perepis' naseleniia rossiiskoi imperii 1897 g. St. Petersburg, 1904.

Programma po antireligioznomu samoobrazovaniiu partiino-politicheskikh rabotnikov i propagandistov Krasnoi Armii. Moscow: Voenizdat, 1940.

Putintsev, F. M. *Proiskhozhdenie religioznykh prazdnikov.* Moscow/Leningrad: Gosizdat, 1925. (10,000 copies.)

——. *Vybory v sovety i razoblachenie popovshchiny.* Moscow: OGIZ/GAIZ, 1938.

Resheniia Iaroslavskogo gubernskogo agitpropsoveshchaniia, 2-3 iiunia 1927. Iaroslavl', 1927.

Resheniia pervoi Iaroslavskoi oblastnoi partiinoi konferentsii. Iaroslavl', 1937.

Sheinman, M. M. *Nravstvennost' religioznaia i nravstvennost' proletarskaia.* 2d corr. ed. Moscow/Leningrad: Gosizdat, 1930.

——, ed. *Krest'ianskii antireligioznyi uchebnik.* 6th rev. ed. Moscow: OGIZ/Moskovskii Rabochii, 1931. (200,000 copies; 274,000 of previous editions.)

Shishakov, V. *Religiia na sluzhbe kapitalisticheskikh elementov v SSSR.* Moscow: Bezbozhnik, 1931. (30,000 copies.)

Spravochnik partiinogo rabotnika. 9 vols. Moscow: Gosizdat, 1921-1935.

Stenograficheskii otchet vtorogo vsesoiuznogo s'ezda Soiuza voinstvuiushchikh bezbozhnikov. Moscow, 1930.

Stepanov, I. O. *Pochemu padaet vera i narostaet bezvirie?* Moscow: Narodnyi Komissariat Iustitsii, 1920.

——. *"Zhivoi tserkvi."* Moscow: Moskovskii Rabochii, 1922.

Struchkov, G. *Antireligioznaia rabota v Krasnoi armii.* Moscow: OGIZ/GAIZ, 1934. (10,200 copies.)

Tan-Bogoraz, V. G. *Tekhnizatsiia tserkvi v Amerike v nashi dni.* Moscow: OGIZ/Moskovskii Rabochii, 1931. (30,000 copies.)

Trinadtsatyi s'ezd RKP(b) (mai 1924): Stenograficheskii otchet. Moscow: Gosizdat, 1963.

Trotsky, Leon. *The Revolution Betrayed.* New York: Pioneer, 1945.

——. *Voprosy byta.* 2d ed. Moscow: Krasnaia Nov', 1923.

Ustav soiuza bezbozhnikov SSSR. Moscow, 1925.

Voprosy propagandy v derevne. Moscow/Leningrad: Gosizdat, 1926.

Vsesoiuznaia perepis' naseleniia 1926 g. Moscow: Tsentralnoe Statisticheskoe Upravlenie, 1928.

Zoeva, M. *Imperializm i reliigiia v koloniiakh.* Moscow: Bezbozhnik, 1930. (15,000 copies.)

Interviews

Grigorii Domashnyi, village of Kurba, Iaroslavl' Oblast, 19 May 1992.

Iurii Fedorovich Oleshchuk, Moscow, 25 May 1992.

Index

Alekseev, V. A., 3, 58–59, 219
Altrichter, Helmut, 89, 97
Anti-Christmas campaigns, 86–87
Anticlerical propaganda, 75–78
Anti-Easter campaigns, 86–87, 115
Antireligion, 8, 10, 119, 151, 173, 175,
  195, 207–211
Antireligioznik (journal), 74
Atheism, 8–9, 21

Barber, John, 136
Battle with Alcohol Society, 63, 66
Berdiaev, Nikolai, 229
Bezbozhnik (newspaper), 2, 43–44, 51, 52,
  55, 73–74, 89, 103, 105, 123, 146, 197,
  201
Bezbozhnik u stanka (Moscow journal),
  48, 74
Bible for Believers and Nonbelievers,
  93–94
Bolshevik Party. *See* Communist Party of
  Soviet Union
Bukharin, Nikolai, 23, 36, 58–59, 63
Burials, 91–92
Bureaucracy, defined, 11

Cadres, 9, 19, 31–40, 157–158, 166–167,
  174–196, 211–216
  training of, 182–187
Calendar, 89–90
Campaignism, 99–101

Census, question of religion on (1937),
  223–224
Central Committee, Communist Party of
  Soviet Union, 38, 64, 77, 175, 199–200
  Antireligious Commission of, 42, 48, 53,
  179
  conference on antireligious policy
  (1926), 54–56, 62
  directives on antireligious work, 30, 32,
  40, 124, 127, 164, 168, 222
Central Trade Union Council, 31, 127,
  159, 165
Church bells, 83, 132–133
Church and state, separation of, 24–28,
  31–32
Church closures, 10–11, 120, 125, 130,
  131, 134–136, 167, 209
Churches, 16–17, 83–85, 130–134, 209
Church valuables crisis, 26–27
Civil War, 25–26, 174, 191
Clergy:
  depictions of, in propaganda, 75–78,
  175–176
  persecution of, 26, 120, 125–126,
  209–210, 222
Cohen, Stephen, 47–48
Collectivization of agriculture, 59–60,
  111–112, 167–169
Commissariat of Enlightenment, 25, 30,
  36, 159, 164, 185
Commissariat of Justice, 25, 32, 73

Communist Party of Soviet Union, 35,
37–39
and League, 9, 150–153, 164–165,
168–173, 180–181
See also Central Committee, Communist
Party of Soviet Union
Constitution, 25, 126, 198, 208
Cultural Revolution, 2, 13, 125, 145, 168,
197
Curtiss, John Shelton, 3, 219

Debates, antireligious, 178–179
Delaney, Joan, 4
Derevenskii bezbozhnik (journal), 74
Dmitriev, Stepan, 193–194
Dues, League, 45, 105, 209

Egorov, Aleksandr Grigor'evich, 121, 161,
178, 188–190, 193

Fainsod, Merle, 4
First Five-Year Plan, 13, 59, 125

Getty, Arch, 199
Godless brigades, 100, 102
Godless corners, 86
Gorev, Mikhail, 51, 79, 82
Great Terror, League during, 14, 210,
219–220
Great Turn, 14, 125, 164

Harvest Day, 88
Hoffmann, David L., 12, 136
Holidays, attacks on religious, 57, 86–90,
217
Hunt, Lynn, 12

Iaroslavl' (city and province), 15–16, 35,
84, 128–129, 161
Iaroslavl' League, 119–122, 124, 127–129,
146, 202–205
Iaroslavskii, Emel'ian, 42, 50–53, 59, 66,
91, 93–94, 156, 159, 165, 167,
169–170, 175, 188, 199–202, 208–209,
221
at Central Committee Conference
(1926), 54–56
life of, 48–49
at Second All-Union Congress (1929),
57, 155–156
Icons, 20, 85–86, 226

Illiteracy, 72
Industrialization, 112–114, 163
International of Proletarian Freethinkers,
6, 109–110

Karasev, Konstantin Evlamplievich, 141,
215–216
Kenez, Peter, 10
Khrushchev, Nikita, 200, 222
Knowledge Society, 222
Komsomol, 38–40, 66, 156, 164, 201, 222
call for antireligious propaganda, 31, 127
conflict with League, 9, 51, 57,
158–159, 166, 208
Kostelovskaia, Mariia Mikhailovna,
48–50, 54–55, 61
and Bukharin, 58–59
and Iaroslavskii, 50–53
Kotkin, Stephen, 199
Krasnyi Perekop textile factory, Iaroslavl',
15, 141–144

Lenin, Vladimir, 22–23, 30, 43–44, 65, 95,
154–155, 228–229
Lenin corner, 86
Lenin levy, 35
Lewin, Moshe, 20–21, 97, 101, 116, 147,
164, 229
Literacy, 16–17, 36–37
Loginov, Anton, 54, 73
Lukachevskii, Aleksandr, 55, 110, 210
Lunacharskii, Anatolii, 22, 57, 114–115,
178
Luukkanen, Arto, 58
Machine tractor stations (MTSs), 137–138
Modernization, 5, 11, 15
Morality, 95–96
Moscow Party Committee, Antireligious
Commission of, 42
Moscow Society of Godless, 5, 41
Museums, antireligious, 69, 129, 206

Narkompros, 159
New Economic Policy (NEP), 13, 29,
47–48, 67–68
New Soviet man (*Homo soveticus*), 5, 39,
71, 78–83, 175, 196

"Octobering," 91, 92
ODGB (Society of Friends of the Newspaper *Godless*), 44, 51–52, 54

Oleshchuk, Fedor, 55–56, 65, 137, 173, 210
Orthodox Church/Orthodoxy, 1, 6–7,
    19–23, 25, 29, 60, 90–93, 125,
    208–210, 222–224

Peasantry, 20–21, 28–29, 74
Pethybridge, Roger, 15
Pius XI, pope, 109
Political culture:
    Bolshevik, 140–148, 153–156, 160, 162,
        176, 226–229
    defined, 11–12
Popov, Fedor Konstantinovich, 191–195
Pospielovsky, Dimitry, 70, 219
Pravda (newspaper), 52, 58, 77, 153, 167,
    172, 201–202
Propaganda, 70–71, 73–75, 158
    anticlerical, 75–78
    antireligious, 2, 9–10, 27–29, 31–33,
        40–43, 69–117, 102–103, 211,
        216–219, 222–223
Propaganda state, Soviet Union as, 10,
    69–70
Pskov (city and province), 16–17, 34–35,
    160
Pskov League, 121–24, 129, 146,
    205–206, 209
Putintsev, Fedor, 87–88, 156

Radonezhskii, Sergei, 27
Red Army, 27, 66, 191
Red weddings, 91
Renovationist Church, 7, 27, 90, 223
Rituals, Orthodox and Soviet, 90–91
Rosenberg, William, 48

Science, in antireligious propaganda,
    94–95
Science and Religion (journal), 222
Second All-Union Congress of
    Godless (1929), 56–58, 118, 153–156

Sects, 29–30, 78
Secularization, 5–8, 33, 60–62, 130–136,
    175, 224–225
Sergei (Stragorodskii), metropolitan, 109,
    125–126, 222
Shalygin, Ivan Alekseevich, 121, 139, 147,
    189, 191
Shuia incident, 3, 23, 26
Siegelbaum, Lewis, 48
Sigov, Ivan Nikitich, 124–125, 160,
    190–191
Sixteenth Party Congress (1930), 169–170
Socialism, 21, 95–96
Stalin, Josef, 39, 77, 169, 221
Stites, Richard, 70, 93
Subscriptions, 103–104

Tax codes, 125–126
Thirteenth Party Congress (1924), 28, 32,
    40
Tikhon (Belavin), patriarch, 25–27, 29
Timasheff, Nicholas, 196
Training of cadres, 182–187
Trotsky, Leon, 23, 41–42
Tucker, Robert, 228
Twelfth Party Congresss (1923),
    31–32, 40

Union of Freethinkers, 110
Varlaam (Riashentsev), bishop of Pskov,
    17, 121
Veniamin, metropolitan of Leningrad, 26
Voluntary societies, 62–65, 67
Vorontsev, G. V., 219

Women:
    as activists, 194–195
    and League, 9
    and propaganda, 79–83

Zhdanov, Andrei, 200, 220